780

A2 Music
Study Guide

OCR

Huw Ellis-Williams
and Gavin Richards

R·

Rhinegold Education

239–241 Shaftesbury Avenue
London WC2H 8TF
Telephone: 020 7333 1720
Fax: 020 7333 1765

www.rhinegold.co.uk

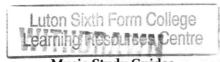
Music Study Guides

GCSE, AS and A2 Music Study Guides (AQA, Edexcel and OCR)
GCSE, AS and A2 Music Listening Tests (AQA, Edexcel and OCR)
GCSE Music Study Guide (WJEC)
GCSE Music Listening Tests (WJEC)
AS/A2 Music Technology Study Guide (Edexcel)
AS/A2 Music Technology Listening Tests (Edexcel)
Revision Guides for GCSE (AQA, Edexcel and OCR), AS and A2 Music (AQA and Edexcel)

Also available from Rhinegold Education

Key Stage 3 Elements
Key Stage 3 Listening Tests: Book 1 and Book 2
AS and A2 Music Harmony Workbooks
GCSE and AS Music Literacy Workbooks
GCSE and AS Music Composition Workbooks
Writing About Music Workbook
Baroque Music in Focus, Romanticism in Focus, Modernism in Focus, *Batman* in Focus, *Goldfinger* in Focus,
Madonna in Focus, *Who's Next* in Focus, Film Music in Focus, Musicals in Focus

Rhinegold also published Classical Music, Classroom Music, Early Music Today, Music Teacher, Opera Now, Piano,
International Piano, Teaching Drama, The Singer, Choir & Organ, British and International Yearbook,
British Performing Arts Yearbook, British Music Education Yearbook, Rhinegold Dictionary of Music in Sound.

Other Rhinegold Study Guides

Rhinegold publishes resources for candidates studying Drama and Theatre Studies.

First published 2009 in Great Britain by
Rhinegold Publishing Limited
239–241 Shaftesbury Avenue
London WC2H 8TF
Telephone: 020 7333 1720
Fax: 020 7333 1765
www.rhinegold.co.uk

You should always check the current requirement of the examination, since these may change. Copies of the
OCR Specification can be downloaded from the OCR website at http://www.ocr.org.uk/ or may be purchased
from OCR Publications, PO Box 5050, Annesley, Nottingham NG15 0DL
Telephone: 0870 870 6622   Email: publications@ocr.org.uk

OCR A2 Music Study Guide
British Library Cataloguing in Publication Data.
A catalogue record for this book is available from the British Library.
ISBN 978-1-906178-75-8
Printed in Great Britain by Headley Brothers Ltd

Contents

The authors

Huw Ellis-Williams was brought up in Bangor and studied in Oxford and Exeter. A pianist, organist and part-time composer, he teaches at a comprehensive school in north Wales where he is head of sixth form. Huw has a particular interest in instrumental music of the early 20th century, and in music for theatre and film. He is an examiner for OCR.

Gavin Richards has been director of music at the Perse School in Cambridge since 2002. He has a music honours degree from Cambridge University and studied piano as a part-time student at the Royal Academy of Music. He has taught piano to students of all ages and has performed widely as a concerto and recital soloist – including a performance of Rachmaninov's Piano Concerto No. 2 at the Symphony Hall in Birmingham. He created the MusicLand website, which has become one of the leading online communities for music education in the UK, and contributes as a freelance writer to Rhinegold Publishing's Classroom Music.

Acknowledgements

The authors would like to thank Alan Charlton for his contribution to the section on Stockhausen, the consultant Paul Terry, Silvia Schreiber and Katherine Smith, who have all been generous in their expert support during the preparation of this book.

The authors and editors are grateful to the following publishers for permission to use printed excerpts from their publications:

Being For The Benefit Of Mr Kite. Words and Music by John Lennon and Paul McCartney © Copyright 1967 Sony/ATV Music Publishing (UK) Limited. Used by permission of Music Sales Limited. All rights reserved. International copyright secured.

A Flock Descends into the Pentagonal Garden. Property of Editions Salabert, Paris. Reproduced by arrangement with G Ricordi & Co (London) Ltd

Stimmung © Copyright 1969 by Universal Edition A.G., Wien. Reproduced by permission. All rights reserved.

Missa Syllabica, Arvo Pärt 'Missa syllabica|für gemischten Chor a cappella' © 1977 by Universal Edition A.G., Wien/UE 31151. Reproduced by permission. All rights reserved.

Eight songs for a Mad King © Copyright 1971 by Boosey & Hawkes Music Publishers Ltd.

West Side Story © Copyright 1956, 1857, 1958, 1959 by Amberson Holdings LLC and Stephen Sondheim. Copyright renewed.

Billy Budd © Copyright 1951 by Hawkes & Son (London) Ltd.

The Confession of Isobel Gowdie © Copyright 1992 by Boosey & Hawkes Music Publishers Ltd.

The Lord Of The Rings: Fellowship Of The Ring (Shore/Walsh) © Copyright 2001 South Fifth Avenue Publishing. South Fifth Avenue Publishing administered by Sony/ATV Music Publishing. Used by Permission of Music Sales Limited. All rights reserved. Used by permission.

The Lord Of The Rings: The Fellowship Of The Ring Theme. Music by Howard Shore © 2001 New Line Tunes. Warner/Chappell North America Ltd. Reproduced by permission of Faber Music Ltd. All rights reserved.

Death On Two Legs. Words and Music by Freddie Mercury © 1975 B Feldman & Co Ltd and Trident Music Ltd. Queen Music Ltd. Reproduced by permission of International Music Publications Ltd (a trading name of Faber Music Ltd). All rights reserved.

Taking Of Pelham One Two Three. Words and Music by David Shire © 1974 Primary Wave Tunes. EMI Music Publishing Ltd. Reproduced by permission of International Music Publications Ltd (a trading name of Faber Music Ltd). All rights reserved.

The Hours. Music by Philip Glass © 2002 MRX Music. Warner/Chappell Artemis Music Ltd. Reproduced by permission of Faber Music Ltd. All rights reserved.

Robin's Theme, *Jollity Theme*, *Robin Fighting Theme* and *King Richard Theme* (from 'The Adventures Of Robin Hood). Words and Music by Erich Korngold © (Renewed) 1938 W B Music Corp. Warner/Chappell North America Ltd. Reproduced by permission of Faber Music Ltd. All rights reserved.

The Voice of Desire (From 'The Voice of Desire'). Music by Judith Weir. Words by Robert Bridges © Copyright 2003 Chester Music Limited. All rights reserved. International copyright secured. Reprinted by permission.

Written on Terrestrial Things (From 'The Voice of Desire'). Music by Judith Weir. Words by Thomas Hardy © Copyright 2003 Chester Music Limited. All rights reserved. International copyright secured. Reprinted by permission.

White Eggs In The Bush (From 'The Voice of Desire'). Music by Judith Weir. Words by Ulli Beier. Music © Copyright 2003 Chester Music Limited. Words: 'Blue Cuckoo' Yoruba hunter's poem, English rendering by Ulli Beier from Ulli Beier YORUBA POETRY, Bayreuth African Studies 62, 2002. All rights reserved. International copyright secured. Reprinted by permission.

Vivaldi: 'The Four Seasons' and other concertos, Op. 8 by Paul Everett (CUP 1996)

Introduction

Course overview

There are three units in the A2 music examination for OCR:

➤ Performing Music 2 (Interpretation)   40%

You should prepare a recital of up to 15 minutes. You may perform as a soloist, in an ensemble or as an accompanist. Your choice of pieces should be linked by a defined style or genre. An examiner will visit your school or college to assess your recital and to discuss your interpretation and the influence of recorded performances on it.

➤ Composing 2   30%

You will complete a portfolio of compositions for your teacher, including exercises in one stylistic technique and a longer composition of up to four minutes.

➤ Historical and Analytical Studies in Music 30%

The listening examination lasts for 2 hours, which includes 15 minutes preparation time for you to listen to the extract of music on the CD. You have to answer questions on the recorded extract, which you are not expected to have studied before. You also have to write two essays from a choice of prescribed historical topics and works that you studied during the course.

The maximum marks for the A2 course is 300. Your marks for A2 are added to your AS level mark (also out of 300), and so the A-level course as a whole will be marked out of 600, divided equally between AS and A2. For a detailed summary of how the marks are allocated for your performing and composing units at A2, go to the relevant chapter in this guide.

These three units continue the work you did at AS and the marks are weighted in the same way.

As in Composing 1 at AS level, your teacher will assess your work and a sample will be sent to the examination board (OCR) to decide if the marks are correct.

Assessment

Historical and Analytical Studies in Music

Section A	**Aural extract (40 marks)**
	An extract on CD and a score of accompanied vocal music 1900–1945 on which you have to answer questions
Section B	**Historical topics (50 marks)**
	There are six topics:
	Song Programme music Music for the screen Music and belief Music for the stage Popular music
	There are three essays on each topic. You are required to choose any two. Each essay is worth 25 marks

The specification lists three works which you are expected to study for the historical topic of your choice (see table overleaf). These are mostly large-scale works, much longer than the works

You can answer both essays on the same historical topic, but it is possible for you to answer questions from different topics if you wish.

You will find a selection of sample questions at the end of each chapter to give you an idea of the type of questions set in the exam.

you studied at AS. However, you are not expected to know these works in the same depth as at AS. In the examination you will not have a copy of a recording or a score to refer to and there are no specific questions on individual details about the works. Instead, you have to write two essays.

It is important to study the prescribed repertoire in enough detail to be able to relate them convincingly to the two Areas of Study – **Tonality** and **Interpretation**. You are not expected to know the whole of a prescribed work, but your choice of passages to study in detail is important. You are expected to use detailed description of selected passages to show your understanding of the important features of the work.

You should apply a similar approach to your study of the related repertoire. Aim to have both a good general knowledge of other related works and a detailed knowledge of certain passages. You should be aware that in this book the authors have limited space to discuss the **related repertoire**. The passages which we have chosen to discuss are intended as a starting point for further study.

The table below lists the six historical topics with their set works and suggested related repertoire.

Prescribed repertoire	Related repertoire	© OCR
Topic 1: Song		
Dowland, *The First Booke of Songes*	English and Italian madrigals, music for solo lute, English consort music	
Schumann, *Dichterliebe*	Early 19th-century lieder, early Romantic character pieces for piano	
Peter Maxwell Davies, *Eight Songs for a Mad King*	Solo songs with piano/instrumental combinations since 1950	
Topic 2: Programme music		
Vivaldi, *The Four Seasons*	Early 18th century programme music (e.g. French keyboard music, Italian instrumental music)	
Berlioz, *Symphonie fantastique*	19th century symphonic poems and programmatic overtures	
MacMillan, *The Confession of Isobel Gowdie*	Descriptive instrumental music since 1950	
Topic 3: Music for the screen		
Korngold, *The Adventures of Robin Hood*	Early film scores by mainstream composers in the post-Mahlerian tradition	
Herrmann, *Vertigo*	Increasing integration between music and dramatic action	
Glass, *The Hours*	Modern adaptations of composing techniques (e.g. leitmotif, minimalist procedures)	
Topic 4: Music and belief		
Byrd, *Mass for Four Voices*	English motets and anthems from the late 16th and early 17th centuries	
Bach, St Matthew Passion	Handel oratorio, smaller scale Baroque works (e.g. cantata, ode) for voices and instrumental combinations	
Stockhausen, *Stimmung*	Music since 1950 which demonstrates the influences of beliefs and/or religious traditions (e.g. Eastern, orthodox, African, Buddhist)	

Topic 5: Music for the stage	
Purcell, *Dido and Aeneas*	Court masque and theatre music in England
Wagner, *Die Walküre*	Contemporary Italian opera
Bernstein, *West Side Story*	Contrasting examples of stage musicals and/or operas since 1945
Topic 6: Popular music	
The Beatles, *Sergeant Pepper's Lonely Hearts Club Band*	British pop music (groups and solo artists) from the 1960s
Queen, *A Night at the Opera*	Examples of 1970s glam rock, music by 'super groups' with international fame
Norah Jones, *Not Too Late*	Examples of music from contemporary singer/songwriters

When you can take the units

The performing and composing units are examined once a year in the summer term. Your performance will be assessed by a visiting examiner and your school or college will let you know the deadline for completing coursework folios. The A2 listening paper however can be taken twice, in January and June. Both papers have the same prescribed repertoire which is listed in the specification. The prescribed works do not change, which allows candidates to sit the paper at any session.

If you wanted to resit any of your AS units, you could retake the listening paper in January, but you would have to wait until the summer session to retake the performing and composing units. If you are taking A2 this would mean preparing for both AS and A2 at the same time. In the case of the performing unit, the visiting examiner assesses both AS and A2 candidates in the same visit. Your teacher will advise you about retaking units in order to improve your mark.

Using this guide

You will have noticed from the 'Course Overview' that the A2 course offers a number of different options in some of the units. This allows you and your teachers more flexibility in choosing parts of the course that suit you, your class and your teachers. In this Study Guide you will find detailed advice about the performing, composing and listening components of the course. There is guidance about the two Areas of Study – **Tonality** and **Interpretation** – which form a consistent theme that runs through the course and a section on each of the historical topics. There are examples, exercises and practice questions which will help you to develop your skills and knowledge.

It is not possible in the scope of this book to cover everything that you will need to know for A2. While as much helpful detail has been included as possible, you will need to continue your own research in order to get a fuller picture of each of the options in the course.

All your activities as a musician are inter-related. Try to **perform** as much as you can: your composing and listening skills will benefit from the knowledge, skills and musical judgement that you develop through practising, rehearsing and performing by yourself and in a group. Your discussion with other musicians about the music you are playing or singing will help you to develop your thoughts about music and the new ideas which you hear from others.

Your **composing** will give you real insight into your performing and listening. The techniques of western tonal harmony are at the heart of much of the music that we hear and play every day. The exploration of exciting new techniques as a composer enhances your ability to perform and to listen perceptively to other music.

Try to **listen** in depth to the music required for this course, but also expand your listening so that it covers a wide range of music. Your performing and composing will benefit from your experiences as a listener. You will find it helpful to keep a diary or log of your listening so that you can use the information for your discussion with the visiting examiner, as part of your commentary on the composition or to answer questions in the listening paper.

If you can, attend as much live music-making as possible. Experience the familiar and the unfamiliar.

> BBC Radio 3 and Classic FM are useful starting points for listening to familiar and unfamiliar works, especially from the Classical and jazz repertoire. The Radio 3 website contains useful information including biographies of composers and musicians. Many broadcast programmes are available on the web for you to listen to again. Particularly useful are the back programmes for the *Discovering Music* series, which discusses a particular work or theme each week.

Areas of study

There are two **Areas of Study** at A2:

➤ Tonality

➤ Interpretation.

These are common elements that link different parts of the course. Their purpose is to give you a focus for your study of music. A detailed understanding of these important elements will help you to develop your overall knowledge of the subject.

Tonality

Tonality was also an Area of Study at AS level. Your previous study at AS should have given you a good grounding in the basics of tonality and harmony:

➤ Primary and secondary triads (chords I–VII), with inversions and added 7ths

➤ Major and minor keys in key signatures of up to four sharps/flats

➤ Cadences (perfect, imperfect, plagal and interrupted) and other standard progressions

➤ Harmony implied in a melody or bass line

➤ Modulation to closely related keys

➤ Tonal devices such as sequence or pedal

➤ Harmonic rhythm (rate of harmonic change)

➤ Melodic decoration: appoggiaturas, auxiliary notes, passing notes.

> If you are unclear about any of the points mentioned here you may find it useful to reread sections in the *OCR AS Music Study Guide* (Rhinegold Publishing 2008), particularly pages 17–18 on tonality to remind yourself of these concepts.

While your previous study at AS focused on music of the late Baroque and Classical periods and on jazz between 1920 and 1960, the course at A2 includes **accompanied vocal music between 1900**

and 1945 and a choice of **prescribed works and related listening**. In some of these works, you will come across increasingly complex tonal harmonies. Your study of a historical topic will demonstrate some of the cultural, artistic and social changes which have happened across a period of time. Throughout history composers have been influenced and have built upon the music of previous generations. They have added new elements, sometimes quite revolutionary, which have changed music for future generations of composers, performers and listeners.

The study of tonality may include music which is not strictly tonal – for example it may be atonal or based on a modal scale. The term tonality should be taken to mean more than the system of western tonal harmony established by the time of Purcell, Vivaldi and Bach. For your study of music for this course you should take tonality to include all forms of harmony and the relationships between pitches in the widest sense.

Interpretation

Interpretation is a new Area of Study at A2, but you will already have considered some aspects of it in parts of your study at AS. At A2 the role of interpretation as an Area of Study is continued in the performing unit as well as playing a stronger role in the composing and listening units. The course asks you to focus more consistently on the issue of interpretation in three ways:

> Your AS performing recital included a viva voce with the visiting examiner where you discussed the decisions you took in interpreting your chosen solo music. The listening paper also dealt with interpretation by including two different performances of an extract from the prescribed orchestral works for you to compare.

➤ **Performing:** The unit is subtitled **Interpretation**, to highlight the importance attached to this element as you improve your skills as a performer. The viva voce continues the pattern established at AS – you are expected to support your recital programme with preparatory listening of performances related to the focus which you have chosen for your recital. You will give details of your listening on the viva-voce preparation form, including brief notes on your observations and the influence which the performances had on your own interpretations. For more information see the chapter on performing.

➤ **Composing:** Section B asks you to interpret a stimulus which is extra-musical, i.e. drawn from outside the music itself – a vocal setting of a text, a piece of instrumental programme music or music for film or TV.

➤ **Listening:** The historical topics are also based on extra-musical stimuli. The setting of text is an obvious point at which the shape of the music is influenced by the words, whether sacred (see Topic 4: Music and belief) or secular (see Topic 1: Song and Topic 6: Popular music). The close relationship of music and drama is explored in Topic 3: Music for the screen and Topic 5: Music for the stage. Composers have also used texts, literature, painting, places, people, ideas and moods as a stimulus for instrumental music, which is discussed in Topic 2: Programme music.

The chapters on the historical topics will set out the techniques and responses of composers to writing music in different genres. The chapter on the listening extract of accompanied song/vocal music 1900–1945 considers in detail the issues of word setting, tonality, accompaniment and interpretation.

Performing

The performing exam is allocated 40% of your overall mark at A2 and is divided into two parts:

➢ **Section A:** Recital (100 marks)

➢ **Section B:** Viva voce (20 marks).

The preparation for your extended recital will take some time. You have to think deeply about what you are performing and undertake some research into performance practice, both by recorded artists and in terms of the performing practices of the past. You should do more than simply select your recital pieces and then practise them all year.

During the course you are expected to build up your experience as a performer. Take advantage of opportunities to perform in a group such as a band, orchestra, choir or chamber group if they are available. Broaden your experience by taking on an unfamiliar challenge: if you are an instrumentalist, join a choir; if you're a singer, learn guitar or bass and form a band; if you play solo piano, learn to accompany. All these experiences will make you a better all-round musician.

Getting the most out of your practice

You will want to practise your recital carefully so that you can perform accurately and confidently. Good practice habits will help you to make progress during this course. Your teacher will tell you how much practice you need to do and how to use your practice time well. If you do not have a teacher for your instrument or voice you should think seriously about how you are developing as a performer. You should work out a strategy that will prepare you for the recital. Talk to your teacher in school or college and ask for their advice.

Here are some tips which you may find useful:

➢ Plan what you want to achieve – set yourself targets for the next few weeks, the next few months, the next few years.

➢ Start your practice with some warm-up exercises – scales and arpeggios, melodic and rhythmic routines – rather than go straight into difficult music without preparation.

➢ Use the warm-up to work on your tone, breathing, bowing, posture or another basic aspect of your playing. It is easier to concentrate on these when you are playing familiar exercises.

➢ Target the difficult passages – play them slowly, working out exactly what's needed, before gradually playing to speed. Just playing through your pieces can be a wasteful way of practising.

If your practice is not helping to achieve your targets then rethink your method of practising. Research ideas on improving your performing. Performers have always experimented with new approaches to the techniques of playing an instrument or singing. Sometimes these are published as 'methods' – books of exercises

At AS you developed the skills and language to discuss your performance with an examiner. These will be developed at A2 by considering the recorded performances of accomplished artists.

and pieces which will develop your playing. Some are intended for beginners, but there are also advanced methods you can follow.

The focus of your recital

Your recital should be no longer than **15 minutes** in length. Time your recital when you practise it so that you know exactly how long it is. There is no specified minimum length, but the examiner will want to be satisfied that it is long enough for you to show a full range of what you can do. You are expected to show your ability to perform an extended recital. Less than 12 minutes will probably be too short.

Choosing your programme

The pieces which you choose to play must be linked by style and genre. You should take some time to develop your ideas about your recital. Most instruments have a huge range of works written for them. You are looking for works which represent a particular style of music which is typical of your instrument or voice. This might be a group of pieces from the work of a single composer, for example solo violin music by J. S. Bach, character pieces for piano by Schumann, songs by George Gershwin, guitar pieces by Joe Satriani.

If you decide to use works by more than one composer, then there should be clear links between them. You should be able to explain the link between your pieces in more than one way. A link of style or genre will be strengthened if there is also a link of time or place. Having the same title does not guarantee a convincing link: there is little connection between the Preludes of Bach and Debussy, which are separated by two hundred years and require very different techniques of piano playing. A better case could be made for preludes and fugues by Bach, Hindemith or Shostakovitch. Here the 20th-century composers pay conscious homage to Bach. The contrapuntal keyboard style presents many of the same challenges to the player, including consistency of articulation in all parts, balance of the voices, and control of structure.

In general it is much better to link pieces which are closer together chronologically, but there should still be a further link of style or genre to give a clear purpose to your recital. Composers who lived and worked at the same time may have explored the same type of music. They may also share the outlook of their particular city or country for example, pieces from the jazz, rock, folk or popular repertoire can be grouped in this way, e.g. West coast jazz.

As a final note of caution, you should avoid vague titles which try to link pieces which are musically too different. 'Dream pieces' or 'Love songs' is too imprecise a link. Whichever pieces you choose, the important thing is that they will demonstrate an aspect of the repertoire for your voice or instrument.

Playing in an ensemble or as a accompanist

You may choose to have your performing assessed as a member of an ensemble. If you play a chordal instrument such as the piano, guitar, lute or harp you may perform as an accompanist. Ask your teacher's advice about selecting pieces for a group. The focus which you choose must still apply to all the pieces in your recital.

If another member of your ensemble is being assessed you must ensure that the recital meets both your needs, i.e. that the pieces are a significant part of the repertoire for your instrument or voice.

Advice from your teachers

You may wish to ask advice from your instrumental or voice teacher about choosing pieces which are suitable for you. You will benefit from their experience as performers and from their knowledge of the repertoire for your instrument or voice. They will be familiar with the standard to which you perform. They are in a good position to suggest pieces which will allow you to show what you can do.

It will help you if your instrument or voice teacher is familiar with the requirements of the examination. You may be tempted to use your latest group of grade examination pieces for your A2 recital as well, but this would be unlikely to produce a satisfyingly focused recital in the way that the OCR examiner will expect. OCR publishes an information sheet for candidates on its website – it would be a good idea for you to print it out and give it to your teacher. You should discuss with them the ideas of a focus for the recital, so that their advice is exactly what you need for this exam.

Web link

Go to www.ocr.org.uk. The information sheet can be found under the 'Pre-release materials' on the page for the new GCE music specification.

Standard

The suggested standard for A2 is **Grade VI** of one of the music examination boards. The specification states that you can access all the grades of the A-level examination by performing music of this standard. Naturally some performers will turn to more challenging music and successful performances at a high level may achieve up to full marks. But, it is important that you perform music which is not too difficult for you. You are expected to play with reasonable fluency. If you have to keep stopping or slowing down for the more difficult sections then the overall flow of your performance will be lost.

You should not play Grade VI music if it is really too difficult or if you are not ready for it. It is preferable to give a balanced and well-presented recital which is within your range. This will be a much more satisfying and enjoyable experience for you and for your examiner.

You are expected to be able to discuss your interpretation of your pieces for your viva voce. Pay attention to the type of language which your teacher uses in discussing your performances. Much of this discussion will be relevant to your own assessment of your recital. You teacher may also know of recorded performances of similar repertoire that have interesting issues of interpretation which you can discuss. Some of these may help to influence you in the way you perform this repertoire.

Section A: the recital

Check the time carefully and make sure that you arrive in plenty of time for the recital.

If you are using an accompanist or if you are part of an ensemble, you need to ensure that the balance of your group is correct. Try to get someone else to listen to your group rehearsing to make sure that the parts which should be heard are not being drowned out. The examiner must be able to hear you or they will not be able to assess your performance properly.

If your performance is amplified, check your levels before you perform. You may get a chance to set up your equipment in the examination room or you may have to move it in when it is your turn. You may be using your own equipment which you know well, or having to adapt to someone else's kit. It is your responsibility to ensure that you know how to set up the equipment correctly – organise a friend to help you move items quickly if you need to.

Tuning is vital. Check this before you go into the exam room. Get someone to check your tuning for you if necessary. You should retune once you are in the exam. The examiner will expect you to check your tuning and they will not mind waiting for you to get it exactly right – they will not want to listen to an out-of-tune performance.

You will be asked to provide a **photocopy of your music** for the examiner. The examiner will use the copy to check that you are playing what is written. There are marks allocated for the accuracy of your performance, so comparing your performance with the printed copy is necessary. The examiner will take the copy away to use when listening again to your recorded performance. The copy will then be destroyed.

You may have learnt your piece from a copy which is not in conventional notation. Guitar players often use tab notation, which is good at recording the positions of pitches in terms of strings and frets, but tends to lack much of the information which candidates are expected to add to achieve a good performance. Examiners prefer if you or your teacher provide additional information about your prepared performance on the photocopy. This might include transcriptions of certain passages in notation, chord symbols, details of the exact rhythm to be used, the addition of dynamic markings and articulation, indications of passages where specific guitar techniques are being used, and so on.

You can perform from memory if you wish. Singers in particular can benefit from communicating their songs more vividly if they are able to perform without a copy. But, if you are not confident you should have the copy on the stand in front of you. Make sure that you have a separate copy for your own use. Give your accompanist and any other players their own copy.

The examiner will record both your recital and the viva voce. This means there is a record of how you performed which can be checked later against the assessments of other examiners. It is also available if there is an appeal about the result. Your school or college can ask for the recording to be returned after the results are published. It can be useful for you to discuss your recorded performance with your teacher to see how you can improve next time.

Nerves are a common problem for performing musicians. Examiners are normally very sympathetic to nervous candidates. They are performers and teachers themselves and understand how difficult performing to an examiner can be. Being nervous is completely natural, and some people react well to the pressure of the situation. It can bring out the best in you. Anybody can miss minor details in a performance which you would never normally miss. Sometimes, however, nerves can seriously inhibit you from performing properly.

Pay particular attention to the volume levels. If the exam is taking place in a small room, adjust your volume to a suitable level. It is hard to assess your performance fairly if the volume level is uncomfortable for the examiner.

Similar information may be needed if you are using a chord grid or improvising from a lead sheet.

Nerves

Allowing plenty of time to practise will help you to build confidence in your ability to perform well on the day. You may find that performing your recital to an audience well before the actual exam reassures you about your ability perform. Some schools like to arrange a concert of exam recitals at lunchtime or an evening concert for parents. In any case the experience of practising your recital beforehand and having it go well is reassuring even if it doesn't completely get rid of your nerves.

You may have an audience present if you wish. Introducing your pieces with a few well-chosen spoken words can help to establish a rapport with your audience and with the examiner. There may be a particular feature of your piece that you would like to mention. If the song is in a foreign language it may be helpful for you to explain what it is about.

> If the audience applauds, acknowledge it in some way – discuss with your teacher how you should do this. A smile and eye contact with your audience really does help.

The accompanist

The accompanist – if you need one – must be provided by you or your school. Arrange to practise with them several times before the examination, if you can on the instrument and in the room which they will be using on the day. They will welcome the chance to get to know the music and to get used to the piano.

This is a chance for you to get used to playing with the accompanist, especially useful if you do not often play accompanied. During your rehearsal time you should establish the tempi you want for the pieces or songs. Don't be afraid to ask your accompanist to play faster or slower. Discuss with them any tempo changes and particular phrasing or articulation that you wish them to use to match your performance. Use the time to establish a mutual understanding of how the performance should sound. If you are comfortable with your accompanist you will worry less about what he or she is doing. You will be able to concentrate better on your own performance.

> If you are singing, the accompaniment must not double the voice. Many songs from musicals are published with the melody in the right hand of the piano as well as in the voice. Ask your accompanist to leave the melody to you and to play only the accompanying chords.

Preparatory listening

When you have decided on your programme, you should begin your preparatory listening and research the focus of your recital. Try to find two contrasting performances of one of the pieces in your programme, if they are available. Comparing the two performances will give you some useful points to think about:

Tempo	Is one performance faster than the other?
	Is there a consistent tempo?
	How much rubato is applied?
	Which performance has the greatest contrast between speeds?
Dynamics	How carefully are dynamic markings observed?
	Are there dramatic contrasts or are the dynamics carefully shaded?
Interpretation	Are there differences in the execution of rallentandi, pauses or silences?
	First impressions – how are the first few bars played?
	How are the final bars played?
	How is the mood of the performance achieved?

Tone	How would you describe the tone produced by the performer?
	Does it suit the music?
	How is it enhanced by techniques such as vibrato?
	Does it vary in different registers?
Phrasing	Are there different approaches to phrasing, breathing or bowing?
	How are rhythmic passages treated?
	Is one player more successful in sustaining a long melodic line?
Articulation	Compare the use of legato and staccato in the performances
	How are faster passages performed?
	Are contrasts of articulation used at points in the music?
Style	Does the style of the performance reflect the genre or period?
	How are performing conventions (e.g. Baroque ornaments, blues inflexions) put into practice?
	Does the playing reflect the influence of a national style or a particular school of playing?
Structure	In which performance are you most aware of the structure of the piece?
	Which performance is more concerned with unity of mood?
	Are the contrasts effective in bringing out the drama of the music or are they exaggerated and unconvincing?

Similar headings and questions can be asked when you consider other recorded performances. As well as recordings of a piece from your recital, you should also choose examples of pieces which are related to the pieces in your recital but which you are not going to play for the exam. The experience of listening to and studying other performers will improve your musicianship, and help you to take more effective decisions about how to interpret your selected pieces.

Section B: viva voce

The viva-voce preparation form should be completed before the day of the examination. The form should summarise the information which the examiner needs to know to begin a discussion with you. It should also show that you have prepared for the recital by undertaking the level of listening and background reading which is expected at A2.

> Take a photocopy of the preparation form to help you remember what you wrote when you are having the discussion.

The form asks you to list:

➤ The focus of your recital, with a brief explanation

➤ The composer, title and length of each piece in your programme

➤ Details of two recorded performances you have listened to, with brief observations on the interpretations

➤ Details of other performances (broadcast, live or recorded) with your observations

> A summary of the way your performance in the recital has been influenced by your listening

> A bibliography of relevant reading (which may include notes from CD recordings and the internet).

Discussing performances

Your teacher will encourage you to use language which is suitable for discussing your performance and those of the musicians you have studied. You should be aware of the technical vocabulary needed to discuss your instrument or voice.

There are many books and magazines available about recorded performances, some specifically dedicated to individual performers or a particular style of music. These will give you a useful insight into the type of language which is needed to discuss interpretations. Magazines such as 'Gramophone' discuss new recordings and contain reviews of past recordings and profiles of recording musicians, mostly but not exclusively in the classical field. If possible find reviews of performances which discuss some of the items in the checklist on the previous page. Some writing on music – particularly on popular music – is very good on the mood of the music or its effect on the listener, but at A2 you need technical detail to explain the effectiveness of the performing. Sometimes magazines or articles written with the performer in mind use more technical vocabulary than popular publications intended for the general listener.

Your discussion with the examiner

Examiners are very experienced in talking to students about their performances. They will be aware that you may be nervous and they are not there to catch you out. They will be keen to discuss your views and to listen to what you have to say about your recital. Their questions are designed to open up areas of discussion so that you can explain about your interpretations and listening.

Ask your instrumental or voice teacher to practise the discussion with you. They will know your pieces well and be able to suggest improvements.

Although the discussion is short, you should prepare what you want to say. It is a good idea to write your preparation form in bullet points. Write clearly so that both you and the examiner can understand what you have written.

Have your photocopied form in front of you to remind you what you decided about your listening and how it related to your performance decisions. The examiner may ask you to illustrate a point by playing or singing a passage from one of your pieces. Select a few passages which are good examples of what you are trying to say and point them out to the examiner when the time comes.

The examiner may well start with a straightforward question to put you at your ease. They may ask you to explain your focus, or they might ask you about the tempo in one of your pieces. From there they will move on to other aspects of the performances. If you have prepared your discussion and thought about what you want to say, the five minutes will go quickly. Try to enjoy the discussion and convey your enjoyment and enthusiasm for the music.

The table below is a summary of what you will have to do for the performing unit and a guide to what is assessed. It also shows how the marks are allocated and lists basic questions to ask yourself as you prepare for this unit.

Performing 2 (Interpretation) – Total 120 marks	
Section A	**Recital (100 marks)**
Aspects which are assessed	Knowledge and fluency of pitch and rhythm (25 marks) *How well do I know the notes and rhythms? How fluent is my performance?* Technical control (25 marks) *How good is my technique of singing or playing my instrument?* Realisation of performance markings and/or performance conventions (25 marks) *How well do I observe markings of tempo, expression, articulation and phrasing? How well am I applying the appropriate performing conventions for my chosen music?* Interpretative understanding and aural awareness (25 marks) *How good is my understanding of the style of the music? How successful am I in judging how my performance sounds?*
Section B	**Viva voce (20 marks)**
	A discussion of about 5 minutes based on your notes on the viva voce preparation form *How much has my listening helped me in deciding how to interpret the works in my recital?*

Composing

There are two sections to this unit. Both are coursework-based, although there is a requirement for a small amount of work to be carried out under timed centre supervision in the first section.

Section A involves creating a portfolio of stylistic techniques. You can choose a style in which to specialise. **Section B** involves submitting one composition lasting up to four minutes. There are some requirements as to what you must create, but you have considerable flexibility to design your own brief for your work. Both sections are weighted equally, at 45 marks – making a total of 90 for the unit.

Section A: stylistic techniques

In this section you are expected to submit a set of no more than **eight exercises**, one of which must have been completed under **centre supervision** towards the end of the course. Your coursework portfolio must be submitted to OCR no later than 15 May in the examination year – therefore much of the harmony work will be carried out in the first two terms.

While this unit is expected to build upon your work at AS (The Language of Western Tonal Harmony exercises), the important difference for A2 is that your exercises must be drawn from just one of the following styles:

a) Two-part counterpoint of the late 16th century

b) Two-part Baroque counterpoint

c) Chorale harmonisations in the style of J. S. Bach

d) String quartets in the Classical style

e) Keyboard accompaniment in early Romantic style

f) Popular song

g) Serial technique

h) Minimalism

The word 'stylistic' is vital for the exercises in this section – a third of the marks (15 out of 45) are available for demonstrating a sense of stylistic integrity. This can be shown by continuing textures appropriately and by using harmonic language sensitive to the style. It is therefore essential that you become familiar with a selection of repertoire from your chosen style through a mixture of playing, singing, listening and score-reading.

Detailed guidance in each of the eight genres is beyond the scope of this book. Early discussion with your teacher in identifying the most appropriate option to suit your skills and interests is encouraged. However, the materials listed over the page (in score and/or CD) may be a useful starting point for background study.

There is also scope for linking your study with the historical topics and this has been indicated below:

		Resources and works
a	**Two-part counterpoint of the late 16th century**	Sacred and secular two-part counterpoint by composers such as Palestrina, Morley and Lassus
		Link to: Music and belief historical topic which includes Byrd's Four Part Mass
b	**Two-part Baroque counterpoint**	Two-part Inventions by J. S. Bach
		Two-part movements from Suites and Sonatas by Handel, and from Violin Sonatas by Corelli
c	**Chorale harmonisations in style of J. S. Bach**	*371 Harmonised Bach Chorales*, edited by Riemenschneider – an invaluable source for this option
		www.jsbschorales.net contains free MIDI files and PDFs of Bach's chorales
		Link to: Music and belief historical topic, which includes Bach's St Matthew Passion
d	**String quartets in the Classical style**	Haydn and Mozart string quartets
		Haydn: String Quartets, Op. 50, by W. Dean Sutcliffe (2008, CUP)
e	**Keyboard accompaniment in early Romantic style**	Schubert and Schumann lieder
		Link to: Song historical topic, which includes Schumann's Dichterliebe, Op. 48
f	**Popular song**	Songs by Gershwin, such as 'Summertime' and 'I Got Rhythm'
		Link to: Popular music historical topic, which includes the Beatles and Norah Jones
g	**Serial technique**	Webern string quartet
		Berg 'Lyric Suite'
h	**Minimalism**	*Clapping Music* (1972) by Steve Reich
		Grand Pianola Music (1982) by John Adams
		Four Musical Minimalists, by Keith Potter (2002, CUP)

You may also find useful:

A2 Music Harmony Workbook by Hugh Benham (Rhinegold Publishing). This book builds on the *AS Music Harmony Workbook* and includes detailed information on some of the most widely offered harmony and counterpoint tasks at A2 level including chorale harmonisations in the style of J. S. Bach, two-part counterpoint, Classical string quartets and Popular Song. The book includes a range of exercises, with step-by-step guidance on how best to complete the textures.

Note: the Popular Song chapter is principally aimed at the Edexcel A2 specification, but you would still find parts of the chapter useful for OCR. The other chapters include exercises specificially designed for OCR A2.

Some general tips for Section A:

> Date each exercise and submit the portfolio in chronological order – the work is marked as a whole, not as a series of individual exercises

➤ Make sure that your work is distinguishable from the given incipit – you can simply put a big asterisk at the point where your own work begins

➤ For options (b) to (f), ensure that you submit work in a mixture of major and minor keys

➤ Check carefully for basic technical errors such as consecutive 5ths or octaves in tonal exercises

➤ Try to demonstrate a range of harmonic vocabulary (particularly in options (c) to (e)) such as chromatic chords suitable to the style

➤ Present your work as neatly as possible, ideally using music technology. If you are submitting hand-written exercises, check your notation very carefully.

Completing an exercise under centre supervision

This is a new requirement for both the AS and A2 composing units – you will need to complete one harmony exercise in your chosen genre under controlled conditions. You should practise this on several occasions before the real assignment and ensure that you are confident in managing your time allocation effectively.

The exercise in the exam will use previously unseen material, but you will have access to any musical instrument of your choice, including a keyboard. You will also be able to use a computer, but not software plugins or other tools to aid working the exercise. The exercise will be of a similar length to those submitted in the portfolio (i.e. 16–24 bars) and you will have 90 minutes to complete the exercise. Following the test, there will be no opportunity to amend or improve the work.

Summary On the following page is a possible plan for managing your time over a 90-minute timed assessment. This is modelled on the chorale option (c) which has consistently been the most popular choice for candidates of OCR's previous composing unit. It should be stressed that not all the strategies here are relevant to other stylistic options. However, you might wish to use this as a starting point to draw up your own strategy for the timed assessment.

Minutes	Action
0–5	Play through the given incipit and the rest of the chorale melody
5–20	**Preparation:** Identify the main phrase endings (often marked with a pause) and work out cadences and any modulations. Remember that interrupted and plagal cadences are rare in the Bach chorale style. Look for possible cadential progressions such as: iib–V⁷–I Look for any points of tension where a chromatic note or more colourful chord might be appropriate Try to identify potential suspensions and mark them in
20–45	**Action 1:** Complete a harmonic plan for the whole chorale (marking it in on your paper) and map out a bass-line for the extract Aim for a mixture of contrary and parallel motion – the latter would tend to use intervals of a 3rd or 6th Try to incorporate some chromatic writing in suitable places
45–70	**Action 2:** Complete the inner parts with the aim of creating a lively texture with passing movement. Take care over good vocal range – tenor parts often move well into leger-line territory Try to avoid consecutives at this stage as they are always hard to remove later The first chord of Bach's cadences is almost invariably decorated while the second is usually a plain chord
70–90	**Checking:** A vital part of the process. Check for: Consecutive 5ths or octaves Unresolved or unprepared dissonance, including suspensions False relations Awkward intervals or overly large leaps within an individual part Accidentals – especially when harmonising in the minor key

This is not a magic recipe for writing a chorale and is no substitute for lots of practice and aural familiarity with your genre. However, you should note the importance of preparation and checking for whatever style you choose. Spending the 90 minutes in a panic, writing lots of harmony from start to finish, will almost certainly lead to haphazard results. A little time building up your own strategy – that is then tested and rehearsed – will pay dividends.

Try to identify the key stylistic features of your genre that you should be focussing on in the preparation and checking phases. Time spent studying the actual music of your chosen genre, and discussing this with your teacher, will be very well invested.

Section B: composition

For the second part of your composing portfolio, you are required to create one composition, lasting no more than four minutes. Your composition must be based on one of the following topics:

> **Vocal composition:** a setting of a poem or text of not more than four stanzas or 120 words

> **Programme music:** a piece for four or more instruments, interpreting a narrative text, character or visual image

> **Film or TV composition:** music to accompany a storyboard, DVD clip, TV theme, cartoon or advertisement.

At the end of your course you will need to submit the following as part of your composing portfolio: a brief (with any texts, translations or other visual stimuli that you have used), a recording and a full score or a detailed commentary on the methods of mixing and producing your master recording.

The brief and commentary

You will need to define your own brief for the composition. A brief is a master plan for your piece and you ought to give it careful consideration before you begin composing. You should also discuss it with your teacher who will be able to advise you on the suitability of your ideas. That said, a brief may well change and develop in the course of the composing process and this is completely normal.

There is no fixed formula for writing a good brief, but it may contain some of the following: your choice of topic and your reasons for this choice – does it overlap with your own particular performing skills or listening interests for instance. The stimulus you are using, for example a poem, a visual image or a film storyboard, what instruments you would like to use and the reason behind this particular combination. It's also worth including a proposed structure of your piece, any musical influences you are drawing on and how you intended to interpret them in your composition.

For this assignment you have considerable flexibility over your choice of instruments as they may be acoustic, amplified or electro-acoustic.

Later in the composing process, you should add the following to your written brief:

> **Documentation of your composing process.** If your ideas changed during the process, or you received inspiration from other sources, mention it at this point. It is a good idea to keep a composing log as you proceed with your work. This could be a simple table with columns for the date, your aims, a review of your work and space for some comments by your teacher.

> **A short appraisal of your composition,** in terms of how it fulfilled the brief. Try to find a midpoint between self-praise and undue pessimism over your work. The examiner will want to see that you are proud of your composing achievements, but they will also want to see that you have thought critically about the outcome. Try to make some detailed analytical comments, for example: 'The use of a low vocal range in bars 23–25 was

particularly effective in suggesting the sombre mood of the text.' Or, 'When I heard bars 33–36 performed by a string quartet, the cello over-dominated the texture and this passage would have benefited from some re-scoring.'

Choosing a topic

There are links between all the composing topics and the Historical and Analytical Studies paper.

You may want to base your choice of composition on the topic that you are studying for Section B of that paper. This will give you a considerable body of music which you can use for background study. You may also take into account your own composing interests and the performing resources available to you at school or college. If you are composing a piece for acoustic or amplified instruments, then the opportunity to hear your music performed live by real players is a hugely valuable one. Can you construct a coherent instrumental ensemble from the members of your class to perform a piece of programme music? Is there a first-study singer who might be willing to demonstrate your song?

Your composition is marked out of 45, in four different categories. These are not completely separate and the quality of one may well influence the quality of another.

Pastiche composition

Writing a pastiche composition (i.e. one based closely upon the style of a particular composer) is allowed. However, you must not overlap with the stylistic techniques chosen for Section A. For example, if you chose option e (keyboard accompaniments in early Romantic style), then your composition should not be a song in the style of Schubert.

How your composition is marked

The effective choice and use of materials *(up to 15 marks)*

➢ Have you chosen a musical language that is appropriate to the stimulus?

➢ Are your musical ideas of a high quality?

➢ Does your composition suggest that you have become familiar with a range of suitable repertoire?

Technical and structural control *(up to 10 marks)*

➢ Does your piece have a logical and coherent structure?

➢ Have you handled technical features such as word setting competently?

Expressive use of medium *(up to 10 marks)*

➢ Have you used instrumental or vocal texture and timbre effectively?

➢ Have you written effectively for instruments?

Communicating your intentions *(up to 10 marks)*

➢ Is your score a clear record of what you intended?

➢ Would someone playing it 'cold' produce the sound you expect?

➢ If you have submitted a production commentary instead of a score, is it comprehensive and detailed?

Writing effectively for instruments

At a basic level, writing effectively for instruments means writing within their playable range. However, instruments have different timbres depending on the range you choose and the kind of material you expect them to play. The effectiveness of what you have written can often only be evaluated by hearing your piece performed by live musicians. Music technology, although a fantastic composing tool, can often disguise the individual character of instruments. For example, consider the following: a flute in the lower part of its range will struggle to play fortissimo; it is not easy for a clarinettist to cross the 'break' repeatedly and rapidly; not all double-stopping for string instruments is practical; wind and brass instruments cannot play chords! You can achieve all of the above in a notation programme, simply by writing it into the score. However, that does not mean that you have written effectively for your chosen instruments.

> It's rewarding to explore these issues by asking friends to play your work on their specialist instrument.

Communicating your intentions

When submitting your portfolio, you need to produce a recording and either a score or a commentary on the recording process. Communicating your intentions clearly is a vital part of the work and is worth nearly one quarter of the available marks.

Producing a score

Many students now produce their scores using notation software. The end results can look highly professional and it is certainly recommended. But it is worth spending time ensuring that you have presented your score effectively. Here are some points to think about:

➢ Make sure you use key signatures correctly to avoid unnecessary accidentals in your score

➢ Check for incorrect accidentals – for example, A♭ instead of G♯ in a piece written in A minor

➢ Make sure it is clear which instruments should be playing your piece – it is very hard to judge the piece under the 'expressive use of medium' marking scheme, unless you have given this some thought

➢ Check for spare bars at the end of a piece, this looks untidy and careless

➢ Ensure that your notation is well spaced on the page – try to compress the number of stave systems per page to an appropriate level

➢ If your piece includes lyrics, make sure they don't collide with other performance directions, with notes or each other

➢ Performance directions and dynamics are expressive instructions and are essential to an interesting piece, but they should serve a musical purpose – they are not purely to decorate your score

➢ If you are using a sequencing package, as opposed to notation software, then you need to take particular care with your score. Initial score print-outs from sequencing software can be highly unreliable. Check, for example, that you have quantised rhythms appropriately and tidied-up any melodic slips originating from your initial recording.

Making the recording

Recording your composition is compulsory and is worth some thoughtful preparation. The task is not set simply to tick a box on the mark-scheme. It is for you, as a composer, to hear and evaluate your work – ideally played by real instruments. You should do it at a stage where there is still time to make further changes to your composition if you are not satisfied with what you hear. If it is going to be played by live performers, they will need time to learn and practise their parts.

Aim for the best recording quality you can get from the facilities available at your school or college. If there is a teacher who specialises in recording technology, try to enlist their help in advance. A recording with proper microphone positioning is likely to be much better than a single microphone in the corner of the room. It's also worth checking the recording environment is suitable – if another rehearsal or a sports fixture can be heard in the background then the quality is going to be compromised. Most students now submit their work on CD, so make sure the disc is finalised and playable on a regular CD player. Submitting your work in MP3 format is not allowed – and the quality is likely to be inferior in any case. Finally, label your CD with your candidate number, name, centre number and the track contents.

Recording production commentary

If you choose not to submit a score, then you must submit a full commentary on the methods of mixing and producing the master recording. This option may well be more appropriate for certain submissions, for example where live instruments are multi-tracked onto a recording of electro-acoustic ones. You may wish to include some of the following: a list of the recording hardware and software; details of the types of microphone used, for example condenser or dynamic, and why you made this choice; the positioning and configuration of the microphones, whether your recording is ambient or multi-tracked; the amount of panning and or compression used; whether you relied on natural acoustics or employed any artificial reverb.

We have so far looked at ideas that are applicable to any composing option. We will now look at some specific suggestions relating to the three different composing topics set by OCR.

Option 1: vocal composition

Before you start this task, it would be a good idea to listen to a number of different composing models. These could range from John Dowland's lute songs to Poulenc's French *mélodies* or Schumann's song cycles or Norah Jones' album *Not Too Late*. Despite the huge stylistic differences between these songs, they all have some common features:

➤ A musically expressive response to their text

➤ A coherent musical structure that may also relate to the chosen text

➤ An imaginative accompaniment that uses instruments in an idiomatic fashion.

Whatever text you choose, and whatever style you decide to work in, you should keep these features in mind as they will determine the success of your composition.

First you need to find some words for your song. Ask your teacher, explore poetry anthologies or adopt the words from a song you know. It tends to be easier to work with poems that have shorter lines, and a clear rhythmic feel, rather than poetry in long free verse.

Let's take some words from a 1794 Robert Burns poem that has already been given a number of musical settings:

> O my luve's like a red, red rose,
>
> That's newly sprung in June:
>
> O my luve's like the melodie,
>
> That's sweetly play'd in tune.

You can find out more about this process by reading pages 61–63 of the *Rhinegold GCSE Music Literacy Workbook* (ISBN: 978-1-906178-59-8).

One of your first tasks is to work out the rhythm of the words – try clapping the text and count how many syllables each word has. Once you have done this you need to decide where the strong syllables fall – try underlining them in the text above. They will often coincide with the beginning of your musical bars. By marking out barlines before the strong syllables you might end up with a sketch like this:

> O my |luve's like a |red, red rose,
>
> That's |newly sprung in |June:
>
> O my |luve's like the |melodie,
>
> That's |sweetly play'd in |tune.

You can then map out a basic rhythmic template for your words, ensuring that the barlines fall in the right place, in relation to the words. A variety of time signatures would be possible, but you do need to ensure that the strong syllables fall on the strong beats of the bar. $\frac{4}{4}$ fits the sense of the words well here. If we use this time signature, notice that the pattern begins on an upbeat or anacrusis:

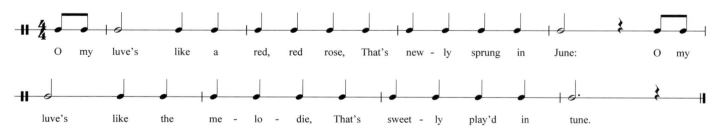

This sketch does very little except ensure that you have captured the natural emphases of your poem. As a piece of music, it is rather dull. Even if it was given a simple melody, the rhythms would become extremely tedious in performance.

Now is the time to make some musical decisions: what sort of vocal setting do you want – do you want to write for solo and accompaniment or for a choral ensemble? For vocal parts, you will need to identify the type of singer (e.g. soprano) and ensure you are using an appropriate vocal range. What key or scale are you going to base your setting upon?

Once these basic musical decisions have been made, it is time to start composing. If you feel comfortable singing, then that is an excellent way to experiment. Otherwise use your musical instrument to begin designing a vocal melody. Look for ways of making the rhythm more flexible than in our previous template. Try to give the melody a good sense of phrase and structure while aiming to incorporate some distinctive intervals. A melody that moves up and down in step for its duration may be rather unimaginative. Look for words that contribute particular meaning to the poem. You may wish to use word painting in some way, to draw attention to, and illustrate, their meaning.

For this setting, we decided that we would write for soprano soloist and add a piano accompaniment at a later stage. Given the traditional Scottish folk-like nature of the words, we are going to use a modal scale – the transposed aeolian mode.

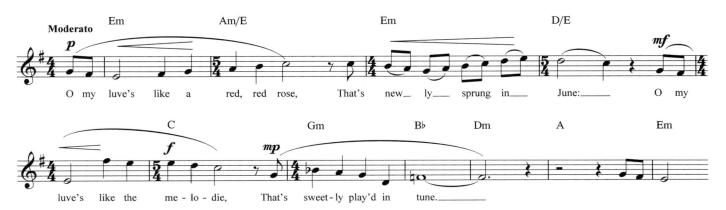

Notice the following:

➤ The greater flexibility in the rhythm than was found in our original template – the alternating time signatures give a dreamy feel to the melody

➤ The use of melisma

➤ The ascending scale on 'newly sprung in June'

➤ The phrase structure – the third line begins in a similar way to the first line

➤ The accidentals in the final phrase that allow a more varied selection of chords.

All these features contribute to a coherent structure and a thoughtful response to the text. There are also some rests (absent from our original rhythmic map) to allow the singer to breathe. The full poem is written in regular stanzas, and the song setting is therefore likely to be strophic. A short piano interlude will be drafted into bars 9–10 and the first three notes of the next stanza sketched in. The notation also includes some harmonic indications and it is a good idea to have a plan for your harmony before you begin writing the accompaniment. We have also added some performance directions, phrasing and the text itself.

> The technical term for the relationship between notes and lyrics is **underlay**. Good-quality notation software will help a great deal with this, but keep in mind the following principles:
>
> Single syllable words should not be split – for example the word 'June' has been written as a single word over two notes, rather than 'Ju-ne'.
>
> Multi-syllable words need to be broken down and you should use hyphens for this. Try to place the hyphen directly before a consonant, e.g. 'me-lo-die' rather than 'mel-od-ie'.

Adding an accompaniment

If you are adding a piano accompaniment to your vocal melody, try to use piano textures which complement the mood of your setting. Block chords filling whole bars tend to be rather unsatisfying on the piano, as the sound decays as soon as you play the note. Equally, remember that the piano has an enormous range – don't just restrict yourself to an octave each side of middle C. When using a small keyboard or midi input at the computer, it can be easy to forget this fact. Also, try to avoid doubling the vocal melody in the right hand of the piano part. This may legitimately happen on occasions but it would be an unimaginative technique to use throughout the whole song. Aim for some dialogue between singer and accompanist, and do exploit the potential of instrumental interludes and postludes (as Schumann and Norah Jones do in some of their songs).

In the example below, the harmonic indications of bars 5–10 have been realised in the accompaniment. Notice:

➢ The use of low notes creating a wide piano range

➢ The use of continuous quavers and a consistent pattern throughout the phrase. Accompaniments tend to be weak if they continually chop and change, never settling on one idea

➢ The addition of pedal markings and other performance directions for the pianist.

The ideas above are intentionally 'work in progress' but show some snapshots of how your piece may evolve. As the piece develops, try out your musical ideas with singers and instrumentalists, and evaluate their success – refining them in the process.

Option 2: programme music

Programme music is a type of music that aims to evoke extra-musical ideas, ranging from stories to portrayals of epic landscapes. It became particularly fashionable in the 19th century and there is a huge wealth of repertoire to study as potential composing models. This topic makes a natural link with the historical topic on Programme Music. Whether or not you are studying this topic, it is recommended that you read the chapter on pages 62–86 in order to familiarise yourself with some of the repertoire.

There are many other works you could look at for further study and inspiration, including Beethoven's Symphony No. 6, the *Pastoral* (1808). This was written at a time when composers did not generally attempt to evoke images through their symphonic movements. However, the *Pastoral* is one of the first examples of a symphony containing descriptive subtitles for each of its movements. Other examples of programme music include Rimsky-Korsakov's *Sheherazade* (1888), which is a four-movement work for solo violin and orchestra based upon a series of episodes from the *Arabian Nights* stories. A lot of programme music is associated with the orchestra but *Pictures at an Exhibition* (1874) by Modest Mussorgsky exploits the descriptive power of the piano alone (although it was later orchestrated by Ravel). *Sleigh Ride* (1948) by Leroy Anderson commonly appears on Christmas compilations, but features various instrumental effects including a range of percussion and a trumpet glissando that imitates a whinnying horse.

> Both option 2 (programme music) and 3 (TV or Film) involve the association of imagery and music. In a piece of programme music, the associations will normally be implicit (that is to say, the listener will not be watching images). In a Film or TV composition, however, the music will accompany action on a screen. Although the end products might be very different depending which option you choose, some of the issues to consider during the composing process may well be similar.

Overture to Shakespeare's 'Midsummer Night's Dream' (1826) by Mendelssohn

An initial composing model

This piece was written by the composer when he was 17, the age of a typical A2 student. Although it is written in the mould of a Classical sonata form, it contains a number of highly Romantic and programmatic features, and evokes a number of elements from Shakespeare's play. Listen to the exposition and notice the following:

Bar	Description
1	A series of chords, with no melody gives a timeless and magical quality to the music. This is reinforced through the ambiguity between the major and minor tonality
6	The first subject, with its busy divisi string writing, suggests the fairies flying around hastily
62	A further theme within the first subject, scored for full orchestra, evokes the grandeur of the royal court
130	The second subject group is more lyrical and is in the dominant key of B major. One of the more pictorial associations can be heard at bar 200 with the repeated interval of a 9th. This is intended to suggest the braying of an ass – in the play Bottom is given a donkey's head by the fairies

When writing a piece of programme music, plan your structure carefully so that you do not end up with a rambling, formless piece. This can be a danger when trying to tell a story through music. You may have some excellent ideas that suggest the different elements in your narrative, but they may sound unrelated and incoherent when they are combined. As you review your work, put the 'programme' to the back of your mind on occasions and ask yourself: 'does this sound like a satisfying piece of music?'

Choosing a stimulus

There are virtually unlimited resources for choosing a piece of programme music. Ideas for inspiration may include:

> A photograph of a landscape

> A short story or fable

> A scene from a play.

It is perhaps best to avoid rather vague stimuli, such as one-word mood descriptors (e.g. happy, sad or excited). Although you may have some excellent ideas based upon these words, it can be difficult to build up a programmatic composition from these alone.

Advice

If you are writing for an instrumental ensemble, try to find a creative and effective combination of sounds. However, don't put dozens of instruments into your score for the sake of it – a small ensemble might be just as worthwhile. Make sure that you use all your instruments in a thoughtful way throughout the piece. If lots of instruments appear only momentarily to provide sound effects, the effect is likely to be unsatisfying. Give lots of thought to the planning of your musical structure and try to pace tension and climaxes effectively.

If you are writing a piece in a tonal style (as many candidates do), ensure that you give it plenty of variety through modulation and contrasting key areas. Avoid excessive repetition that may evoke your subject matter but is not musically interesting in itself. Try to avoid well-worn musical clichés that examiners are likely to hear on a regular basis. These include long drum-rolls to depict a storm or a trombone glissando to demonstrate someone falling.

Option 3: film or TV composition

If you choose this option for your composing portfolio, it is recommended that you read the chapter on Music for the screen. This will give you a number of ideas for preliminary study and listening.

This option gives you an opportunity to write music for a sequence of visual images. Although you do not need to submit the visual images with your composition (as a video), it is best to work in close association with them. Music is fundamental to film and television. However, in these contexts, good music often doesn't draw attention to its presence. You may have watched a film and barely noticed the music. However, if you were to remove it, the experience would be greatly impaired. Although the great fight and love scenes may contain music of a suitably epic quality, other passages may be much more restrained. The old adage 'less is more' is worth bearing in mind – a simple monophonic violin melody might be more haunting than crashing chords scored for full orchestra.

Getting ideas and choosing a stimulus

Listen to a range of music from film and television. Film score writers such as John Williams, James Horner and Danny Elfman are obvious starting points but there are many other composers worthy of exploration.

Here are some further suggestions which could become compositional models for your own work:

➢ *Pirates of the Caribbean* (2003) score by Klaus Badelt – this encompasses a huge range of music from the lyrically haunting to the epic.

➢ *Scott of the Antarctic* (1948) score by Ralph Vaughan Williams – this is highly descriptive music from a mainstream British composer of the 20th century. Vaughan Williams recast much of the music into his seventh symphony (*Sinfonia Antarctica*). Listen for the composer's use of instrumental timbres and textures to evoke the cold and barren landscapes of the film. The 17th scene (The Deaths of Evans and Oates) also contains a wordless chorus which adds further pathos to the music.

➢ The Lloyds TSB advert from 2007, which features the Tasmanian Symphony Orchestra, is composed by Elena Kats-Chernin – there are more ideas relating to TV advertisements on www.tvadmusic.co.uk.

The Snowman (1982) by Howard Blake

Although cartoons and animations themselves are generally associated with younger children, setting music for one would be a worthwhile activity and one encouraged by the specification. Howard Blake's setting uses melody, harmony and instrumentation in a particularly evocative manner. Watch the passage where the snowman comes to life, setting a timer to 0:00 at the point where the snowman glows on the strike of midnight.

An initial composing model

Timing	Musical description
0:00	Percussion timbres, trills and chain of descending major 3rds give the music an exotic and magical feel as the snowman comes to life
0:07	A unison descending minor scale played on the bassoons and cellos match the footsteps of the young boy. The exotic flavour is continued by the flattening of the second degree of the scale
0:13	The music settles on a major chord as the snowman makes a gesture of greeting. This is followed by more descending minor scales (as above) to match the snowman's walking
0:23	A short melodic fragment on the piccolo is heard as the snowman looks uneasy and anxious about entering the house. After he enters, a theme is heard on the xylophone and pizzicato strings. This is developed sequentially
0:46	A dramatic chord featuring a tritone is heard. This also contains brass effects followed by tremolo strings to illustrate the snowman's fright

Although the music is based on a series of short cues, the overall effect is totally coherent. Blake does not simply string together a series of unrelated sound effects. If the music was heard on its own, it would still sound satisfying and you need to apply this test to your own composition.

This type of composition is called a **storyboard** and it will commonly feature in film and television music, where the music is written to match a series of precise cues. Finding a suitable storyboard is perhaps the best stimulus for this composition.

It allows you to demonstrate the specification requirement of controlling a musical structure around a series of given timings. You can either devise your own storyboard or base one upon a scene from a film, TV programme or cartoon. Your brief will then show this as a sequence of timings and the description of accompanying action.

Exercise 1

Try analysing some other appropriate music in a similar way. Listen for how the composer uses melody, harmony, rhythm, instrumentation, texture and timbre to reinforce the action on the screen.

When you have assembled your storyboard, take time trying out ideas before committing immediately to the composition itself. Jot down features that you would particularly like to include in a planning grid. It's important to work hard at your musical themes to ensure they are strong and striking. Aim to develop them as you would in an ordinary composition, and don't just use them as one-off sound effects. You may want to use themes to represent different characters or objects as they appear in the action – John Williams uses a similar technique in his *Star Wars* scores.

Try to make your scoring imaginative – look for ways you can use texture and timbre creatively. Consider the use of range, dynamics, instrumental effects (e.g. muting) and unusual combinations.

Aim for a wide harmonic vocabulary and try to incorporate some dissonance, rather than just working with standard chord patterns. Avoid clichés – some of these are illustrated in the section on programme music (page 30)

Examiners are particularly impressed when candidates arrange live performances of their storyboard music – while still maintaining the given timings. However, a computer-based recording is absolutely fine. Less impressive is when candidates artificially manipulate their music simply to fulfil the storyboard timings. A meaningless ritardando or accelerando inserted to keep the music on track can be quite a giveaway.

Summary   The table on the following page is a summary of what you have to do for the composing unit and a guide to what is assessed. It also shows how the marks are allocated and lists basic questions to ask yourself as you prepare for this unit.

Composing 2 – Total 90 marks	
Section A	**Stylistic techniques (45 marks)**
Complete at least eight exercises in one of the styles listed opposite	Two-part vocal counterpoint of the late 16th century
	Two-part Baroque keyboard counterpoint
	Chorale harmonisations in the style of J. S. Bach
	String quartets in the Classical style
	Keyboard accompaniments in early Romantic style
	Popular song
	Serial technique
	Minimalism
Aspects which are assessed	Language (15 marks)
	How familiar am I with the chords and notes that suit the chosen style?
	Technique (15 marks)
	How well do I use the chords and notes to create the typical features and textures of the style?
	Stylistic understanding (15 marks)
	How well does my piece demonstrate my knowledge of the style?
Section B	**Composition (45 marks)**
Complete one composition, lasting no more than 4 minutes, based on one of the types of composition listed opposite	**1. Vocal composition**
	A short poem or text, no more than four stanzas or 120 words
	2. Programme music
	An instrumental composition for four or more instruments, interpreting a narrative text, character or visual image
	3. Film/TV composition
	Music for a storyboard, DVD clip, TV title theme, cartoon or advertisement
You should hand in your brief, a recording (either in full or reduced/synthesised instrumentation), and a full score (or a detailed commentary on the mixing and producing of the recording)	
Aspects which are assessed	Materials (15 marks)
	How successful is my musical material? Am I familiar with the musical language from other listening?
	Technique (10 marks)
	How well have I used my material to construct a successful composition?
	Use of medium (10 marks)
	How well does my piece suit my choice of instruments/voices/technology?
	Either Notation and recording (10 marks)
	Is my piece well presented through its score and recording?
	or Recording and commentary (10 marks)
	How successful is my control of production techniques? How detailed is my commentary?

Listening

The first section of your written exam is a listening assignment. For this part of the paper, you will need access to your own CD player in order to hear a recording of the aural extract. You may play this recording as many times as you wish (pausing wherever necessary) and you are advised to spend around 30–40 minutes on this section of the paper.

The aural extract is drawn from the repertoire of **accompanied vocal music composed between 1900 and 1945**. If the text of the piece is in a language other than English, you will be given a translation on the paper. You will also have a copy of the score (in complete or near-complete form) on a separate insert.

The format of the paper will be a mixture of short questions (such as identifying a key, chord or cadence) and longer questions demanding a paragraph of prose in response (for example commenting upon the use of texture in the music and how it impacts on the word setting).

You may be asked to relate the aural extract to another relevant piece of vocal music. This necessitates familiarity with a range of different examples and you may wish to draw upon some of the extracts in this chapter. The following study areas are identified by the specification as being the focus of this section: **Word setting, Tonality, Accompaniment** and **Interpretation**.

For the first three concepts listed above we will look briefly at two contrasting works from the period. We will also consider key language and issues, study ideas relating to the two works and offer one or more further listening ideas. For the topic of 'interpretation' we will consider what might be expected from you in the exam and how best to structure your answer, using a musical extract.

It should also be noted that the sections are not mutually exclusive. For instance, there may be lots of further tonal interest in a piece that is considered under 'word setting'.

Word setting

The way in which a composer sets the text is of fundamental importance to vocal music. Here are some points to consider when listening to vocal music:

➤ Is any speech or narration introduced beyond the vocal line itself?

➤ Is the word setting lyrical or more declamatory?

➤ Does the composer make use of melisma?

➤ Is there any vocal writing that resembles recitative?

➤ Are there any word-painting effects, where the composer has used a musical technique to highlight part of the text expressively?

Works to explore

Oedipus Rex (1926–1927, revised 1948) – an opera-oratorio by Igor Stravinsky

Peter Grimes (1944) – an opera by Benjamin Britten

Stravinsky, although born in Russia spent the central part of his life working in Paris. *Oedipus Rex* was premiered in this city and stems from the time when he took particular interest in Neoclassical ideas. Britten was an English composer who made a conscious attempt to distance himself stylistically from other British composers such as Holst, Elgar and Vaughan Williams, whom he regarded as rather staid and traditional. *Peter Grimes* is the first of a series of operas written by Britten, the others coming after the period defined by this question. Both *Oedipus Rex* and *Peter Grimes* are based upon tragedy.

Oedipus Rex

Six solo roles, plus a male chorus of relatively small size make this a work of modest scale, typical of neo-classical thinking. It is also less than an hour in length. Additionally, there is a narrator who explains aspects of the plot at regular intervals – the libretto itself is written in Latin which gives the opera a ritualistic quality.

'Caedit nos pestis' (chorus)

Following the narrator's initial explanation, the chorus implore Oedipus to deliver them from the plague and the musical setting heightens their pleas. The music opens in a dramatic and flamboyant fashion with full orchestra and chorus. The texture is homophonic, with the same rhythms in both the chorus and the orchestra. Dramatic pauses and dynamic contrasts separate the phrases.

'Liberi, vos liberabo' (Oedipus)

The syllabic chanting of the chorus in the previous movement contrasts with the florid writing given to King Oedipus in this passage. He boasts that he can save his people and his vanity is characterised by ornate melodies, a wide vocal range and extensive melismas in the word setting.

Peter Grimes

This work employs 13 solo roles, chorus and large symphony orchestra as well as various off-stage instruments and a dance band. The orchestra's role is emphasised with the interludes that occur throughout the opera, better known in the concert hall as Britten's *Four Sea Interludes*.

End of the Prologue: The truth – the pity – and the truth (Peter Grimes and Ellen Orford)

In this duet, written in a recitative style, Ellen is showing compassion towards Peter. The first section of the duet consists of separate vocal phrases in dialogue (some of which slightly overlap). Peter's initial phrase is based around a narrow vocal register though this widens as his mood becomes increasingly animated. The initial separation of the characters is implied through the

Available on: Stravinsky: The Essential Stravinsky (Disc 5), Chandos: CHAN6654-58.

Listening selections

Available on: Britten: Peter Grimes, Chandos: CHAN9447-48.

Listening selection

Further listening

Facade by Walton: an extract of this may be found on *Favourite English Songs*, sung by Felicity Lott, Chandos CHAN6653.

bitonal relationship of their melodies – Peter's is focused on F minor and Ellen's on E major. However, their increased mutual understanding sees them singing together in octaves for the final section of this duet, a passage that contains some highly expressive melodic intervals, such as the minor 9th.

Tonality

The early 20th century saw a variety of approaches to tonality. Some composers continued to write in the major and minor keys that had been used in the past, but many extended these with increasing amounts of chromatic writing, more discordant harmonies and more unusual modulations. Some explored alternatives to tonality, such as music based on modes or whole-tone scales. Some abandoned tonality and wrote entirely atonal music. All of these trends happened in the same few decades, so we cannot trace a neat line from the beginning to the end of the period. Here are some questions to consider:

➤ Is the harmony mainly dissonant or often consonant? If consonant, does it sound Romantic in style?

➤ Is the musical language diatonic, chromatic, modal or atonal?

➤ Is there a key centre? How strongly does it govern the piece?

Works to explore:

Hymnus Paradisi (1938) by Herbert Howells

Erwartung (1909–1913) by Arnold Schoenberg

Howells (1892–1983) was an English composer who wrote an enormous amount of music for the Anglican Church liturgy. Schoenberg (1874–1951), an Austrian composer, is most often associated with 12-tone technique (serialism) following the First World War. You may find it surprising to learn that *Erwartung* was composed nearly 30 years prior to *Hymnus Paradisi*, although it is not a 12-tone work.

Hymnus Paradisi

Available on: Howells *Hymnus Paradisi*, Naxos 8.570352.

This work employs soprano and tenor soloists, mixed chorus and orchestra. Based upon elements of a traditional Requiem Mass, Howells wrote this piece following his own personal tragedy – the death of his son.

Listening selection

Requiem aeternam

Howells' compositions were often influenced by traditional Church modes and the opening of this movement suggests the dorian mode based upon E. This use of modality can be heard throughout the work, including in the opening 'Preludio'. Other features include the use of the pentatonic scale at the end of the 'Sanctus' and the chromatic alterations in the tenor solo at the opening of 'I Heard a Voice from Heaven'.

Erwartung

Erwartung is a one-act opera in four scenes, lasting around half-an-hour. It employs a large orchestra and solo soprano.

'Da kommt ein Licht!' (Scene 3)

Schoenberg's harmonic language in this work is atonal – there is no governing key centre. It marks an extreme point in his development of a style that later became known as expressionism. Listen to the opening of this track, and note the thin, ethereal textures of the strings and woodwind accompaniment. This helps depict the woman approaching the edge of the forest. Her terror is reinforced by the highly 'athematic' sense of the vocal melodies – not only do they lack a tonal shape, but the composer avoids any discernible repetition or logical structuring of ideas. Listen also for hints of *Sprechstimme* (around 0:22 on the Naxos recording), a vocal technique that characterised *Pierrot Lunaire*.

Available on: *Schoenberg: Pelleas und Melisande/Erwartung*, conducted by Robert Craft, Naxos 8.557527.

Listening selection

Further listening

George Gershwin: *'S Wonderful – Songs Of George Gershwin*, Naxos Nostalgia, 8.120828.

Sprechstimme is a vocal technique which falls between speaking and singing.

Accompaniment

The works considered thus far have used orchestral or large instrumental ensembles as their accompaniment. However, composers used a range of other accompaniment resources in the repertoire of this period. The accompaniment has the power to add a great deal of expressive colour to vocal music, and you should look carefully for instances of this in your exam extract.

Here are a number of questions to consider:

➢ What instrument(s) are in the accompanying texture?

➢ Is the accompanying texture homophonic or contrapuntal and does it change?

➢ How does the accompaniment use musical features such as melody, harmony, dynamics, and timbre to convey expressively the sense of the text?

Works to explore:

On Wenlock Edge (1909) by Ralph Vaughan Williams

Chansons Gaillardes (1925–1926) by Francis Poulenc

Ralph Vaughan Williams (1872–1958) was an English composer who made a particular feature of native folk music in his work. Francis Poulenc (1899–1963) was a French composer and member of a group of French and Swiss composers called 'Les Six'.

On Wenlock Edge

This works employs a solo tenor, piano and string quartet.

'From far, from eve and morning'

This is the second song in this cycle of six settings. Listen to the way in which Vaughan Williams uses the instruments of the accompaniment. The poem is in three stanzas; the first stanza and the second half of the final stanza feature the tenor and

Available on: *On Wenlock Edge / Five Mystical Songs* (English Song, Vol. 3), Naxos 8.557114.

Listening selection

pianist alone. At these points the vocal style is recitative-like with the piano adding occasional arpeggiated chords by way of accompaniment. The second stanza employs the full string quartet and the instruments are used to create a continuous veil of sound which is suddenly broken at the word 'say'.

Chansons Gaillardes

This work uses a voice (normally baritone) and piano.

'Madrigal'

The third song in this cycle of eight, *Chansons Gaillardes* (Ribald Songs) is a mixture of tongue-in-cheek reverence and downright bawdiness. This very short poem contains both and Poulenc produces a concise setting that lasts just over 30 seconds. Listen for the instrumental effects used in the piano. These include scalic flourishes, staccato chords, trills, grace notes and rapid repeated notes – all across a wide range of the instrument, which emphasise the irreverent and witty nature of the text.

Available on: *Poulenc Melodies*, Naxos, 8.553642.

Listening selection

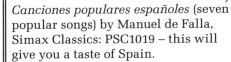

Further listening

Canciones populares españoles (seven popular songs) by Manuel de Falla, Simax Classics: PSC1019 – this will give you a taste of Spain.

Interpretation

As part of this task, you may be asked to comment upon the performers' interpretation of the piece you are given. This relates synoptically to your own performing awareness and your ability to make critical judgements about the performances of others. For this type of exercise, you should study as much detail in the score as possible, and then evaluate how the performers interpret it. Try to become familiar with the main score terminology (for example, dynamics, tempo markings and other performance directions) as this will help you tackle this question more confidently. Here are some issues to consider:

➤ The tempo markings – look at the initial one and notice if it changes

➤ Do the performers use any rubato?

➤ Look at the dynamics and other performance markings – how do the performers respond?

➤ Does the singer use tone quality in an expressive way?

➤ Does the singer highlight or dwell upon any words – perhaps for expressive effect?

➤ Does the singer bring anything else to the performance that is not explicitly instructed in the score?

Further reading

The Pimlico Dictionary of Twentieth-Century Composers by Mark Morris (ISBN: 978-0712665681, Pimlico 1999).

The World of Twentieth-Century Music, edited by David Ewen (ISBN: 978-0709043980, Hale publishing 1991).

Exercise 2

Look at the following vocal extract from the beginning of the fifth movement of Mahler's *Das Lied von der Erde* (The Song of the Earth). This is a large-scale work for two vocalists and orchestra written in 1908–1909.

Try to absorb as much detail as possible from this vocal part. Then aim to listen to one or two recordings to observe how they differ in interpretation and consider the questions listed *opposite*.

Two contrasting ones would be:

➤ Charles Kullman's 1930s recording, available on the Naxos Historical label, 8.110850

➤ Thomas Harper's more contemporary Naxos recording, 8.550933.

A translation of the text is given below:

If life is only a dream,	And when I can drink no more,
why then the misery and torment?	because my stomach and soul are full,
I drink until I can drink no more,	I stagger to my door
the whole, dear day!	and sleep very well!

The melody of this drinking song contains a wealth of dynamic, articulation, and tempo detail. However, there is also considerable opportunity for singers to demonstrate a personal approach through their interpretation. For example, note the differing approaches to bars 9–10 in the two recordings above. Kullman's interpretation is far broader and more emphatic of the words 'I drink until I can drink no more'; Harper meanwhile does not make a great deal of the accents marked on each note.

Topic 1: Song

Song refers to a piece of music for a single voice or multiple voices which may also be accompanied by one or more instruments. There is evidence that song (at least in some form) existed in the ancient cultures, for example those of Rome, Greece and Mesopotamia. However, prior to the advent of notation systems, these existed in a purely oral context – passed down from generation to generation by word of mouth. The development of notation enabled composers to produce a written record of their work, but inevitably this led to a divergence between the 'folk-song' and 'art-song' repertories – the latter tending to become increasingly sophisticated.

The selection of works defined by OCR for this topic gives us a series of snapshots across nearly four hundred years. First, into Elizabethan England at the end of the 16th century with songs by Dowland; secondly, German Romanticism in the 19th century with Schumann's masterpiece *Dichterliebe*. And finally, 1960s England with Peter Maxwell Davies, and the various theatrical associations that he encompasses within his work, *Eight Songs for a Mad King*.

All three of the set works demonstrate a sympathetic relationship between music and words – albeit in very different ways. The musical interpretation of the text therefore becomes a starting point for our study of song and the specification outlines a number of ways in which this may be observed. You are expected to look at different ways in which the voice is used – something that becomes particularly fascinating with Maxwell Davies' composition. The role of the accompaniment is also singled out for study and the three set works are equally diverse in this area. We move from Dowland's lute, through Schumann's piano, to Maxwell Davies' more esoteric ensemble of wind, string, keyboard and percussion instrumentalists.

The Scottish essayist and historian Thomas Carlyle suggested that 'all deep things are song. It seems somehow the very central essence of us.' The considerable inspiration that can be derived from a good text has fuelled composers' musical imaginations for at least three thousand years.

> If you have chosen this topic, you may also wish to relate it to your composing unit of study. An obvious link would be to explore the 'Keyboard accompaniments in early Romantic style' option and this would give you first-hand experience of the tonality and keyboard textures as a background to Schumann's output.

The First Booke of Songes

John Dowland was an English composer and lute player born into the Elizabethan period – probably in 1563 – though this cannot be verified for certain. His admiration for Queen Elizabeth I led to a number of attempts to gain patronage at her royal court. However, he did not achieve such a post in London until 1612, when he was offered work as a lutenist for James I. Much of his life was spent working in various aristocratic appointments in France,

> A lute is a plucked string instrument which has six strings or pairs of strings known as *courses* and frets a semitone apart. It was one of the most popular instruments in the late Renaissance and early Baroque periods.

Germany and Denmark. It was shortly before his offer of work in Denmark that he published *The First Booke of Songes or Ayres of Foure Partes with Tabelture for the Lute* in 1597, and it was an outstanding success, confirming his position at the forefront of English musical life.

The First Booke was reprinted at least four times between its first publication and 1613, and was published in a style used by later sets of lute songs. Previously, a composer may have compiled four separate partbooks, with each separate book containing the music for one voice or instrument. However, the 'table-book format' solved the problems of combining lute and staff notations in a printed collection and allowed for a variety of different domestic performance possibilities (see example *right*). They can be performed by one person singing the vocal line while accompanying themselves on the lute. Alternatively, they can be sung by a group of singers (as a part-song), with instruments such as viols replacing or reinforcing any of the vocal parts.

The edition that you use should show the lute tablature underneath the vocal part. It would be helpful to use an edition that also shows a piano version of the lute part, so that you can easily play and sing through some of the songs. While you will not be expected to interpret lute tablature, it is useful to understand how the notation works.

The beginning of the first song in your edition may look similar to the example shown *right*.

There is a C clef printed before the vocal stave. This shows that Dowland's original manuscript used this clef and that the music has therefore been transcribed into the more familiar treble clef by a modern editor. These 'movable C-clefs' work in exactly the same way as the modern alto and tenor clefs: the middle point of the clef (where the two semi-circles join) indicates middle C.

The lute part looks rather more formidable but it is not hard to understand. Like guitar tablature, the lute tablature tells you which string and fret to play. Dowland, in his youth, would have learned to play a lute with six pairs of strings (called *courses*) that would be tuned to the notes shown *right*.

Each line on the lute tablature represents one of the six courses, the top line showing the highest-pitched course. A seventh course sometimes appears below the tablature (Dowland's songs often require this seventh course), using what you would recognise as a leger line. The letters 'a' to 'f' tell the lute player which fret to put their finger behind. The letter 'a' means that the string should be played unfretted, 'b' is the first fret, 'c' is the second fret and so on. In older editions, the 'c' may look like an 'r'.

Finally, the flags above the lute tablature show the relative rhythms used in the piece. A single flag represents a note that has been transcribed as a minim; two flags shows a crotchet and a three flags indicates quavers. (If there is no flag, then the previous note length is repeated.) This is not an exhaustive guide to lute tablature, but should allow you to gain a basic understanding of the notation.

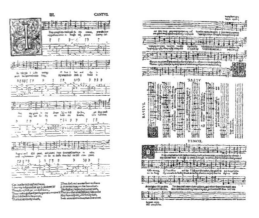

Understanding the score

The edition used for this study is published by Stainer and Bell, edited by Edmund H. Fellows and revised by Thurston Dart.

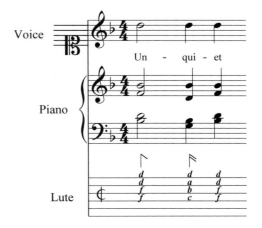

Pitches of the six courses

Structure All of Dowland's songs in *The First Booke* are strophic, that is they use the same music for each verse. Song composers of the time favoured a simple verse structure that was effectively AABB. The second half of the song was normally enclosed by repeat marks, which often resulted in the final couplet being sung twice. While Dowland ventured beyond this simple structure on occasions, it can be seen clearly in the 13th song 'Sleep Wayward Thoughts'. The first two lines of the stanza are set to the following musical idea:

Sleep Wayward Thoughts

The third and fourth lines use the same music as above. The fifth and sixth lines of the stanza are set to a fresh musical idea, but are repeated to give the feel of an eight-line verse.

In contrast, in the first song of the collection, 'Unquiet Thoughts', the first half of the verse is set in a more through-composed manner. There is no repetition of musical ideas, forming one longer A section. The second half follows the convention of repeating the fifth and sixth lines of the verse.

Rhythm and dance forms Many of Dowland's songs use elements from contemporary dances, such as the Galliard, for example in the fourth song of the collection, 'If My Complaints Could Passions Move'. The clear triple-time metre, regular four-bar phrases and the stereotypical dotted rhythm in bar 3 (all features of the Galliard) can be heard in the opening to this song. However, if we are expecting Dowland to be entirely predictable in his approach to rhythm, then the second line comes as a surprise.

If My Complaints Could Passions Move

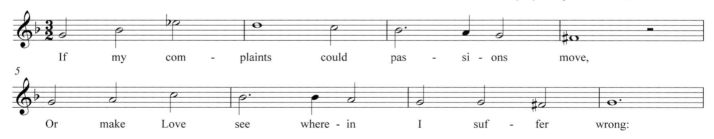

In bars 6–7, the natural emphasis on the first beat of the bar is disrupted, creating what modern ears would hear as a hemiola. Effectively, bars 6–7 are articulated as if they were notated as three bars of duple metre, instead of two bars of triple metre.

Dowland's manipulation of rhythm in this way gives rhythmic variety to his songs and becomes strongly characteristic of his style. Although time signatures were rarely used to indicate changes, duple or quadruple rhythms were often inserted into a triple-time metre, to reflect the natural speech rhythms of the words. The effect occurs in the first phrase of 'Sleep, Wayward Thoughts' (see example *opposite*) and, perhaps more dramatically in the eighth song 'Burst Forth, My Tears':

Burst Forth, My Tears

Burst, burst forth,___ my tears, as - sit my for - ward grief

And show what pain im - pe - rious Love pro - vokes,

The song begins with a duple metre, though this is immediately destabilised with the syncopation of the second bar. Bars 3–4 insert a triple metre into the song; these rhythms reflect the natural stress of the text suggesting Dowland's sensitivity to the word setting.

The word-setting convention of the time was to set text line by line, and Dowland does not break this mould. His musical phrases largely correspond to the lines of the stanzas, but his rhythmic inventiveness take us beyond mere predictability. The second half of the first song, 'Unquiet Thoughts', contains two such rhythmic features:

Unquiet Thoughts

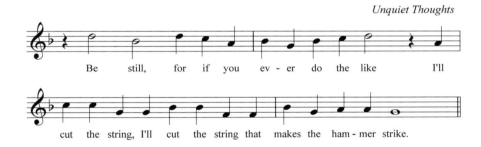

Be still, for if you ev - er do the like I'll

cut the string, I'll cut the string that makes the ham - mer strike.

The words 'be still' appear on two minims, syncopated across the prevailing metre and the four crotchets on 'makes the hammer' are expressively descriptive of the text.

Harmony and tonality

Although Dowland's songs pre-date the establishment of the tonal system, which governed music from the late 17th century onwards there are chord progressions and cadences that define major and minor keys. However, modal touches are still prominent as well as the use of false relations and tierce de Picardie.

Although 'Unquiet Thoughts' is given a key signature of a single B♭, the music leans towards the key of G minor. Up until the 18th century this was common practice: in minor keys the sixth (in this case the E♭) is usually indicated by accidentals rather than in the key signature. Consequently, minor keys have a signature of one less flat than we would use today. The feeling of ambiguity between tonic major and minor is created by his use of false relations and tierce de Picardie – two of the most common features of the late Renaissance style.

False relation: is a chromatic contradiction between two notes sounded simultaneously and in different parts. For example a G♮ against a G♯.

Tierce de Picardie: is a major 3rd in the final tonic chord of a passage in a minor mode.

Come Heavy Sleep

Texture and lute accompaniment

The accompaniment is shown as a piano score, so you can easily play through and understand the different textures.

The penultimate song of the collection 'Come Heavy Sleep' refers to a plea for 'Sleep' (a metaphor for death) to come and release the protagonist's 'tired soul'. It is the movement between G major (at the end of the first section) and B major (at the start of the second), which is dramatically effective. If the point has not already been made to the listener, Dowland makes it even more insistent by strumming the B major chord seven times in this bar see *left*.

There is a wealth of interest in Dowland's lute accompaniments, and his mastery of the accompaniment is generally sympathetic to the melodic line, his lute parts show varying degrees of intricacy. 'Now, O Now, I Needs Must Part' is largely homophonic, and the melody and chords move in similar rhythms:

Now, O Now, I Needs Must Part

'Come, Heavy Sleep', which has already been discussed for its tonality, has a much more intricate accompanying lute part. There is real independence in each line of the lute texture and this can be heard in the first two bars. Later in the song, Dowland introduces a rhythmically recurring idea that drives forward the second section of the stanza:

Come, Heavy Sleep

Related repertoire

Your choice of related repertoire should be drawn from the considerable body of music produced by Italian and English madrigal composers. It should also extend to music for the solo lute and English consort music. You are expected to show an awareness of the influence exerted on the English madrigal tradition by its Italian counterpart.

Madrigals are musical settings of secular Italian or English verse, often about love or in a pastoral setting. The lute song is effectively a simplified version of the madrigal. It attempts a more lyrical rendering of the text than the madrigal could achieve with its more intricate polyphonic textures. In England, the lute song eventually superseded the madrigal in terms of its popularity in the 17th century. The madrigal, however, enjoyed a spectacular flowering in the 16th and early 17th centuries, especially in Italy and England.

The relationship of the lute song to the madrigal

In Italy, Andrea Gabrieli (c. 1532–1585) and his nephew Giovanni (c. 1555–1612) were both important exponents of the form. Their composition led to a visual form of word painting on occasions, where the notation suggested something about the text. For example, a pair of consecutive semibreves might be used to depict 'eyes' or the use of 'white' or 'black' notation to suggest a particular mood. As none of this could be detected aurally, it suggests an emphasis on a performing culture for the repertoire, rather than a purely listening one. Infact, most Italian madrigals were written for professional singers, while the English tended to write for the amateur market.

The Italian madrigal

Although Carlo Gesualdo (c. 1561–1613) had a reputation that partly rests on his fame as a murderer, he is also remembered as a highly original composer. His experiments with chromatic juxtapositions, particularly in his madrigals, can be as striking today as they were unorthodox for the time. They are almost always related to his concern for expressing the text, and these unrelated chords can often be found under words such as 'pain' and 'death'.

Gesualdo

Gesualdo's madrigal, *Moro, lasso, al mio duolo* (1611), is a striking example of the composer's use of chromaticism. The opening phrase moves in homophony through a series of harmonically unrelated chords: C♯ major – A minor (first inversion) – B major – G major (first inversion) with some passing dissonance in the inner parts – G major root position – E major. The meandering harmonic juxtapositions effectively paint the text which refers to 'death' and 'suffering' at this point. This is contrasted with more playful, imitative, diatonic writing where the text moves to the words 'and she who could give me life'. The relationship between these two different musical textures and harmonic styles is then developed through the remainder of the madrigal.

In England, Henry VIII's Act of Supremacy had divorced the country from the Papacy in 1534. Its religious isolation from Rome was also reflected musically and there was little continental

The English madrigal

influence upon England at this time. However, by the 1580s there was a renewed interest in Italian music, and it was in England that the Italian madrigal was to have its greatest influence. An important English publication of this time was a collection of madrigals known as **Musica Transalpina**. It was published in 1588 by Nicholas Yonge of St Paul's choir and contained a number of madrigals by Marenzio, Palestrina and others. Crucially, it also provided English translations to the verse, which became a great stimulus to composers who may have otherwise been deterred from setting the texts.

Two of the most important exponents of the English madrigal were Thomas Morley (c. 1557–1602) and Thomas Weelkes (c. 1575–1623). We will use a madrigal by each of these composers to give an overview of the English madrigal tradition:

My Bonny Lass She Smileth by Thomas Morley

In Pride of May by Thomas Weelkes

Morley's *My Bonny Lass* is a lighter type of madrigal that again originated in Italy and that was known in England as a **ballett**. It is characterised by a light, dance-like style and fa-la-la refrains. This particular example comes from a collection of balletts published in 1595 (in both English and Italian versions) that Morley adapted from a set by the Italian composer Gastoldi, published four years earlier.

Scores for both of these works can both be found in *Invitation to Madrigals 7*, edited by E. H. Fellowes (Stainer and Bell).

Ballett is pronounced like cassette, not like ballet (bal-ay), even though both words are clearly related to dancing.

My Bonny Lass She Smileth

The dance rhythms are immediately apparent from the opening with the rhythm of the first two bars repeated in bars 3–4. The opening texture is homophonic and the rhythm of the music imitates the natural accentuation of the words.

The structure of Morley's ballett is uncomplicated with two sections, both repeated, forming each stanza. The ballett as a whole is strophic. But one of the hallmarks of the genre is the 'fa-la-la' refrain and this dominates the second half of each section. It also provides contrast in the texture, with Morley employing a more contrapuntal style at this point. The final 'fa-la-la' refrain of the stanza is significant in its change of metre, moving from duple to triple time.

Tonally, the madrigal is rooted in G major, but there are many splashes of modality and frequent false relations between F♮/F♯ and C♮/C♯. In fact, the original would have been written without a key signature, the sharps inserted as required by the performers – a practice known as **musica ficta**.

Weelkes' madrigal *In Pride of May* (1598), also in the ballett style, shows a more sophisticated contrapuntal style. The opening four bars use two different motifs, the first imitated between the two soprano parts and the second imitated from tenor to alto:

Musica ficta is a highly complex subject, but in its simplest terms refers to the fact that musical sources pre-1600 rarely indicated all the intended accidentals and it was up to performers to insert them. Modern editors will frequently show their 'best guess' over the accidentals in the music. Sometimes they will be inserted as sharp/flat/natural symbols above the note, rather than to the left of it.

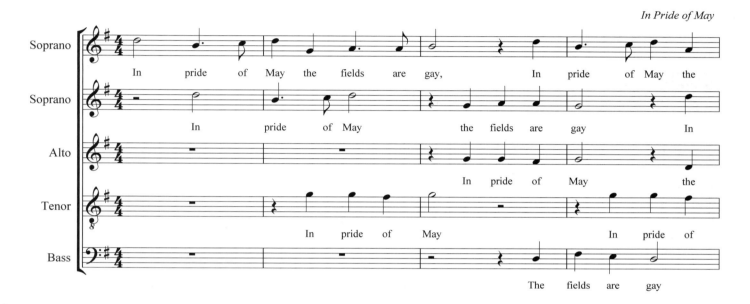

In Pride of May

The bass finally joins these two motifs together in bars 6–9. Weelkes shares Morley's enthusiasm for rhythmic shifts – the second half of the stanza has two bars inserted in triple time.

Both Morley and Weelkes use dissonance in a highly expressive way to illuminate words within the text and to drive forward the harmony through the use of suspensions. The perfect cadence at the end of Weelkes' ballet shows the characteristic use of a suspension in this later Renaissance style. The note G in the second part down is 'prepared' (marked P) by sounding as part of a chord of G major. This note hangs on while the chord changes, creating the suspension (marked S) – notice the prominent clash between G and A in the two upper parts. This dissonance resolves (marked R) when the G falls to the F♯, where it forms part of the chord of D major.

The specification suggests you listen to some examples of English Consort Music. The term consort music refers to music for vocal or instrumental 'consorts' (collections of a particular instrument, for example a consort of viols).

English Consort Music

Although Byrd is most renowned for his religious works, he also produced a large body of instrumental work and secular song, perhaps driven by a burgeoning demand for domestic music. Byrd – who held a patent for publishing his own music – produced a set of *Psalmes, Sonets and Songs* in 1588. Although they were scored for a solo singer and consort of four viols, the composer later rescored them for a vocal consort of five – perhaps jumping on the bandwagon of the madrigal's popularity.

One of Byrd's better-known individual consort songs – *Fair Britain Isle* (1612) – was written as an elegy to mourn Henry, Prince of Wales, the eldest son of King James I. The song is written in two fairly lengthy verses and the latter section of each is repeated. The contrapuntal dexterity of Byrd's Mass is also evident here. The polyphonic texture of the accompanying viols is sophisticated and frequently gives them great independence from the solo voice. However, they also come together in support of the soloist at crucial moments of the text, for example 'by Death's', 'in moment of one hour', 'of virtues', and 'that with thee died'. This serves to highlight the key words of the text and reinforce its gravitas.

Further listening

A recording of *Fair Britain Isle* is available on*: Byrd: Consort and Keyboard Music / Songs and Anthems*, Naxos 8.550604.

Exercise 3

1. In what ways did Dowland's accompaniments help express the sense of the text?

2. How did the English madrigal composers differ in style from their Italian counterparts during this period?

Further reading

John Dowland by Diana Poulton (ISBN: 978-0520046498, University of California Press 1992).

English Song: Dowland to Purcell by Ian Spink (ISBN: 978-0800823962, Taplinger Publishing Company 1986).

Dichterliebe

The song cycle became an increasingly important genre for 19th-century Romantic composers. It was distinct from earlier song collections, in its grouping of songs by a common theme, the verse usually written by one poet. Coherence could also be given through the use of poetic narrative, planned key schemes and repetition of material. The first important song cycle to achieve this was Beethoven's *An die ferne Geliebte* (1815–1816) and it was quickly followed by others, with particularly important contributions from Schubert and Schumann.

Schumann finally married his long-term love, Clara Wieck, in 1840 and he composed a spectacular number of songs in the same year – around 150 in total. Schumann's output in this industrious year (sometimes called his *Liederjahr* – 'Year of Song') included his great song cycle *Dichterliebe* ('A Poet's Love') set to verse by Heinrich Heine (1797–1856). The song cycle tells of a love that fails, and Schumann seemed to find a natural affinity in Heine's pained poetry. In fact, the composer's own personal life had been far from straightforward: syphilis, deep depression, suicidal tendencies and a refusal from Clara's father to give consent to their marriage. Having composed very little in 1839, it seemed natural for the realisation of his marriage to coincide with such a creative surge.

As a music critic, Schumann had regular opportunity to articulate his own aspirations as a composer. With Lieder, his emphasis was firmly upon the expression of the text and in his opinion a song should strive 'to recreate in a subtle musical realisation the most delicate effects of the poem'. There are many instances in *Dichterliebe* where Schumann uses musical means to highlight poetic imagery. He may achieve this through the shape of the vocal line, his use of tonality, musical structures, the piano accompaniment – or a mixture of all of these.

Tonality

Schumann's adventurous use of tonality can be seen in the first song of the cycle, 'Im wunderschönen Monat Mai', where the fragmentary sense of the poem is mirrored in what sounds like an incomplete musical structure. The song ends on an unresolved dominant-7th chord, and Schumann's lack of closure leaves Classical traditions firmly behind.

Listen carefully to this first song, and consider the following points about the tonality:

➤ The opening key is not clearly established. Although F♯ minor might be suggested by the key signature and early appearance of the E♯s, the music has no perfect cadences in this key

➤ The opening arpeggio figure is based around chord IVb, but is decorated by an appoggiatura and an augmented 5th within it (the A♯). It then moves to an unresolved dominant 7th in bar 2 (C♯–E♯–G♯–B)

➤ The vocal phrases are short and many sound unresolved (e.g. bar 10 and bar 12)

Dichterliebe opens with the poet's declaration of love in springtime, but this love is rejected and the latter part of the cycle deals with his exclusion from all things beautiful in nature. The final song refers to him burying his love and sorrows in a coffin and hurling it out to sea.

> The final vocal phrase also seems unresolved and the brief piano postlude further undermines the harmonic stability.

The words at the end of the poem 'Mein Sehnen und Verlangen' (My longing and desire) suggest an open-endedness that Schumann reinforces with his choice of harmony:

Im wunderschönen Monat Mai (bars 22–26)

The lack of clear-cut tonality in this first song contrasts markedly with the apparent decisiveness of the sixth song, 'Im Rhein, im heiligen Strome'. This song begins with the tonic (E) sounded in both the vocal line and piano accompaniment, followed by the outline of the tonic arpeggio, suggesting a more diatonic approach. The song also contrasts from earlier Lieder in the cycle with its lower vocal range, louder dynamics and fewer suspensions and appoggiaturas:

Im Rhein, im heiligen Strome (bars 1–4)

The text of this song is about the mighty river Rhine that flows past the great cathedral of Cologne, which Schumann depicts with solemn dotted rhythms in E minor, and sonorous octaves in the bass of the piano part.

Although there is a good deal of diatonic harmony in the song, there are also glimpses of Schumann's more adventurous chromatic style. The move from a root-position G major chord to a second-inversion E♭ major chord in bar 27 is striking. This is followed by a series of chromatic shifts in the right hand of the piano, above pedal notes in the bass.

There is also a mixture of diatonic and chromatic writing in the final song of the cycle, 'Die alten, bösen Lieder'. The song opens with a tonic chord in the key of C♯ minor, followed by octaves in dotted rhythms that perhaps refer back to 'Im Rhein'. It is noteworthy that the harmony of the first stanza is restricted to the primary triads – chords I, IV and V. A significant turning point in the harmony are the striking diminished-7th chords in bar 39 and 40. This change in rhythm, piano texture and harmony perhaps suggests the casting of the coffin into the sea.

Following the perfect cadence in bars 42–43, the harmonic language is not 'functional' in the traditional tonal sense. Schumann alternates dominant 7ths and diminished 7ths in unorthodox inversions, while the bass line of the piano follows the vocal part in octaves. The contents of the coffin, hinted at in the second stanza are now revealed (the poet's 'love and suffering') and the dark, directionless quality of the harmony seems entirely fitting for the poet's renunciation of love. Schumann again uses an appoggiatura at a key textual moment – this time to highlight the word 'Liebe' (love) in bar 49. This device has also been used to highlight the word 'Herzen' (heart) in the first song.

The final section, with its fifteen $\frac{6}{4}$ bars of solo piano writing, demonstrates Schumann's innovations in the role of the accompaniment. A passage of music for piano at the end of a song is known as a piano postlude, and Schumann frequently places great emphasis on their importance. They may have a role in providing some commentary or after-thought on the song or indeed, as in this case, on the whole song cycle.

The music of this postlude is not new to listeners of the whole cycle. In fact it is closely based upon the 12th song 'Am leuchtenden Sommermorgen' (On a radiant summer morning). In this song, the poet walks sadly in a garden and imagines that the flowers are whispering to him not to be angry with 'our sister' – a reference to the poet's beloved. Therefore the return of this music at the end of the cycle evokes further yearning memories that suggest Schumann's own interpretation of the poetry. It also shows the importance placed upon the piano as an equal in the partnership between vocalist and accompanist.

Dichterliebe's composition falls towards the end of a period that had seen considerable advances in the development of the piano. Both composers and performers wanted a more powerful, sustained sound and increased range that was made possible

The role of the piano and text expression

by technological developments precipitated by the industrial revolution. The piano also became a popular piece of domestic furniture and many sociable evenings of song, chamber and piano music were enjoyed around the instrument.

Schumann uses a wealth of piano textures in *Dichterliebe* and it is the accompaniment that frequently aids the illustration of the poem's text. Song No. 7, 'Ich Grolle Nicht' is one of the most immediately appealing of the cycle and its repeating quaver pattern sets up a piano figuration that is maintained throughout the song – a common technique for Schumann. The boldness of the piano part conveys the apparent confidence of the poet, claiming that he 'bear[s] no grudge'. However, Schumann's decision to repeat these words six times (compared to twice in the poem) suggests a level of irony in the composer's interpretation of the text. Perhaps he feels that the poet really does bear a grudge after all, given his need to express the line repeatedly.

The piano adds a good deal of chromatic colour and sonority to this song. For example, the word 'Herz' (heart) in bar 3 is coloured by a chromatic chord, which makes it stand out from the surrounding diatonic harmony. The left hand is mostly written in octaves, using some of the lowest notes available on the piano – exploiting rich sonorities that were still a novelty in the first half of the 19th century. In fact the accompaniment is so rich that you should be careful not to overlook the melodic line itself. Melodically, it is one of the highpoints of the cycle and many recordings will utilise the ossia in bars 27–29. This takes the melody to its highest range in the cycle and it is a dramatic moment of musical climax.

Schumann's instincts as a composer for the piano can also be seen in the next song, 'Und wüssten's die Blumen die kleinen' ('And if the flowers knew...'). The images of nature become comforters in the poet's grief and they are seen as decorative pictures to which Schumann responds with broken, fluttering chords and a quaver melody in the right and left hands:

Und wüssten's die Blumen (bars 28–29)

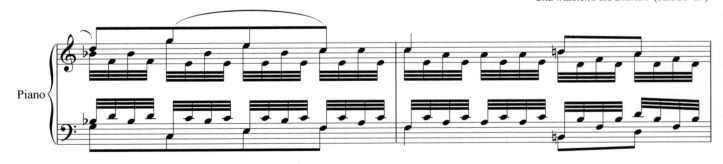

This shows the increased capacity of the piano's tone production – a melody can be projected from within this busy broken chord figuration.

Schumann once suggested that 'simpler feelings require simpler keys'. The profound emotions of the 13th song, 'Ich hab' im Traum geweinet' (I cried in my dreams) have a musical setting in the suitably complicated key of E♭ minor. However, perhaps the most dramatic feature of this song is its relationship between vocalist and pianist. The two do not perform together during the first two stanzas, instead alternating short musical fragments, separated by rests and occasionally a fermata (pause):

Ich hab' im Traum geweinet (bars 1–7)

The vocal range is narrow and the piano part is written at a low tessitura. The overwhelming mood is one of pessimism, despair and bitterness. The singer and pianist are not joined harmonically until the third stanza and this change in texture coincides with the briefest moment of optimism in the poem ('I dreamed that you still loved me'). Schumann does not include a fully worked-out postlude in this song. Instead there is some 'residue' of the preceding material separated by dramatic moments of silence.

> The first vocal motif of song No. 13 covers a range of just one semitone. Compare this musical idea with the opening of Song No. 2, 'Aus meinen Thränen spriessen' and note also the similarity of the subject matter. Song No. 2 refers to 'tears' while in song No. 13 the poet 'cried in my dream'.

Related repertoire

Your related repertoire should be drawn from the huge wealth of Lieder composed in the early 19th century and should also include some character pieces for piano from the same period.

The other dominating force in Lieder during this period was **Franz Schubert** (1797–1828) who, despite his short life, composed over 600 Lieder. They demonstrate his supreme ability as a melodist, his harmonic imagination and his skill for writing highly inventive piano accompaniments. A number of his songs are organised into song-cycles, examples being *Die Schöne Müllerin*, *Winterreise* and *Schwanengesang*, a collection published posthumously. Other songs stand alone as individual masterpieces, an excellent example being *Erlkönig*, which is a vivid dramatic rendering of Goethe's poem.

Winterreise (Winter Journey*)*, composed in 1827, is a cycle of 24 songs for tenor voice and piano, using poetry by Wilhelm Müller. The poet tells the story in the first person and he describes a long and woeful winter journey where the cold and barren landscapes mirror the feelings of his own heart. The themes of lost love,

Winterreise

loneliness and landscapes are fundamental to the cycle, as they are within much German Romantic Lieder.

As you listen to this song-cycle, consider Schubert's approach to word setting, tonality and the role of the piano accompaniment. An example for each of these is given as a starting point for your exploration.

The third song of the cycle, 'Gefrorne Tränen', uses a wide vocal range, with different tessituras representing the different moods of the narrator. 'El Tränen, meine Tränen' (O tears, my tears) is set at the lowest point of the range and uses just two notes, a semitone apart. This suggests the bleakness and despair in the poet's mind and the piano reinforces this by tracking the vocal line in octaves:

Gefrorne Tränen (bars 20–21)

A greater sense of determination is seen at the end of the poem with the words referring to the melting of 'des ganzen Winters Eis' (all winter's ice). Not only does Schubert repeat the text several times, but he sets the final part of the vocal line at the top of the singer's range.

'Auf dem Flusse' (No. 7) contains some striking harmonic innovations. The song begins in E minor, but at the mention of the 'stillness' of the river, the key slips effortlessly into D♯ minor. Schubert further highlights this anomaly by using a second-inversion chord (bar 9). This song also contains one of Schubert's favourite devices – shifts between major and minor tonality. The third stanza 'In deine Dekke' sees the introduction of the poet's lover into the narrative, and the music fittingly moves into the tonic major. The piano accompaniment is also particularly imaginative in this song. The figuration becomes increasingly complicated as it proceeds.

The relationship between singer and pianist is crucial to Romantic Lieder and Schubert's *Winterreise* is a highpoint in this. In the final song of the cycle ('Die Leiermann' – No. 24), the poet describes a lonely hurdy-gurdy player grinding out sad songs. Schubert uses the piano to play a drone bass (a 5th interval on the notes A and E) throughout the whole song, in order to evoke the sound of the hurdy-gurdy. The vocal phrases are all short and interspersed with a repetitive wistful 'hurdy-gurdy' tune in the piano part. The alternation between singer and pianist draws parallels between the hurdy-gurdy player and the sad, lonely narrator – no one is listening to either of them singing their sad songs in the cold. Schubert's piano postlude is economical and gives an unfinished feel, entirely in keeping with the lonely wandering of the singer throughout the cycle.

For a more in depth study on the use of vocal range to suggest mood or character, listen to *Erlkönig* by Schubert.

To explore Schubert's use of tonality further, listen to 'Der Doppelgänger' from *Schwanengesang*. Schubert uses an unorthodox harmonic progression as a repeated ostinato for the accompaniment. His piano textures are sparse and ghostly, in keeping with the supernatural sense of the poem.

Exercise 4

1. Comment on Schumann's expressive use of accompaniment in *Dichterliebe*.

2. Compare and contrast Schumann's word-setting techniques with one other 19th-century composer of Lieder.

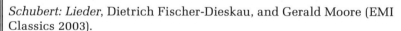

Further reading

Schumann: Dichterliebe (ISBN: 978-0393099041, Norton Critical Score 1971), edited by Arthur Komar – an authoritative edition for study of the song cycle, with a good deal of introductory material and commentary on the individual songs.

Nineteenth-century German Lied by Lorraine Gorrell (ISBN: 978-1574671230, Amadeus Press 2005).

The Cambridge Companion to Schubert (ISBN: 978-0521484244, CUP 2008) by Christopher H. Gibbs.

Schumann's Dichterliebe and Early Romantic Poetics: Fragmentation of Desire, by Beate Julia Perrey (ISBN: 978-0521042451, CUP 2008). A very in-depth and philosophical account of the song cycle for students who want to explore the set work deeper.

Further listening

Schubert: Lieder, Dietrich Fischer-Dieskau, and Gerald Moore (EMI Classics 2003).

Schumann: Carnaval; Papillons; Kinderszenen; Arabeske, Nelson Freire (piano) (Decca 2003).

The latter CD contains recordings of three of Schumann's most important collections of piano miniatures. In some ways, these might be considered a form of song cycle without words.

Eight Songs for a Mad King

Eight Songs for a Mad King is a piece of music theatre for male voice and ensemble. The songs are entitled:

1. The Sentry
2. The Country Walk
3. The Lady-in-Waiting
4. To be Sung On The Water
5. The Phantom Queen
6. The Counterfeit
7. Country Dance
8. The Review

The London premiere in 1969 caused something of a scandal in the musical world, not least through its extraordinary use of the human voice.

Peter Maxwell Davies (b. 1934) composed *Eight Songs for a Mad King* in 1969. Like the other two set works within this topic, it is a collection of songs in one volume. However, it is certainly not in a form or style that would have been recognisable to Dowland or Schumann. Normally described as a piece of music theatre – or a monodrama – its libretto was written by Randolph Stow and draws upon quotations from George III. It stems from a period in the composer's life when he was increasingly attracted towards drawing on theatrical elements in his music.

George III's reign of nearly 60 years (October 1760 to January 1820) was only exceeded in length by Queen Victoria, although the last ten years of his reign were spent in seclusion suffering from insanity (his son, later George IV, acted as monarch under the terms of the Regency Act). His latter years were made famous by the 1994 film *The Madness of King George*.

In his introductory note to the work, the librettist, Randolph Stow, describes how the text was inspired by a miniature mechanical organ, once owned by the King. The organ played eight different tunes and was used by George in an attempt to teach his bullfinches to sing. The songs become the King's monologues while he listens to the birds performing, and there are many references to these throughout the work. At its culmination, the drama depicts the King smashing a violin into pieces.

Maxwell Davies' use of vocal technique has precedents in a 1912 work by the German composer, Schoenberg, called *Pierrot Lunaire*. In this work, Schoenberg uses a technique called *Sprechstimme*, (speaking voice) where the voice is no longer used exclusively for the singing of notes. In *Pierrot Lunaire*, the notes are replaced by marks to indicate the pitch of speech. Maxwell Davies goes a number of steps further in his work, employing a notation to depict the effects of speaking, half-speaking, harmonics, chords and overtones. Amid all this is a huge range of whining, screeching and screaming across a range of more than five octaves, which relied heavily on the vocal skill of the actor Roy Hart, for whom the piece was written.

Word setting and vocal techniques

Maxwell Davies employs a wide variety of expressive vocal effects in this work and he developed his own notation for representing them. These notational symbols are shown in the preface to your score and it would be worth becoming familiar with them. There is a close relationship between the vocal setting and the language of the text. Listen for the following examples, and then try to find other instances of expressive word painting yourself:

➢ No. 2: the word 'strangling' (shortly after figure H) is set to a long melisma over a very wide vocal range.

➢ No. 4: a lyrical approach is used for the words 'Sweet Thames flow soft'.

➢ The text 'Deliver me from my people' (also in Song No. 4) uses one of the lowest vocal tessituras in the work.

The range lies well below that of a conventional bass and its anguished, syllabic quality evokes a despairing tone:

To Be Sung On The Water (Song No. 4)

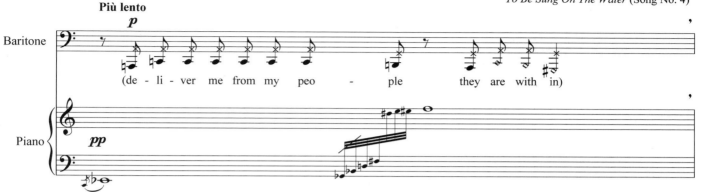

> ➤ The words 'I am all alone' (Song No. 4) have an obvious expressive quality in that there are no accompanying instruments at this point. The vocal line is marked pianissimo and Maxwell Davies indicates that it is to be sung without vibrato. The simplicity and small vocal range suggests the King's loneliness.

> ➤ No. 5 asks the vocalist to 'ululate like a dog'.

> ➤ No. 6 uses a rapid breathing effect in its first words 'I am nervous' to suggest the anxiety of the King.

> ➤ The opening of Song No. 7 uses a further range of theatrical effects where the vocalist is instructed to adopt the manner of a 'female vocalist' and also sing 'like a horse':

Ululation is a long, high-pitched, wavering sound that is practised in various cultures, sometimes for the expression of celebration or grief. It can also be heard in some African music and appears in David Fanshawe's popular choral work *African Sanctus*.

Country Dance (Song No. 7)

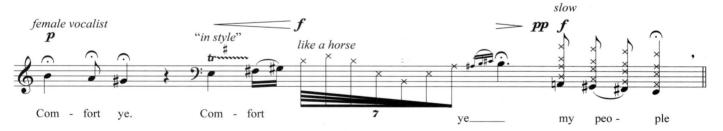

> ➤ There is dramatic irony at the end of Song No. 7. The words 'I shall rule with a rod of iron' is sung in a high-pitched, thin voice.

Instrumental techniques

Maxwell Davies' instrumental textures, techniques and colours contribute vividly to the dramatic effect of this work. It is scored for flute (doubling piccolo), clarinet, piano (doubling harpsichord and dulcimer), violin, cello and percussion. The choice of instrumentation creates further links with Schoenberg's *Pierrot Lunaire*, which as an accompaniment to the voice, used flute/piccolo, clarinet/bass clarinet, violin/viola, cello, and piano. This combination of instruments became known as a 'Pierrot ensemble' and in 1967 Maxwell Davies and Harrison Birtwistle, another contemporary British composer, founded the Pierrot Players. This led to further compositions for this type of ensemble.

The Pierrot Players were renamed The Fires of London in 1970.

Maxwell Davies uses a range of instrumental effects in the *Eight Songs*, including flutter-tonguing on the flute and various imitations of birdsong in Song No. 3, and note clusters for the keyboard in Song No. 6. Another keyboard device can be found in the first song shortly before figure E. The piano is instructed to play a chord 'silently'. The notes are therefore not heard literally, but the dampers are removed from the strings – allowing harmonics to vibrate in sympathy with other notes being played.

One of the most fascinating aspects of this piece is the way in which Maxwell Davies uses the keyboard instruments in such a versatile manner. The keyboard part ranges from a harpsichord, used to provide a continuo (for example the recitative in Song No. 6) to a piano providing its own percussive effects (for example the repeated note clusters in Song No. 7 just before the King destroys the violin).

One of the best examples of this type of dialogue is Song No. 3 – notice the interaction between flute and singer.

Another important element is the interaction between the singer and the instrumentalists. The composer, in his explanatory note, suggests that the instruments can also represent the bullfinches that the King was teaching to sing. This is in addition to their purely accompanimental role. A number of the songs also portray an extended dialogue between the King and individual players.

Drama, quotation and parody

Maxwell Davies himself acknowledges a range of musical quotation used in *Eight Songs*. He refers to aspects of styles of composers 'from Handel to Birtwistle'. The following paragraphs are some examples of quotation or parody that heighten the sense of the drama.

In Song No. 5, Maxwell Davies creates a historically authentic sound, with the harpsichord parodying the Baroque dance styles of the Allemande and Courante.

The Allemande and Courante were standard movements of the Baroque instrumental dance suite. The Allemande was in duple metre and a dance of moderate tempo. The Courante is a triple-metre dance and is normally at a quick tempo – its name literally means 'running'.

Following a highly dissonant recitative (Song No. 6) that uses note clusters on the piano, 'Country Dance' (Song No. 7) is written in a much more tonal style than we have come to expect from this work. The latter borrows a number of elements from Baroque opera, such as the 'chugging' quaver continuo accompaniment and the melismatic vocal line. There are also a number of modern elements such as the chromatic bass line prior to the entry of the vocalist, and the metrical disruption with a $\frac{7}{8}$ bar at the same point. The synthesis of these different historical styles becomes increasingly absurd at the end of the song, when the vocal line parodies an Italian tenor aria:

Country Dance (Song No. 7)

The words 'comfort ye' at the start of Song No. 7 are a direct quotation from Handel's *Messiah* (the aria 'Comfort Ye, My People'). The vocal styles that then transform this passage however, would not have been recognisable to the Baroque composer. This song is perhaps the most eclectic of the entire work. Following the line of vocal recitative, the piano plays a page of pseudo-cocktail lounge music, followed by a country foxtrot which leads to the climax of the piece – the King's smashing of the violin.

The smashing of the violin represents the moment when the King becomes overwhelmed by his own insanity. The final song begins with straightforward rhythmic values for the vocal part leading up to the moment when the King announces his own death. The King is then instructed to recite an extended passage of text 'extremely sanely' and there eventually follows the realisation that he is not dead after all.

The final song makes one further link (through a performance instruction) to the dialogue held with the bird in Song No. 3. The caged birds have been a central dramatic theme for this work; at the original performance this was highlighted by the instrumentalists performing within bamboo cages. This striking piece of theatre suggests that the birds (and hence ensemble) have a dual function – both as captives of the King and as keepers for him in his own 'trapped' condition.

Maxwell Davies' own preface to the edition is essential reading and it will enable you to gain a first-hand awareness of the composers' intentions. This highlights, for example, his attempt to create a 'schizophrenic' effect in Song No. 5 and the rationale for the visual elements in the score. The most obvious manifestation of this is the 'bird-cage notation' in Song No. 3. Perhaps there is an interesting comparison to be made with the visual notation that the early madrigal composers tried to bring to their music.

Related repertoire

Your choice of related repertoire should be based upon songs for solo voice and piano (or instrumental combinations) composed since 1950.

Judith Weir (b. 1954) can be linked with Peter Maxwell Davies in their enthusiasm for Scottish traits in their music (although both composers were born in England, Weir was of Scottish parentage and Maxwell Davies moved to the Orkney Islands in the 1970s). Her song cycle *The Voice of Desire* for mezzo-soprano and piano was composed in 2003. It makes further links with Maxwell

Davies' *Eight Songs for a Mad King* in that all its songs are based upon conversations between humans and birds.

The Voice of Desire

The Voice of Desire is a song cycle containing four songs. Unlike Schumann's *Dichterliebe* it does not use a single poet's collection as its text. Instead, Weir draws upon four different poets: Robert Bridges (1844–1930), a traditional African poem translated by Ulli Beier, Thomas Hardy (1840–1928) and John Keats (1795–1821).

The lack of a common tonal language among composers in the 20th century means that we can expect very different outcomes between Judith Weir's song cycle and Maxwell Davies' *Eight Songs*. Weir draws on a more tonal style throughout the cycle and although there is some dissonance in the final song ('Sweet Little Red Feet'), it is written exclusively using the notes of the aeolian mode.

Weir uses a variety of vocal styles in the song cycle. There is a strong sense of lyricism in the first song ('The Voice of Desire'), and some extensive use of melisma:

The Voice of Desire (bars 25–27)

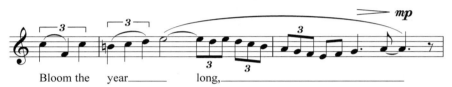

This contrasts with the more syllabic and declamatory style of the final song, while the third song, 'Written on Terrestrial Things', provides a further area of vocal contrast. The performance instruction for this song is 'freely, reflective, thoughtful' and Weir complements this with a recitative-like vocal line. In the first section, the voice is either singing without accompaniment or above a long held chord in the piano. This fits well with the evocation of a barren wintry landscape:

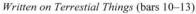

Written on Terrestial Things (bars 10–13)

The use of idiomatic intervals and note-patterns is also worth exploring in this song cycle. It frequently appears to relate to Weir's absorption of the Scottish folk style. Features of traditional Scottish music include the use of 4th intervals, the pentatonic, hexatonic and heptatonic scales and the inclusion of drones (for example in the piano part within song No. 2 – 'White Eggs in the Bush').

A **pentatonic** scale is a five-note scale, most commonly represented by the black notes on the piano keyboard.

A **hexatonic** scale is a six-note scale. This can be created by alternating minor 3rds and semitones within the octave, for example: C–E♭–E–G–G♯–B.

A **heptatonic** scale is a mode or scale based upon seven pitches within the octave, the most common being the major and minor scales.

The use of the 4th interval (and its inversion, the 5th) is particularly distinctive in the first song. It is used to build up chords (for example, the first chord of the song) and also melodic ostinati in the piano accompaniment. The pentatonic scale is also used in the first song and can be seen on the long melismatic setting of the word 'come' (see example *right*).

The Voice of Desire (bar 9)

The hexatonic scale can be found in the third song, for example in bars 22–23. The notes used in these bars are based upon the pattern of alternating minor 3rds and semitones within the octave. The inclusion of the E♮ in bar 24 shifts this towards a heptatonic pattern:

Written on Terrestial Things (bars 22–24)

The accessibility of the tonal language, and the dramatic use of both vocalist and piano accompanist make it an enjoyable starting point for further study around this topic. A particular dramatic highpoint is the second song, with its wide vocal range and exciting rhythmic effects (note the syncopation in the vocal part and the use of hemiola effects interspersing a $\frac{3}{4}$ feel into a $\frac{6}{8}$ time signature).

> Weir's highly approachable song cycle is performed fairly regularly and a recording is available within the Naxos Online Music Library.

Exercise 5

1. A review in the Sunday Telegraph of the first performance of *Eight Songs* read: 'composing madness into the actual technique of music is artistically as self-defeating as portraying a boring operatic character by writing boring music.' Do you think this is a fair assessment of Maxwell Davies' piece?

2. Comment upon ways in which the composers from this topic employ instrumental techniques to complement their word-setting.

3. How do Dowland, Schumann and Maxwell Davies compare and contrast in their approach to word-setting?

Further reading

There is limited reading material available specifically on the *Eight Songs*. For some general perspectives on Maxwell Davies, you could use the following:

Max: The Life and Music of Peter Maxwell Davies by Mike Seabrook (ISBN: 978-0575058835, Weidenfeld & Nicolson 1995).

Peter Maxwell Davies by Paul Griffiths (ISBN: 978-0860511380, Robson Books 1982).

Topic 2: Programme music

The term programme music is used to describe pieces in which the composer sets out to portray a story or a specific image through music, unlike absolute music (works such as sonatas, concertos and symphonies) in which the music rarely refers to anything specific beyond itself.

The first of the prescribed works for this topic comes from the Baroque period. Vivaldi's *The Four Seasons* is a set of four violin concertos that are linked by a programme in the form of four sonnets, possibly by the composer – one for each season of the year.

While programme music has been less dominant at other times in musical history, non-musical stimuli are plentiful in dramatic music (such as opera or oratorio) or in song, where there is a text to prompt a musical response.

Programme music was relatively rare in the 18th century but it became very popular in the Romantic period as the range of tone colours available from the large orchestras of the 19th century allowed composers to imitate effects ranging from birdsong to storms. The most common type of Romantic programme music was the **symphonic poem** (or **tone poem**) – an orchestral piece in a single movement. For example, *The Sorcerer's Apprentice* by Dukas tells in music the well-known children's story about a magician's lazy assistant who creates havoc with spells that he has not yet mastered. However, the second of the prescribed works is more unusual – Berlioz's *Symphonie fantastique* is not a symphonic poem but an entire 19th-century symphony based on a programme written by (and about) its composer.

The third prescribed work, *The Confession of Isobel Gowdie* by James MacMillan, was written in the late 20th century and was inspired by the case of a 17th-century Scottish woman condemned for being a witch.

Composers of programme music face the challenge of telling the story while at the same time producing a composition that is satisfying in structure. All three of these works have been constructed as carefully as any other piece by their composers. Vivaldi adapts the form of the Baroque solo concerto. Berlioz's *Symphonie fantastique*, inspired by the example of Beethoven's symphonies, adopts a revolutionary approach to writing a programmatic symphony in five movements. James MacMillan writes what the 19th century would have regarded as a symphonic poem, inspired by an event in Scottish history, which has contemporary relevance for the composer.

The Four Seasons

Antonio Vivaldi (1678–1741) was for much of his working life associated with the Pio Ospedale della Pietà, an orphanage where the illegitimate daughters of the wealthy families of Venice were brought up. The girls were given an excellent musical education, achieving high standards on the violin and in orchestral playing. Even though Vivaldi took holy orders, he led the life of a violinist, composer and director of music at courts and opera houses, writing over 600 concertos, other instrumental works, sacred music and operas. While travelling to promote his own works he was obliged by his terms of employment to send regular concertos to the Ospedale.

The Four Seasons is the name given to the first four of a set of 12 concertos, *Il cimento dell'armonia e dell'inventione* ('The Trial of Harmony and Invention') published as Vivaldi's Op. 8 in Amsterdam in 1725. Earlier in 1711, Vivaldi's 12 concertos *L'estro armonico*, Op. 3 had been published in Amsterdam, facilitating the dissemination of the composer's music outside Italy – Bach even transcribed some of the Op. 3 concertos as a means of studying their techniques of composition.

Publication

The first four concertos in the set are:

Op. 8 No. 1	RV269	La Primavera – Spring	E major
Op. 8 No. 2	RV315	L'Estate – Summer	G minor
Op. 8 No. 3	RV293	L'Autunno – Autumn	F major
Op. 8 No. 4	RV297	L'Inverno – Winter	F minor

The published version didn't include a full score: instead the concertos were issued as a set of six parts (solo violin, violin 1 and violin 2, viola and two sets of bass parts). Vivaldi also included the four sonnets, which explain the programme of *The Four Seasons* and added letter cues to link the lines of the sonnet with the corresponding passage of music. He also added occasional extra descriptions for some passages.

Most of Vivaldi's concertos are untitled, but there were three other concertos with descriptive titles in the Op. 8 set. His publication title, 'The Trial of Harmony and Invention', seems to represent no more than the attempt of a canny businessman to market his compositions more effectively. While in some of the concertos the title attached to the work appears largely unconnected to the musical content, the type of detailed programme outlined for *The Four Seasons* is unusual.

The concertos are in a standard three-movement form. The outer movements are in **ritornello form**, which in Vivaldi's hands became a highly successful and much imitated structure for the Baroque concerto. Before Vivaldi, composers were familiar with contrasting sections of tutti (all the players) and solo or ripieno (a group of solo players), but Vivaldi's achievement in his Op. 3 concerti was to strengthen the function of the tutti ritornello sections, by repeating the main thematic material, and to establish the tonal structure of

Ritornello form is a structure used for many large-scale movements in the late Baroque period. An opening instrumental section (called the ritornello) introduces the main musical ideas. This is followed by a contrasting texture featuring solo writing. Sections of the opening ritornello, often in related keys, then alternate with the solo textures until, at the end, the complete ritornello (or a substantial part of it) returns in the tonic key. The fragmentary nature of most of the ritornello sections in the middle of the movement gives the form its name – ritornello means a 'little return'.

the movement. The first and last ritornello would be in the tonic, the others in related keys, separated by varying episodes for a soloist or group of players (ripieno). The strong melodic profile and the emphasis on tonic and dominant (I and V) in the opening ritornello created a clear point of return that the audience could not miss.

In *The Four Seasons*, the virtuoso solo violin part and the programmatic element of the concerti required that there should be longer solo episodes. Vivaldi constructs the ritornelli from separate sections of musical material. The later ritornelli tend to use just a few of the separate sections, with a fuller repeat of the opening left to the final tutti. The flexibility of this scheme allows a much greater focus on the solo or programmatic passages.

The sonnets The authorship of the sonnets is unclear – they may be by Vivaldi himself. The amount of guidance they give about the programme varies. The cheerful pleasures of the country are depicted in Spring and Autumn, while Summer and Winter present the more threatening aspects of nature. There is more descriptive variety in the outer movements, in which the structure of alternating ritornelli and solo episodes provide the framework for describing a sequence of events. The middle slow movements illustrate a single picture:

➢ Spring: the sleeping goatherd and his dog in the meadow

➢ Summer: rest disturbed by flies, wasps and distant thunder

➢ Autumn: the sleeping drunkards

➢ Winter: by the fireside while it rains outside.

Apart from Autumn, the slow movements are aria-like melodies for solo violin. Like a soloist in an opera, the violinist would have been expected to add their own ornamentation or embellishments to the melody.

The Baroque violin Vivaldi's career as a composer coincided with the great era of violin making in Italy. The violins of the great families of violin makers – in Venice this meant Guarneri – were highly prized for their tone and some are still in use to this day. The 18th-century violin had a shorter fingerboard than the modern violin, and the bridge was usually lower, flatter and narrower. The strings were made of gut, so the brighter sound of the modern metal E string was not available, but the low G string was beginning to be wound with silver or copper wire. The Italians liked the violin to sing out and to project, and so used a longer bow than the modern violin bow. The singing style of violin playing, modelled on the operatic aria, was much in vogue – it can be seen in the concertos and sonatas of Corelli, the most influential of Vivaldi's Italian predecessors.

Italian violinists were familiar with a range of common techniques used by modern violinists such as pizzicato (plucking), tremolo (rapid repeated notes) and sul tasto (playing over the fingerboard). A little vibrato was used on longer notes and the mute was available (marked con sordino). Vivaldi also regularly uses double-stopping (playing more than one string at a time).

Other virtuoso violin techniques include:

➤ Ondeggiando (ondulé) – alternating between two strings

➤ Arpeggiando – arpeggiated passages, sometimes written out for a few bars as an example for the remaining bars:

L'Autunno, 3rd movement (bars 59–62)

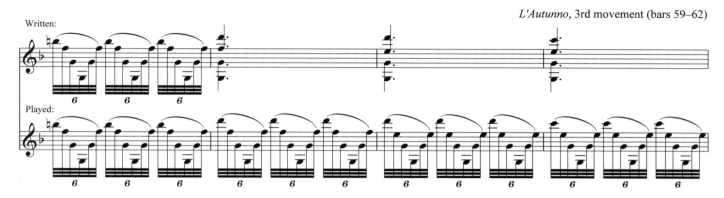

➤ Bariolage – rapid alternation between a recurring pitch on an open string and one or more pitches on an adjacent string:

L'Estate, 3rd movement (bars 51–53)

Concerto No. 1 in E major, Spring

In the **first movement** the joys of spring are illustrated with cheerful simplicity. The three-bar sections are made up of repeated phrases, with the sections repeated in an overall AABB pattern. There are simple harmonies over a heavy tonic pedal. Despite the instant memorability of the first six bars, the A section returns only once at bar 66, otherwise it is only the B section with its return to the tonic, which is used in subsequent ritornelli. In the first episode the three violin parts imitate birdsong, elaborating the notes of a chord of E major for 14 bars. The bass and continuo stop playing: there is no change of harmony to take the music forward. The music is static, as if everything has stopped to listen to the birds. The tutti is only three bars in length (bars 28–31) with a fully scored episode to follow representing the breezes and the murmuring of the streams. The passage manages to combine the constant gentle movement of the semiquavers in 3rds with the slow, unhurried pace of harmonic change between chords I and V.

Another three-bar ritornello is followed by the more dramatic image of thunder in the repeated demisemiquavers. After rapid scales representing lightning, the solo violin reverts to the more usual virtuoso arpeggios for the rest of the episode, answered by the continuing thunder of the demisemiquavers, modulating to the key of the relative minor, C♯ minor. The next birdsong episode

> The **continuo**, short for basso continuo, is the group of instruments that form the accompaniment in Baroque music. It may include instruments such as the harpsichord and a cello or bassoon.

(bars 59–65) uses an ascending chromatic phrase over a C♯ pedal in the bass. The solo violin's tonic to dominant melody is answered by the first violin's dominant to tonic. The imitative style is effective in creating the effect of a small flock of birds rather than just one. The final episode (bars 70–75) is for solo violin and continuo only, typical of Vivaldi's practice of writing a more thoughtful episode to precede the final ritornello. The solo violin's pairs of semiquavers are derived from similar figures in the earlier episodes.

The portrait of the sleeping goatherd and his dog in the **slow movement** is in the relative minor, C♯ minor, an unusual key for Vivaldi but one which he regarded as particularly expressive. The bass is tacet, the lowest notes of the texture being provided by the gruff bark of the viola (marked in some editions 'strappato' – suggesting a rough pulling of the bow against the strings). The solo depicts the sleeping goatherd, the violins' 3rds in a gentle dotted rhythm representing the rustle of the leaves and plants. The music unfolds beautifully, with the sequence in bars 8–13 leading to a modulation to the dominant minor, G♯ minor.

In the **final movement**, the drone in the bass of the opening tutti depicts the shepherd's bagpipe. The gentle compound metre (a $\frac{12}{8}$ time signature) is often associated with pastoral scenes in the music of this period (the Pastoral Symphony in Handel's *Messiah* is another example). The flexibility of Vivaldi's ritornelli can be seen by comparing the melodic material in the four tutti sections. Each ritornello begins with the same melodic material, taken from bars 1–3, but the material from bars 4–12 is not used again until the last ritornello. The simple structure of melodies, which are based on pairs of repeated four-beat phrases, adds to the rustic feel of a country-dance, celebrating the joys of spring.

Although the programme is not outlined in detail, the use of minor keys as subsidiary keys in the structure seems to hint that not all country life is idyllic and trouble-free. The second tutti is in the relative minor (C♯ minor) – a key which has already played a significant role in this concerto. The third tutti (bars 58–71) begins in the tonic major but switches unexpectedly to the tonic minor after only three bars. The material in the tonic minor tutti is organised in a different way: descending sequences of bars instead of the pairs of repeated bars used in the first tutti. The bass is strikingly different too. No longer the static pedal bass of the opening of the movement, in the minor tutti the bass imitates the rhythm of the melody (bars 62–63), before presenting its own agile line of quavers (bars 64–67), followed by descending chromatic dotted crotchets. This expressive passage is a departure from the predictable country mood of the rest of the movement, another demonstration of Vivaldi's flexible, developmental approach to the ritornello.

The final episode – still in the minor key – is played over a dominant pedal, with highly expressive touches such as the F♮ and the leap of a major 7th from E to D♯. The sudden return of the tonic major for the final tutti is refreshing, but the minor key episode means that the joy of the dance is no longer quite the same.

Third movement		
Tutti 1	Bars 1–12	Tonic
Episode 1	Bars 13–21	Solo and continuo
		Sequential passage modulating to relative minor
Tutti 2	Bars 22–34	Relative minor, modulating to dominant
Episode 2	Bars 35–57	Bars 34–48: double stopping – a succession of modulations through the cycle of 5ths, returning to the tonic
		Bars 48–58: new material accompanied by repeated notes in the upper strings, modulating to the dominant
Tutti 3	Bars 58–71	Tonic, then tonic minor
Episode 3	Bars 72–78	Chromatic, cadenza-like passage over a dominant pedal in the tonic minor
Tutti 4	Bars 79–89	Tonic

Concerto No. 4 in F minor, Winter

This concerto has the most detailed indications of the programme in the score. The possibilities of winter bring out Vivaldi's resourcefulness in using the solo violin and strings to convey the icy elements of the programme. The key of F minor suits the coldness and discomfort of the season. By contrast, the second movement is in a heart-warming E♭ major, a carefully crafted combination of a beautiful melody and an elaborately textured accompaniment.

The translation of Vivaldi's Winter sonnet is taken from *Vivaldi: 'The Four Seasons' and other concertos, Op. 8* by Paul Everett (ISBN: 13 978-0-521-40692-5, CUP 1996).

First movement		
A	*To shiver, frozen, amid icy snows,*	Repeated notes, with trills on each
		Dissonant entries (G in viola, D♭ in second violin), building diminished chord against F pedal
		Diminished 7th in bar 5, followed by tonic F minor for first time
		Chromatic chords (F^7, G^7/F) over tonic pedal
		Chromatic shift in bass to F♯ with diminished 7th chord (bar 10).
		L'Inverno, chords in bars 1–12
B	*at the harsh wind's chill breath;*	Solo demisemiquaver descending arpeggios and scales
		Accompaniment continues with shivering **A** music
C	*to run, stamping one's feet at every moment;*	F minor tutti – harmonic sequence
		Energetic rhythmic figure, repeated demisemiquavers and semiquavers
		Stamping semiquaver chords, repeated pairs of descending chords, octave leaps in the bass

D	*with one's teeth chattering on account of the excessive cold;*	Repeated semiquavers in violins, with quavers in the viola as the lower part
		Double-stopping with suspensions causing dissonances of 2nds and 7ths.
		Solo repeated demisemiquavers

Second movement

E	*to pass the days of calm and contentment by the fireside* *while the rain outside drenches a hundred others;*	Elaborate texture, different rhythmic movement in each part
		Contented cantabile solo melody
		Pizzicato rain in continuous semiquavers
		Sustained harmony notes in the viola
		Repeated quavers in the bass, a calm steady pulse

Third movement

F	*to walk on the ice, and with slow steps*	The ice represented by a sustained tonic pedal (dominant pedal from bar 21)
		Fast solo semiquaver melody representing sliding, repeated phrases, combining stepwise movement with leaps of a 5th or 6th
G	*to move about cautiously for fear of falling;*	Slower, quaver movement
		Stepwise movement continues, inching up chromatically in bars 30–35
		Range of the melody in bars 25–39 restricted to a 5th
H	*to go fast, slip, fall to the ground;*	More rapid descending phrases
I	*to go on the ice again and run fast*	Bolder semiquaver movement
		Adventurous wide leaps using the open D and G strings
L	*until the ice cracks and breaks open;*	Full ensemble in octaves
		Rhythmic continuity is broken by sudden movement and rests
		Descending melodic figures
M	*to hear, as they sally forth through the ironclad gates,*	Slower, quaver movement for warmer wind
		Major key – E♭ major – contrasting with the chilly key of F minor
N	*Sirocco, Boreas, and all the winds at war.* *This is winter, but of a kind to bring joy*	Rapid demisemiquaver passage-work in solo
		Rapid repeated notes in the accompaniment
		Predominant use of minor chords – B♭ minor (bar 124), F minor (bar 127), B♭ minor (bar 129), C minor (bar 131)
		Antiphonal contrasts between solo violin (or full violins) and full orchestra
		Low registers predominate from bar 140 to the end

Related repertoire

In addition to *The Four Seasons*, you are expected to study other early 18th-century programme music. The specification mentions Italian instrumental music and French keyboard music as examples.

François Couperin (1668–1733) is sometimes known as 'Le grand' to distinguish him from the rest of his musical family. He worked at the court of Louis XIV at Versailles. Couperin's keyboard technique is rooted in the tradition of the French lute composers, in which melody and bass notes were often not plucked simultaneously, creating an arpeggiated texture.

Couperin

Couperin's *Treizième Ordre* (13th Suite) for harpsichord was published in his third volume of *Pièces de Clavecin* in 1722. The suite comprises 16 pieces in B minor, the longer at the beginning and end. Allegedly the subject is Louis XIV's nephew Philippe d'Orléans, a sad, frustrated man who consoled himself for his unsuitable marriage and lack of promotion with parties and a dissolute lifestyle. The Ordre is dominated by a sequence of 12 variations on the **La Folia bass**, with the title *Les Folies Francaises ou Les Dominos*.

The La Folia bass and its associated melody was used as the basis variations by many 17th- and 18th-century composers, including Corelli and Bach:

Each variation represents different characters at a masked ball, the 'domino' of the title being the coloured cloak worn by each guest as they arrive. The variations (the French title is 'couplet') are only 16 bars each, a complete performance lasting no more than 8 minutes. The ornamentation is an integral part of the style, lending a grace and precision to the expressive melodies and their dance-like rhythms. While Vivaldi's music sets the seasons in the country, Couperin's music is sophisticated, civilised and courtly – the music of the town and society.

Titles of variation	The guests	Their cloaks
1. La Virginité	Virginity	Invisible
2. La Pudeur	Modesty	Pink
3. L'Ardeur	Ardour	Flesh
4. L'Espérance	Hope	Green
5. La Fidélité	Fidelity	Blue
6. La Persévérance	Perseverance	Flaxen grey
7. La Langueur	Languor	Purple
8. La Coquéterie	Coquetry	Different colours

9. Les vieux Galants et les Trésorières surannées	Old Roués and Pensioned-off Courtesans	Crimson and verdigris
10. Les Coucous bénévoles	Benevolent Cuckolds	Yellow
11. La Jalousie taciturne	Silent Jealousy	Moorish grey
12. La Frénésie, ou le Désespoir	Frenzy, or Despair	Black

A brief portrait of each character is quickly drawn. Languor appears with the slow rhythm of four equal notes in each bar – marked *également* so that the player is not tempted to interpret the notation by allowing *notes inégales* (uneven or dotted rhythms). The flirtatious Coquette in her cloak of different colours cannot settle on one time signature, cheerfully darting through three different metres in the first four bars of each eight-bar section:

La Coquéterie (bars 1–8)

Dotted rhythms feature for the Old Roués, attempting to leap vigorously between registers but ending in a tired lower octave. The Cuckolds are represented by the sound of the cuckoo in 3rds in the left hand. Silent Jealousy moves slowly through lower registers, its stepwise movement and suspensions suggesting barely suppressed emotion. The rapid semiquavers of Frenzy bring the variations to a close.

The final number of the ordre – *L'âme en peine* (The Soul in Torment) – is a more extended piece in binary form. The slow dance rhythm in triple time and the frequent use of gradually descending phrases in thirds brings the set to an expressive and sombre conclusion.

Exercise 6

1. Explain how Vivaldi uses instrumental resources to interpret the programme in *The Four Seasons*. Use detailed examples from at least three movements.

2. How did composers of instrumental music before 1750 use tonality and harmony to express a non-musical subject? Illustrate your answer by referring to at least one work by two different composers.

3. Describe the use of programmatic elements in French keyboard music before 1750. Use examples drawn from the keyboard works of one or two composers.

Further reading

Vivaldi: 'The Four Seasons' and other concertos by Paul Everett (ISBN: 13 978-0-521-40692-5, CUP 1996). A short, readable and scholarly account of the Op. 8 concertos, including a useful line-by-line translation of the sonnets for *The Four Seasons*.

Vivialdi by Michael Talbot (ISBN: 978-0198164975, Master Musicians Series OUP 2000)

Resources

Scores of *The Four Seasons* are readily available. Bärenreiter publish an edition edited by Christopher Hogwood (2002), based on the Manchester version of the score but incorporating some elements of the Amsterdam (Le Cène) version.

There are many fine recordings of *The Four Seasons*. Jeanne Lamon's recording with Tafelmusik (Sony SMK89987) is a spirited and beautifully ornamented performance.

Angela Hewitt has made a series of Couperin's Keyboard music for the piano. The *Treizième Ordre* is in Volume 3, Hyperion Records CDA67520.

Symphonie fantastique

Hector Berlioz (1803–1869) conceived the *Symphonie fantastique* in the wake of a series of profound, personal and artistic experiences. He had discovered Shakespeare performed in Paris by an English touring company, fallen in love with its leading actress Harriet Smithson (whom he was later to marry), heard Beethoven's symphonies for the first time when they were conducted by Habeneck at the Paris Conservatoire, and he had read Goethe's *Faust*. For a person of Berlioz's emotional susceptibilities these events had a powerful impact.

Berlioz's *Symphonie fantastique* is in five movements:

I	Rêveries – Passions	Reveries – Passions
II	Un bal	A Ball
III	Scène aux champs	Scene in the Country
IV	Marche au supplice	March to the Scaffold
V	Songe d'une nuit du sabbat	Dream of a Witches' Sabbath

It was first performed at the Paris Conservatoire on December 5th 1830, conducted by Habeneck.

The programme

The title 'fantastic' is to indicate that the work is based on the imagination. The story is of a musician who becomes obsessed with a woman, represented by a musical theme, the *idée fixe*. Whether at a ball or in the country, his thoughts of her are inescapable. He is convinced that his love is not returned and takes opium. Under the influence of the drug, he imagines his own execution for killing the woman he loves and then his own funeral and Witches' Sabbath, surrounded by a dancing orgy of ghosts, witches and the beloved herself.

Although later in his life he suggested that it was not strictly necessary, in his original preface to the score Berlioz writes: 'The distribution of this programme to the audience [...] is indispensable for the complete understanding of the dramatic plan of the work'. The programme is like the text of an opera, explaining the instrumental drama. Conventional Parisian musical opinion regarded purely instrumental music as inferior to vocal music and opera. Even Beethoven's symphonies met with incomprehension from the public and the critics, except from Berlioz and like-minded younger musicians. For Berlioz and his contemporaries the expressive power of instrumental music was precisely that it was not restricted by the words. New techniques of melody, harmony and tone colour enabled music to express much more than words could say, while remaining poetic and indefinable.

Love, which cannot be fulfilled, and the feeling of yearning for the unattainable are typical themes of early Romantic artists. Schumann explores the same themes in his song cycle *Dichterliebe* (see the chapter on Song). By the time Berlioz came to write the *Symphonie fantastique* he had become disillusioned by Harriet Smithson's indifference to him. Some of the symphony can be traced back to other compositions – the *idée fixe* itself to his cantata *Herminie* (1828), the 'March to the Scaffold' from his unfinished opera *Les Francs Juges* (1826). Both the new material and the recycled are made to serve the artistic vision of the composer. The autobiographical element in the work and the composer's success in finding new means of expression for his programme made an immediate impact. Schumann wrote approvingly about it and Liszt (who had been at the first performance) made a transcription for piano. Berlioz rewrote several sections and continued to programme the work in his concerts.

Thematic transformation

The transformation of the theme which represents the beloved is a key musical device in telling the story. It is heard in full at the beginning of the fast section of the first movement. The first phrase can be seen below:

1st movement (bars 72–79)

1st movement (bars 3–4)

But, there was a hint of it in the opening of the introduction. Compare the phrase in the first violins in bars 3–4 *right* with bars 3–8 of the *idée fixe above*.

The 40 bars of the complete *idée fixe* is made up of the irregular lengths of melodic phrases (8+7+4+4+4+5+2+2+4), which so perplexed his critics. For Berlioz, the melody was the main means of expression. The semitone motif – marked in the example above – pervades the score. In a diatonic context – E and F in C major – the effect is beautifully expressive, but it also has a more emotional chromatic context, for example in bars 15–16 of the melody (bars 86–87 of the score), where the semitone is from G (the dominant) to A♭ (the flattened 6th). The shape of the melody, with its climbing, short, repeated phrases is mirrored in the similar structure and phrasing of the melody of the 'Scene in the Country'.

Berlioz's focus on long melodies contrasts with the more Germanic, Beethoven-influenced technique of motivic development, with its emphasis on tonality and structure. This style became influential throughout Europe. For its use in Tchaikovsky, the most mainstream of the Russian composers, see *Romeo and Juliet* later in this chapter.

The *idée fixe* appears more or less complete in the second, third and fifth movements, but assumes a completely different rhythmic identity each time. In 'The Ball' it appears in the form of a graceful dance in triple time, but the repeated short motifs in the cellos and basses suggest that the image of the woman 'troubles the soul'. When it appears on solo clarinet at the end of the movement, only a frantic, faster resumption of the dance can banish the thought of unrequited love.

Second movement (bars 121–128)

In the 'Scene in the Country', it appears before the climax of the movement, alternating with increasingly passionate phrases first for the cellos and basses (doubled by the bassoons) and then for the full strings, building up to a fortissimo diminished-7th chord in bar 106. The passion subsides with expressive syncopated chords, dying away (morendo) to pianissimo.

Oboe (flute 8ve higher)   Third movement (bars 90–92)

The orchestra

Berlioz was a master of the use of the orchestra. His treatise on orchestration (*Grand Traité d'Instrumentation et d'Orchestration Modernes*, 1843) became the standard textbook on the subject. As one of the few composers not to play the piano, he was free of the influence of piano music in constructing orchestral sonorities. Influenced by the virtuoso achievements of Paganini on the violin and Liszt on the piano in discovering new possibilities for their instruments, Berlioz wanted to do the same for the orchestra. His orchestration is not a matter of orchestral display but of carefully selecting the sounds he needed in order to achieve a precise expressive effect.

Large bands of woodwind and brass were a standard feature of public music in post-revolutionary France, but Berlioz adapted these forces to symphonic music for the first time. As a conductor he insisted that the brass and woodwind should be balanced by an appropriately large string section. He uses four bassoons with the double woodwind section. A piccolo (played by the 2nd flute) is used in the first, second and last movement; there is an important cor anglais solo (in the rôle of the shepherd's pipe) in the 'Scene in the Country'; and a clarinet in E flat is used in the last movement.

The brass employs four horns, two trumpets, two valved cornets (cornets à pistons), three trombones one ophicleide and one serpent (precursors of the tuba as the bass of the orchestral brass). Some modern performances and recordings include the part for a single cornet, which Berlioz added to his manuscript score but did not include in the published version. The percussion also increases in importance – becoming more of a section in its own right – with detailed instructions for the players and unusual effects such as the rolled chords on four timpani (requiring four players) at the end of the 'Scene in the Country'.

First movement: Reveries – Passions

The artist's dreamy restlessness is suggested in the succession of short phrases for the strings, each avoiding settling on a perfect cadence in C minor, preferring to end on the dominant. His unfinished thoughts are broken up by the pauses, before the music continues. Only in bars 13–14 is a phrase repeated, but it is harmonised differently, as if the thought is being considered in a different way. The following semiquaver sextuplets begin a 'surge of passion', the music gathering speed with the cross-rhythms against the triplet quavers suggesting a turbulence of emotion. There are constant surges of dynamics from piano to sforzando and back, reinforced by the ascending arpeggios in the violas and cellos. The opening melody returns at bar 28, more fully orchestrated with a sextuplet arpeggio figure in flute and clarinet.

With the pedal on A♭ starting in bar 46 the music goes into different harmonic territory. The A♭ is harmonised with a D♭ chord in bar 49, followed by chords of A♭–E⁷–C♯m–G♯m. The remoteness of the chords from the tonic symbolises how far the artist's thoughts have taken him out of the real world. The return of the key of C (this time C major) brings the tremolo strings, woodwind and horns together for the first time. Note Berlioz's carefully notated dynamic markings, – mezzo forte, diminuendo to pianissimo, crescendo to fortissimo, and suddenly *ppp* – all in the space of two bars (61–62).

The Allegro section is in a loose type of sonata form. There is an exposition repeat, with a modulation to the dominant (G major), but the second subject – if it can be called that – is a development of the opening phrase of the *idée fixe* with a new answering phrase (bars 156–160), itself related in its stepwise falling 4th to the second phrase of the *idée fixe*. The expressive *idée fixe* phrase is met by the disturbed forte of the answering phrase, its rhythm underlining the emotional turbulence with the accompanying quavers on second and fourth beats and sforzando accents in the melody on the fourth beats.

The development continues to exploit the contrasts in mood. Bars 198–228 use first-inversion chords ascending and descending chromatically, the semitone motif derived from the *idée fixe* in the woodwind and horns. A dramatic three bars of silence is broken by a single horn note, then a build-up of an accompaniment texture in the strings (from bar 234). Berlioz uses the subtle rhythmic effect of having the bass note of the chord on the fourth quaver of each group (marked *mf* in cellos and basses), avoiding the more obvious placing of the bass on the stressed beat. The woodwind have the full G major *idée fixe* in octaves, doubled by the first and second violins on the first quaver of each group of quavers.

MacMillan uses a similar technique to highlight the *Lux aeterna* melody at a point of climax in *The Confession of Isobel Gowdie*, bars 275–295.

Having found a way back to the tonic of C major (bar 329), there is still no rest. The chromatic notes continue to disturb the harmonies and the music takes a turn into the very low sounds of the cellos, basses and bassoons, modulating into A major with a perfect cadence (bar 357–358). From this low point the oboe solo begins a passage of searching. The scoring is delicate, with the low sounds of the clarinet and bassoon chords, and the inter-twining countermelodies of the violas and cellos. The bright sound of the violins is held back until bar 384. The harmonies are based on the chromatic rising and falling first-inversion chords heard earlier, but Berlioz creates a constant mood of ambiguity and emotional turbulence by alternating major and minor versions of the same chord. In bar 372–373, for example, F♯ minor is followed by F♯ major, moving up chromatically to G minor (the violas have the B♭ as an A♯), followed by G major. The 3rd of the major chords become the 3rd of a minor chord at each chromatic shift, creating series of subtle and emotionally disturbing harmonic changes.

After the return of the *idée fixe* in an exciting and energetic C major, the movement ends with the 'consolations of religion' – quiet sustained diatonic chords and peaceful plagal cadences.

Fourth movement: March to the Scaffold

Public execution was not uncommon in early 19th-century France, and the mass executions of the terror which followed the Revolution were not too distant a memory. Berlioz's music conveys the tumult of the crowd and the inevitable forward momentum of the march to the execution. From the opening bars his attention to the details of the orchestration is evident. The timpanists are instructed to play with sponge-headed beaters, playing the first of each group of sextuplets with both sticks, the rest with the right hand stick alone. The pizzicato double basses are divided in four.

From bar 164, the artist's last thoughts of the beloved, represented by four bars of the *idée fixe* in the clarinet, are cut off by the short G minor chord in the full orchestra. The percussion are instructed to damp the sound of their instruments to make the chord as short as possible, allowing the descending pizzicato strings to suggest the fall of the head from the moment of execution.

Fifth movement: The Witches' Sabbath

The last movement gives Berlioz the opportunity to give full expression to the macabre proceedings over the artist's grave. The pianissimo tremolo on a diminished-7th chord sets the mysterious night scene. The effect is enhanced by the unusual use of divisi violins and violas in eight separate parts, muted (con sordino) and playing at the point of the bow (the part most suited to playing a quiet tremolo). In bar 4, the diminished 7ths descend in parallel staccato chords to a C major chord in the following bar, with the violins and violas switching to pizzicato and both cellos and basses divisi to create a rumbling effect of four-note chords. The piccolo, flute and oboe call on a repeated 'C' ends with a strange glissando to the lower octave, a difficult effect to achieve on woodwind instruments.

After the slow introduction there is a brief hint of the distorted *idée fixe* in the clarinet, which causes an outbreak of the full orchestra on an unexpected chord of E♭ major. The violins are divided into ten overlapping parts and there are trumpet triplets in cross-rhythm with the quavers in the rest of the orchestra. At bar 39 the dominant chord of B♭ major prepares us for the return of the distorted *idée fixe*, this time properly established in the new key of E♭ major.

The 'Witches Sabbath' *idée fixe* is 'a vulgar dance tune, trivial and grotesque'. This once beautiful theme is distorted by the acciaccaturas and trills; the piccolo adds to the shrillness of this melody. The squareness of the rhythm is underlined by the repeated chords of the oboes and clarinet, its crudeness by the arpeggios starting on the beat in the four bassoons in unison.

Fifth movement (bars 41–44)

Clarinet in E♭

From bar 127 he introduces the *Dies Irae* melody, which would have been well known to Berlioz's Roman Catholic audience as the plainchant melody for the Requiem Mass:

Di - es i - rae di - es   il - la, Sol - vet____   saec - lum____ in fa - vil - la

The ophicleide had a much rougher sound than the tuba, which is usually heard in modern performances. Also the bells would have been different to modern tubular bells – Berlioz specified a much deeper sound, but even he had to compromise by allowing grand pianos to be used if real bells were not available.

Related repertoire

You will need to listen to symphonic poems and programmatic overtures from the 19th century. The concept of the symphonic poem was developed by the Hungarian composer **Franz Liszt** (1811–1886), who began a sequence of 12 such works when he settled in Weimar in 1848, including *Les Préludes* and *Prometheus*. These were in one movement, similar in scale to the first movement of a symphony. They were inspired, like Berlioz's programmatic overtures, by literary works (including Victor Hugo and Shakespeare), either following a detailed narrative or giving an impression of a character or creating a scene or mood.

In Russia the group of composers known as 'The Five' was attracted to the symphonic poem as a useful means of promoting a nationalist style of composition. The group's leader Balakirev suggested that the 29-year old **Tchaikovsky** (not part of the group) write *Romeo and Juliet* (1869, revised 1870 and 1880), providing an outline of the elements of Shakespeare's play to be included and suggesting keys for the various themes. Tchaikovsky subtitled the work 'Fantasy Overture after Shakespeare'. The work is in sonata form, with three groups of themes, their rhythmic identity quite distinct:

➤ Slow introduction (F♯ minor) – Friar Laurence: minims, homophonic, hymn-like

➤ First subject (B minor) – the conflict between the Montagues and Capulets: faster rhythms (quavers and semiquavers) and syncopation

➤ Second subject (D♭ major) – the Love theme, crotchet movement.

The Love theme demonstrates Tchaikovsky's melodic gift and his command of the Romantic style. The melody is constructed from short motifs, moving mostly in step but with highly expressive wider leaps. The example on the next page shows his use of appoggiaturas and dissonance (marked *) and the strong harmonic framework – note the bass line moving in 5ths and 4ths. The horn's sighing ostinato figure grows out of the mysterious augmented chords in the muted strings in the bars after the first hearing of this theme. The A♭ bass in bar 219 is used in the following bars as a dominant pedal, over which the melody is extended in a series of six-note phrases. The combination of falling phrases and the slow climb to a climax creates a suitably sexually charged mood, which will be even more passionate when the theme is repeated in the full orchestra in the recapitulation.

The development section contrapuntally combines motifs of the three themes, conveying the conflict in the story. The contrasts between the rhythmic elements of the themes are used to exciting

Romeo and Juliet

The group of composers belonging to 'The Five' were Mily Balakirev, César Cui, Modest Mussorgsky, Nikolai Rimsky-Korsakov and Alexander Borodin.

Further reading

Berlioz's own writings offer an excellent insight into the state of music at this time. Often humorous and ironic, sensitive and observant, his *Memoirs* (translated by David Cairns) and *Evenings with the Orchestra* (translated by Jacques Barzun, Chicago University Press, 1999) also record his frequent exasperation at the low standards and shallowness of the French musical scene.

Resources

The score of *Symphonie fantastique* is available in the inexpensive Eulenburg audio and score series, which includes a CD recording of the work. There are many recordings available, including Colin Davis' splendid recording on the London Symphony Orchestra label (LSO 0007CD).

Other related repertoire

Prometheus (1855) by Franz Liszt.

Night on a Bare Mountain (1867, revised by Rimsky-Korsakov 1886) by Modest Mussorgsky.

Tod und Verklärung (Death and Transfiguration) (1889), *Don Quixote* (for cello and orchestra, 1897) by Richard Strauss.

effect. The nervous energy of the action is represented by the constant semiquaver movement or long passages of syncopated accompaniment. In bars 334–341 he uses the full orchestra playing the three-note semiquaver motif of the first subject syncopated with the minims of the Friar Laurence theme. The following bars have the strings in octaves playing the semiquavers against the exciting and unpredictable syncopated chords for the rest of the orchestra. The B major epilogue sums up the tragic conclusion to the play.

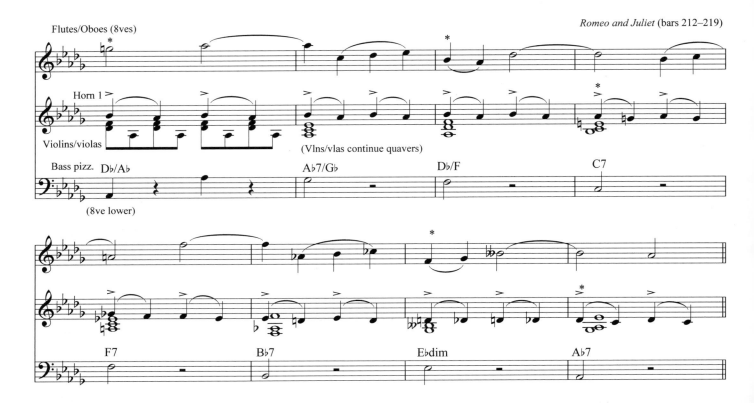

Romeo and Juliet (bars 212–219)

Exercise 7

1. How did Berlioz use instrumental texture and timbre to interpret the subject matter of the *Symphonie fantastique*?

2. Compare the approaches of Vivaldi and Berlioz to writing descriptive music.

3. Using examples from extended passages of two works by different composers, show how 19th-century composers of programme music used new techniques in harmony and tonality.

4. Explain the popularity of symphonic poems or programmatic overtures in the 19th century, using examples from the works of at least two different composers.

The Confession of Isobel Gowdie

The Scottish composer James MacMillan (b. 1959) wrote *The Confession of Isobel Gowdie* for the BBC Scottish Symphony Orchestra to perform at the BBC Proms in 1990. The work was an immediate success and has been performed all over the world.

Like Vivaldi and Berlioz before him, MacMillan lays out the programme of *The Confession of Isobel Gowdie* at the front of the score. The story is taken from a period of Scottish history when over 4000 were killed as part of the mass hysteria which surrounded the persecution of witches. Isobel Gowdie was from Nairn in the north of Scotland. In 1662 she confessed under the severest torture to belonging to a coven of 13 witches, to having been baptised and raped by the devil and to various other devilish crimes. She was strangled at the stake and burned in pitch. Although the story is colourful and dramatic the composer does not tell the story in the sense of depicting a sequence of events. Instead MacMillan describes the work as 'the Requiem that Isobel Gowdie never had'. He uses elements of Scottish religious song to ask for forgiveness on behalf of the Scottish people for the murder of Isobel Gowdie.

Like the symphonic poems of the 19th century, the work is in one movement. It divides into three sections:

A	Bars 1–129	Opening section (Largo) Ends with 13 chords
B	Bars 130–344	Middle section
A	Bars 345–426	Final section: recapitulation

Other works by MacMillan include a percussion concerto *Veni, Veni Emmanuel* (1992), *The World's Ransoming* (1995–1996) for cor anglais and orchestra, and a choral setting of the St John Passion (2007).

Tonality and harmony

Although the music is tonal, this does not mean conventional tonality with a system of modulations. Instead it uses a modal scheme with contrasting groups of pitches for the different sections of the work. The opening and closing sections use the sound of the lydian mode, with its sharpened 4th of the scale (B in the example below). The sharpened 4th also is a feature of the Latin chant *Lux aeterna* (Let eternal light shine on them, Lord), which is part of the setting of the Requiem Mass:

Lux aeterna is the most significant of the chants used in this piece. Immersed in the traditional music of Scotland and Ireland, MacMillan also quotes modal and pentatonic melodies from Gaelic religious and folk music, and makes up other melodies of his own in the same style. While Berlioz quotes the *Dies irae* in a way that would be immediately obvious to a listener familiar with the chant, in the opening and closing sections of this work MacMillan integrates various chants into a complicated texture. The overlaying of many chants, which are unified by a common melodic style, symbolise the people of Scotland.

The overall tonal scheme of the work is based on C. The opening dissonant interval of a 2nd between D and C is resolved on a unison C at the end of the first section (bar 62) and in the final bars of the work.

The structure of the work has a strong programmatic feel. The opening section's use of woodwind and strings has a feeling of prayer and mourning. The faster central section uses brass, woodwind and percussion to represent the confession itself, growing in violence and hysteria. The return of the *Lux aeterna* melody in a rich string chorale brings the tragedy to a conclusion and a desire for forgiveness. The repeat of the opening section at the end is not exact: the prayers have been altered by the experience of the violence in the middle section. The return to middle C represents a complicated resolution of the strands of the story, in which peace and forgiveness is achieved by both the victim and the persecutors.

> The 'confession' of the title is not simply Isobel Gowdie's; it is also that of the Scottish people. The audience is invited to identify with the story and to apply its message to modern political situations in which innocent people are persecuted by fascist regimes.

Orchestral techniques

MacMillan is resourceful in the wide range of orchestral timbres and textures he uses to interpret the story and contribute to the work's emotional impact on the audience. There are specific effects for individual sections or instruments:

➢ Wailing glissandi on the strings

➢ Violent slapping of the fingerboard of the double basses in free rhythm

➢ Rapid grace notes on the horns

➢ Antiphonal placing of the two percussion players

➢ Double glissandi on tubular bells, played by two hammers starting from opposite ends of the range.

The outer sections are predominantly for the strings, with the woodwind, brass and percussion playing a greater role in the more violent middle section.

Opening section

The first 13 bars are scored for clarinets, bassoons and horns only, beginning on middle C and D – a tone apart, and one by one introducing G, F♯ and E to cover the first five notes of the lydian scale. The C and D are held throughout the passage in the horns, the 1st and 3rd horns alternating with the 2nd and 4th so that there is no break in the sound. Any feeling of a definite beat is disguised by the slowness of the pulse and the use of syncopations in triplets and quintuplets in order to avoid placing notes directly on a stressed beat.

Lydian scale

At bar 14 (letter A) the strings begin to be added to the texture. The marking 'divisi' means that the section of players divides the parts between them, with the outer player of each desk on the upper part and the inner players on the lower. This allows MacMillan to build up a web-like texture of ten independently moving string melodies. Each part has a chant-like melodic character of its own, restricted to a small range of neighbouring pitches, and together create a complicated texture of interweaving chants and litanies.

With the introduction of the strings the pitches used begin to fan out: the second violas introduce the note A in bar 17, the first group of second violins the higher B and C (bars 21–22), the second cellos introduce the lower B and begin to work down to E and D (bars 18–19). By the time the first violins enter (bar 33, letter B) the texture already spans four octaves. The violins take the upper part even higher.

A closer look at the string writing shows the use of the same rhythm in pairs of string parts, with intervals of 3rds and 6ths contributing to the richness of the sound. For example, in bars 44–47 there are five pairs of melodic lines:

➤ Upper violins I and II: triplet minims and sustained notes

➤ Lower violins I and II: sustained notes and triplet minims

➤ Upper violas and cellos: short phrases in 3rds and 6ths, accented semiquavers in bar 46

➤ Lower violas and cellos: short ascending figure, repeated/varied in syncopated triplet rhythm

➤ Basses: pedal D in octaves

➤ In bar 47 the wailing pitch bend in the 1st violas introduces B♭ for the first time.

The rhythmic character of the melodies begins to change, with held notes elaborated at the end in a flurry of semiquavers, a type of ornamentation found in Gaelic psalm singing. Glissandi are used between repeated pairs of adjacent notes, creating a feeling of wailing. There is the mood of a threnody – from the Greek words *thrēnos* (wailing) and *ōidē* (ode) – a song of lament at a death. The music is in the Gaelic tradition of the funeral lament, known as *corranach* in Scotland. The first use of the *Lux aeterna* melody in the second double basses (at bars 25–26) is largely hidden by the rest of the texture, but the moving notes of the melody are emphasised by the crescendo to *mf*.

The elaborations of the melodies become more intense. At bar 50–53 the burst of semiquavers appear three times, each group longer than the preceding one, before disappearing into the string texture 'like a sigh'. The climactic *fff* chord at bar 54 is spread over five octaves, with a bass pedal on C, its lowest string. Over the next nine bars the texture is reduced to unison middle C, the dynamics to *pp* – with glissando sighs each time a part moves from D to middle C.

From bar 65 (letter D) the music changes to a more violent, painful mood. The contrast is established by:

➤ The change of tonality, with the use of B♭ and F♮ (instead of the previous F♯)

➤ The change of instrumentation – the brass and woodwind are used as sections for the first time

➤ Snare-drum rolls accompany the crescendos

➤ The change to more dissonant chords, made up of semitonal clashes

➤ The parallel 5ths in the violins, starting *pp*, ending with a *ff* glissando on an upward semitone, marked 'like a scream – molto vibr., tutta forza.'

The complex orchestral texture is achieved by combining a number of strands:

➤ Chords that crecendo in the brass, built up by the separate entry of each note of the chord, prominently using the figure of a descending semitone and a 3rd (see *left*)

➤ The highest part – in the first trumpet – begins with two notes, with each subsequent phrase an extended repeat of the previous phrase. The outline of the four descending stepwise notes is related to the descending three-note cell of the brass chords (see *left*)

➤ The rest of the orchestra plays a sustained chord, with a crescendo from *pp* to *sfz*.

As the tension increases, the music shifts up a tone (bar 80, letter E), with the G–F♯–D–C cell sound prominent. The percussion players play two pairs of congas, two timbales and a snare drum. The strings' wailing pitch bends are followed by complicated descending passages, successively using faster groups of tuplets to make the descent gather speed as it reaches the bottom. The pitches used are a variation of the lydian cell used at the beginning. The horns elaborate the sound of this chord with angular grace notes (to be played on the beat) before the sustained note or with semiquaver nontuplets at the end of the note.

At bar 112 (letter G) a new syncopated figure is introduced. The phrase is five quavers in length at first. The use of the same rhythm in large groups of instruments is a clear contrast with the dense polyphonic textures used so far. Again each time the phrase is repeated it is extended by a few more notes (the bar 115 phrase lasts for 8 notes; bar 118 lasts a whole bar; bar 121, a whole bar and a beat; and bar 124 one and a half bars).

The homophonic use of the orchestra is more a feature of the middle section of the work. The 13 chords at bars 127–129 represent the 13 witches of the coven in Isobel Gowdie's confession. The chord is highly dissonant – it uses 11 different pitches – but carefully spaced so that the strings are using the weight of sound of their lower strings. Only the third trumpet (on B) has a note in the mid-treble clef range. The high woodwind and trumpets 1 and 2 are in a high or very high register.

Discussion

There is scope to discuss MacMillan's response to the witch element of the story. In a radio interview with Stephen Johnson for the BBC, the composer is reluctant to be drawn on the precise programmatic details of the music, preferring to leave the listeners to draw their own conclusion. Compare his approach to that of Berlioz in the Witches' Sabbath.

Middle section

In the middle section the tempo gradually increases using a technique known as **metric modulation**. At each tempo change the new pulse is two-thirds of the previous crotchet beat. For example, at bar 156 look at the snap-pizzicato in the cellos and basses (it is doubled by bassoons, tuba and timpani). The crotchets at the new speed are continuing at the same pace as the triplet crotchets of the previous two bars. This process is repeated at bars 182, 211 and 247, by which point the music is very fast.

Each change of tempo introduces a new melodic and rhythmic variant of the most important pitches of the *Lux aeterna* melody.

Lux ae - ter - na lu - ce - at e - is, Do - mi - ne

In this middle section, the *Lux aeterna* melody has been transposed down a fourth (compare with page 79).

These four notes have already played a significant role in the cells used in the previous section. The melodies in the middle section continue to have a strong motivic element. The example from bars 151–152 use octave displacement to invert the interval: the semitone E♭ to E♮ becomes a diminished octave. The interval of the second can also be replaced by a 7th or a 9th. The melody is made up of pairs of tones and semitones or their inversions. In bars 166–167, which are at a faster tempo, the melodic profile of the four notes has been retained, but the leap of a 4th between the D and G has been stretched to a 6th (D to B). The repeated notes at the end of this phrase become an increasingly significant feature of this section.

Vlns. I
(bars 151–152)

Violins
(bars 166–167)

The *Lux aeterna* melody is used in a slower harmonised form, using the melodic technique discussed earlier of extending the melody each time it appears:

Bars 155–157	2 notes	Woodwind/brass *ff*
Bars 181–184	5 notes	Full orchestra *fff*, with pulse of metric modulation in percussion/violas
Bars 246–256	Full melody	Suddenly *ppp*, sustained notes, contrasting with previous loud, rhythmic passage for brass. Timpani plays pulse of metric modulation
Bars 275–295	Full melody to bar 286, then extended	Trumpets, first flute/oboe/clarinet (piccolo from bar 293), violins' arpeggios highlighting melody and rhythmic accompaniment

The brass writing is highly rhythmic and dance-like, combining quavers in unpredictable patterns of twos and threes. The music gets faster, building up to the eight bars of repeated crotchet Bs at bars 329–336. The accented quintuplets in the brass are marked 'frantic, like an eruption'. At the most violent point in the music, when the brass, woodwind and percussion are silent, the lower strings are revealed playing the lamenting chant of the opening.

Related repertoire

You will need to be familiar with other descriptive instrumental music written since 1950. In the immediate aftermath of World War II many composers wanted a complete break from the past. Few were interested in programme music, preferring more abstract compositions. The music of Anton Webern, with its intense expression and mathematical manipulations of a 12-note series, proved a starting point for Europeans such as Karlheinz Stockhausen (1928–2007) and Pierre Boulez (born 1925), and for the Japanese composer **Tōru Takemitsu** (1930–1996). In American-occupied Japan, composers were discouraged from developing a national style of music, and music students were exposed to European and American music. Takemitsu's music was profoundly influenced by Messiaen and Webern, but the greatest influence was the avant-garde experimental composer John Cage (1912–1992).

Takemitsu

Takemitsu led a busy career as a composer of over 90 film scores, which allowed him the financial independence to continue writing for the concert hall. It is worth listening to his 1985 score for Akira Kurosawa's *Ran*, a film based on Shakespeare's *King Lear*. His later concert works saw him move from the experimental, atonal style into a more sensuous approach based on manipulations of pentatonic scales, with more consciously Japanese elements than he had allowed in his early works. Many of these works are inspired by rain or water; others have parallels with the stylised formal arrangement of a Japanese garden. The use of pictorial titles and the approach to creating a musical sound is reminiscent of the French composer Claude Debussy (1862–1918).

A Flock Descends into the Pentagonal Garden (1977) was written for the San Francisco Symphony Orchestra. It was inspired by a dream in which the composer saw a flock of white birds led by a black bird descending into a pentagonal garden. The tempo is very slow, typical of Takemitsu, with value attached to individual gestures or silences. The opening bars feature an oboe solo (occasionally in unison with a second oboe). The first chord consists of the five notes of the pentatonic scale, a sound that returns at various points in the score to give a mood of rest in between more active, dissonant passages. The oboe represents the birds, the repeated notes played normally (marked N) or as harmonics (marked with a circle), using the note C as a reference point. The phrasing and dynamic markings are highly detailed. The accompanying chords grow more dense with clusters of seven or eight notes.

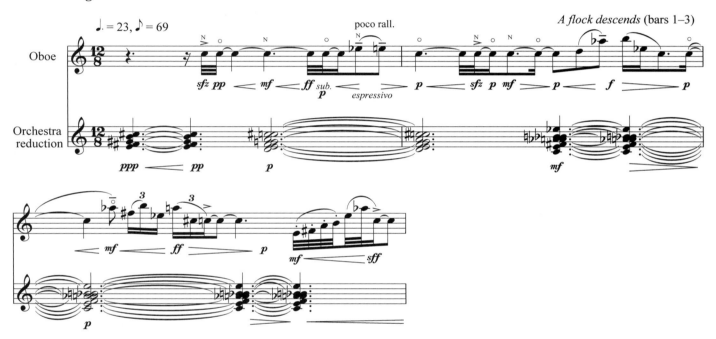

The composer tended to be secretive about his methods but insisted that this work was strictly controlled by a system of 'magic squares' that determined which notes were to be used. Even so, it is his sensitivity for orchestral textures which is more apparent.

Elements of aleatoric music are used at letter J of the score, where the strict tempo is abandoned. The vibraphone, tubular bells, marimba, celesta and the two harps have notated phrases which they are instructed to repeat many times, but at their own tempo over sustained harmonics in divided desks of cellos and basses. The conductor is given an approximate timing for each passage before adding the next group of phrases in the build up of texture. At the entry of the brass, the instruments listed are instructed to 'play only twice, then stop playing', and the texture dies down to *ppp*, followed by a silence of one or two seconds. As the music reaches the end the final chord is built up of the pentatonic notes heard at the beginning with some added pitches.

Exercise 8

1. Compare the use of harmony in two contrasting works of descriptive instrumental music composed since 1950.

2. Describe how James MacMillan uses instrumental timbre to illustrate the subject of *The Confession of Isobel Gowdie*. Discuss detailed examples from two extended passages.

3. James MacMillan describes *The Confession of Isobel Gowdie* as 'the Requiem that Isobel Gowdie never had'. Assess to what extent he was successful in this aim. Illustrate your answers with a detailed discussion of at least two extended passages from the work.

Further listening

You can listen to James MacMillan discussing *The Confession of Isobel Gowdie* on http://www.bbc.co.uk/radio3/discoveringmusic/pip/7j5qe/.

Other related repertoire

Threnody for the Victims of Hiroshima for 52 solo strings (1960) by Krzysztof Penderecki.

Different Trains, for string quartet and tape (1988) by Steve Reich.

Further reading

The Music of Tōru Takemitsu by Peter Burt (ISBN: 978-0521026956, CUP 2001).

Resources

The full score of *The Confession of Isobel Gowdie* is published by Boosey & Hawkes.

A number of recordings are available, including Sir Colin Davis' excellent recording, coupled with *The World's Ransoming*, on LSO Live (LSO0124).

Seiji Ozawa and the Boston Symphony Orchestra have recorded Takemitsu's *A Flock Descends into the Pentagonal Garden* (DG 00289 477 5381).

Topic 3:
Music for the screen

Music accompanied the on-screen action from the early days of the cinema. The makers of Hollywood's major silent movies employed their own composers to write or arrange accompanying music. This was printed and circulated with the film to cinemas, where it was played by live musicians. For low-budget films, a pianist or organist in the cinema would improvise suitable music, sometimes using ideas from books of 'mood music' that were produced for the purpose. When the technology of talking pictures was invented, the film studios adapted quickly to the demand for a pre-recorded soundtrack of specifically composed music.

In the 1930s, film companies set up their own music departments to cope with the huge numbers of films being made. There was intense pressure on film composers to finish their work in a matter of weeks so that the film could be released as soon as possible. Studio bosses wanted composers who would work quickly and adapt their methods to the requirements of film-making.

> The ability to work as a collaborative member of a team was essential. Teams of musicians supported the work of the credited composer of the film, particularly in the time-consuming process of orchestrating the music. Sometimes the collaboration extended to composing uncredited additional sections of music.

The three prescribed film scores in this topic are the work of composers who were well-known as composers outside the film studio. Each film demonstrates a different approach to the art of providing a score for a film.

The Adventures of Robin Hood (1938) is by the Austrian composer Erich Korngold, who in the early 1930s moved from his homeland to the United States and as a result escaped Hitler's occupation of Austria. As a Jew he knew that his music would be banned in his own country and that his life would be in danger if he returned. He brought to film music a symphonic approach to writing music, influenced by the operas of Richard Wagner and the orchestral music of Gustav Mahler and Richard Strauss. This style fell out of fashion in the 1950s but was revived and modernised by composers such as John Williams in the 1970s.

Vertigo (1958) was one of Bernard Herrmann's well-known scores for the British-born director Alfred Hitchcock, whose films are renowned for their suspense and mystery. Herrmann's economical approach is more concerned with reflecting the inner feelings of the characters, than providing illustrative commentary on the action, which the audience can see for themselves.

The Hours (2002) score is composed by the leading minimalist composer, Philip Glass. In choosing a composer for a film, producers and directors have a wide variety of compositional styles available to them. The choice of Philip Glass was a response to the artistic challenge of a story about the parallel lives of three women connected by one of the masterpieces of the English novel.

While using a CD recording is convenient and helpful, you will only get a full picture with a DVD of the film itself.

The OCR specification states that film scores should be studied in the context of the film, not as a separate score (if these are available) or a concert version of highlights. The relationship between the dramatic action and the accompanying music is an important part of one of the Areas of Study, Interpretation. You are expected to know about how the music is used to enhance the action of the film.

The Adventures of Robin Hood

The Adventures of Robin Hood

Warner Brothers, 1938

Directed by Michael Curtiz and William Keighley

Starring Errol Flynn (Robin Hood), Olivia de Havilland (Maid Marian), Basil Rathbone (Sir Guy of Gisbourne), Claude Rains (Prince John)

Music by Erich Wolfgang Korngold

Orchestrations by Hugo Friedhofer

Korngold's first feature film was *Captain Blood* (1935), the film which established Errol Flynn as a star.

Erich Wolfgang Korngold (1897–1957) was a child prodigy. The son of a leading Viennese music critic, the famous musicians of Austria and Germany lined up to hail his genius and perform his works. By the time he was 23 he was sufficiently established as a composer to have his first full-scale opera, *Die tote Stadt*, premiered both in Cologne and Hamburg, followed shortly afterwards by performances in London and New York.

In the 1930s, Max Steiner's scores for films such as *King Kong* persuaded the Hollywood film studios of the advantages of engaging composers, trained in European techniques of composition, to write the music for their films. Korngold had successfully arranged the music of Mendelssohn for a film of *A Midsummer's Night Dream* (1935), following which he was invited to work for Warner Brothers in Hollywood. Warner Brothers were well aware of the prestige of having Korngold composing for them. His contract was to produce music for three films every two years – much less than other film composers – and was guaranteed that his name should have a separate credit in the titles and would also be included in any advertising in which the director was mentioned.

The Adventures of Robin Hood represented a big financial investment for Warner Brothers. It was filmed in Technicolor, which required expensive cameras and lighting to capture the colourful scenery and costumes. Although they had Max Steiner as the company's main composer, Warner Brothers wanted Korngold's music for this film. Korngold resisted at first, arguing that the action sequences were not really suited to his style of music. The company persisted. When Hitler marched his armies into Austria in 1938, the situation for Jews in Austria changed overnight: Korngold realised that he and his family were safer in the United States, and he temporarily abandoned his concert and opera career to compose film music.

In all Korngold wrote scores for 16 films, seven of which starred Errol Flynn. When the war ended he returned to Austria and attempted to revive his career as a composer of serious works, but he found that his late Romantic style was regarded as outdated and conservative. At the time of his death his reputation rested mostly on the fine quality of his film scores, but there has since been a serious reassessment of his work as a whole, with many of his concert works and operas receiving performances all over the world.

The pressure to produce film scores to a tight deadline meant that few Hollywood composers orchestrated their own work. For *The Adventures of Robin Hood* Korngold wrote his music in short score, leaving the task of producing a full orchestral version to

Hugo Friedhofer and Milan Roder. For the recording of the cues onto the finished film, Korngold conducted the orchestra himself. Korngold also saved time by adapting themes from some of his previous works. For example, Robin Hood's theme is taken from his overture *Sursum Corda* (1919). There is a full discussion of Korngold's borrowings from his own music in Ben Winters's study of the music for the film (see further reading at the end of this section).

European composers working in Hollywood brought to films the style and techniques that they had learned from studying and working in Europe. Their style of dramatic music was principally derived from the symphonic style of German opera pioneered by Richard Wagner (for a discussion of his opera *Die Walküre* read the relevant section in the chapter on Music for the stage). Instead of using separate numbers (songs, arias, choruses) in which the singers were accompanied by the orchestra, Wagner's operas linked scenes into a continuous orchestral texture. He also developed the system of leitmotifs, where a theme or motif became associated with a character, event, object, idea or emotion. The repeating, developing and combining of leitmotifs was used to integrate the music and drama. When composers such as Korngold came to write film scores they tended to approach the task as if they were writing an opera without words.

Film music however is not continuous in the sense of opera, but composed of a series of individual numbers (known as cues), which vary in length from a few seconds to a few minutes. Korngold was highly adept at using his various themes in different forms each time they were heard. His techniques included reorchestrating and reharmonising according to the mood of the scene, and cutting down themes into smaller motifs, which allowed them to be repeated and developed more flexibly. He also linked themes melodically and rhythmically which increased the feeling of continuity and allowed dramatic ideas to be linked in the music. For example, the tonic-dominant leap at the beginning of the **Robin**, **Jollity** and **Fighting themes** make links (see below) to different aspects of Robin's character and personality. The ascending leap of a minor 9th in 'Robin fighting' theme is also a feature of Sir Guy's theme – they are both fighting men and the fight between them is one of the most important elements of the story.

Friedhofer orchestrated almost all of Korngold's films and established a good understanding of his style and methods of composing.

Musical style

Wagner's works exerted a powerful influence on European music, particularly in Germany and Austria. Composers such as Richard Strauss and Korngold developed this style further in their own operas and orchestral works.

Beginning of the film

Timing	Action on screen
0:00–1:28	Title music
1:45–1:54	Cut to interior, Prince John and Sir Guy
2:28–4:05	Norman oppression, Robin's theme, Much is caught
4:36–5:42	Robin and Sir Guy
6:03–7:58	Banquet at Nottingham Castle, Prince John and Maid Marian
9:08–10:03	Robin's entrance with deer, Robin and Prince John
14:02–18:10	Fighting, Robin's escape, chase on horses
18:23–18:47	Scene change to Priest blessing the Norman dead
19:26–20:25	Forest scene, entrance of Little John
20:38–21:58	Quarterstaff fight, Will Scarlett's lute accompaniment
22:02–23:18	Merry Men formed: 'Meet Robin in Sherwood at Gallow's Oak'
23:54–25:40	Swearing the oath, Norman oppression, the Black Arrow

Title music

Timings are for guidance only. Different DVD editions can produce different timings for the same film.

The title music introduces three themes in the film: the **March of the Merry Men**, **King Richard's theme** and the **fanfare** that is associated with Prince John. It opens with the March, which features a melody in 3rds and is in clear four-bar phrases. This is followed by a bridge section, notable for its curious melody in parallel 4ths and use of the whole-tone scale. Korngold uses the repetition of the octave leap motif at the end of this bridge section as a transition into King Richard's theme, its noble character fitting the historical nature of the narrative on screen. The title music ends with the fanfare, which, as noted below, creates a seamless link into the first scene.

King Richard's theme

Diegetic music is music in a film which forms part of the action (i.e. played or heard by the characters), not part of the underscore.

There is very little directly diegetic music in *The Adventures of Robin Hood*. Little John whistles 'Sumer is Icumen In' when we see him for the first time. Otherwise the musical elements in the story are imitated by the orchestra:

➤ At the end of the **title music** the tonic-dominant timpani of Prince John's fanfare provides a neat transition into the mounted timpani at the proclamation

➤ At the **banquet** the introductory music for the scene is well under way as the camera pans over the band. The added flute sound suggests the woodwind instruments being played

➤ In the **fight at the stream** between Robin and Little John, violin pizzicato (in places strummed across all four strings) is used to imitate the sound of the lute, which Will plays while the fight goes on.

The fanfare is repeated quietly, as if offstage, at the beginning of Prince John and Sir Guy's scene. When the Prince knocks over the goblet, the chromatic descent of the bass clarinet and cellos reinforces the symbolism of the blood red wine being spilled. This passage is an introduction to a more extended section of music – an expressive minor-key theme representing the Norman oppression of the Saxons.

At the beginning of the first forest scene, the leaping major 7ths and minor 9ths of Sir Guy's theme are introduced followed in sharp contrast by the first appearance of Robin's cheerfully heroic theme in C major. Much, the Miller's son, hunts the deer to the sound of parallel 3rds similar to the Merry Men's theme. As Sir Guy and his men chase after Much for his crime Sir Guy's theme is repeated, but the subsequent dialogue is unaccompanied by music. As he raises his baton to strike Much the first three notes of Sir Guy's theme are heard, cut short by Robin's arrow and the full restatement of Robin's theme as he rides over to confront Sir Guy. The underscore for their verbal duel makes use of the 3rds motif. Sir Guy rides off to the sound of his own theme.

The courtly theme that starts the Banqueting scene only appears here. It is characterised by fussy chromatic harmonies, suggesting the artificial formality of Prince John and the nobles who are after his favour. Following Prince John's fanfare (the camera tellingly focuses on the dog attacking its meat) a formal woodwind variation accompanies Prince John's speech. By contrast, Maid Marian's theme is harmonised much more simply, suggesting her beauty and honesty.

Even in the action scenes Korngold attempts to shape his material in a satisfying musical pattern. The chase on horseback uses galloping dotted rhythms for the horses, setting up a consistent rhythmic background throughout the sequence. When the horses are not in shot the use of the same tempo maintains the tension. As the Norman soldiers ride away from the camera the music diminuendos, but he returns briefly to the same music to end the scene when Much rides away with his message.

In places a clear musical structure is encouraged by the repetition of similar scenes, particularly action sequences which switch rapidly between contrasting scenes. In the scene with the black arrows, each instance of Norman oppression leads to a death by Robin's black arrow. The music alternates between the Oppression theme and the Fight motif, creating a musically effective ABABAB structure, which builds in tension as the sections are repeated.

Prince John and Sir Guy

Banqueting scene

The black arrows

The attack on Sir Guy's men in Sherwood Forest

Timing	Action on screen
32:02–36:19	Preparations for the ambush, the attack
36:55–40:46	Escort to the camp, clothes for Sir Guy, the banquet
41:32–46:30	Captured treasure, the victims of oppression, farewell

The Sherwood Forest scene uses three more extended passages of music, each lasting 4–5 minutes, breaking off for Robin's speeches. The March of the Merry Men is made more amusing by the use of the bassoon to double the violin melody, with prominent use made of trills. The March rhythm is used to give continuity to the changes in shot. As the Norman party approaches, the melody stops but the rhythm continues with Sir Guy's ascending leaps on the violins. As the horses rest to take water the march continues but the tempo is slower, building up the tension as we wait for the Merry Men to jump out. The fight is not as serious as the earlier fight in the castle. No one is killed, and the music is a light, scherzo-like version of the March. The jumping down out of the trees is represented by the descending scales in the violins and the harp glissandi. The good-natured aspect of the ambush is underlined by the Jollity theme (at 35:34, after the Sheriff and Sir Guy realise they are being attacked).

The waltz was a common feature in classical and popular music of the time. Its flowing melodies were widely used in American stage musicals and European operettas, so its use in dramatic film music was unsurprising.

A waltz provides the continuity for the second passage of music. It provides a romantic element to the story as Robin and Marian get to know each other (with Much and Bess providing a comic equivalent). The melody of the March is turned in to a waltz in the scenes with the men. The original waltz returns at the end as Robin and Marian sit together at the banquet.

After Robin's speech the music starts again as the captured treasure is revealed, leading to the waltz version of the Merry Men theme. The use of the King Richard theme as Robin asks 'What shall we do with the treasure?' tells us the answer before his men do.

Korngold's skill in adapting his themes to different dramatic situations is demonstrated by his slow, lamenting version of the Oppression theme over a bass pedal, as Marian is shown the homeless families which Robin is sheltering in Sherwood Forest. Richard's theme is also used in the underscore, beautifully scored for solo cello, as Robin explains his hatred of injustice and Marian begins to understand him. The romantic richness of the string underscore comes from the chordal writing in the violins, the expressive chromatic harmonies and the use of portamento (sliding between notes), which was more widely used as a technique of orchestral violin playing than it is today. The waltz completes the scene as Marian rides away.

Exercise 9

1. Make notes on the music for the Archery contest. Explain how Korngold combines new material for the contest with the themes of the characters. How is the March of the Merry Men changed to suggest their disguise?

2. Compare the 'fighting' music in the film. Apart from the examples in the scenes discussed here, there is a dramatic duel between Robin and Sir Guy at the climax of the film. How is the seriousness of this fight to the death apparent in the music?

Related repertoire

You should be familiar with at least one film score by a composer with a similar background to Erich Korngold. Like Korngold, **Max Steiner** (1888–1971) was a Vienna-trained child prodigy, but he emigrated to the United States as a young man. He spent some time working in the theatres of New York before moving to Los Angeles to compose for Warner Brothers. Initially film producers and directors were unsure of the precise role music should play in a film. Earlier films with sound tended to use music where there was a clear musical link to what was on screen – similar to the ensemble playing in the banquet scene in Robin Hood or the lute accompaniment as Robin and Little John fight with the quarterstaffs. The concept of an **underscore** – music which accompanied or represented the action on screen without being part of it – took some time to gain acceptance.

King Kong

Steiner's score for *King Kong* (1933) became a model for the successful use of originally composed music in a film. He exploited the new technology of recording the music separately from the sound for the action. He pioneered the technique of writing music cues that were the correct length for the dramatic action, conducting the orchestra to fit in with the film. He introduced the practice of assigning musical themes to the characters and situations in the manner of operatic leitmotifs. His success in matching the action to appropriate music was highly influential. He was a highly prolific composer, who had a long career, writing music for hundreds of films.

Gone with the Wind

Gone with the Wind (1939) is an epic movie based on the novel by Margaret Mitchell, which follows the life of its main character, Scarlett O'Hara, from her privileged background in the southern state of Georgia through the disaster of the Civil War and her unhappy marriage afterwards to Rhett Butler. The music uses leitmotifs for the main characters and their relationships, but the most memorable music is Tara's Theme (representing Scarlett's home and the land on which it stands), the title music for the film. In the final scene, after Rhett has left her, she hears in her mind the overlapping voices of other characters talking of Tara. The music uses a wordless chorus to create a dream-like atmosphere. As she realises that Tara is where she should be, the music modulates to a major key and the motifs of the Tara theme are transformed into the full theme. The wordless chorus gives a final lift to the music to achieve a typically optimistic

Further reading

Erich Wolfgang Korngold's The Adventures of Robin Hood, by Ben Winters (ISBN: 13-978-0-81088-5888-6, Scarecrow Press 2007). A detailed treatment of the subject, including the background to Korngold's film music, collaboration with others, analysis of the score and numerous examples.

Hollywood-style ending. Scarlett's silhouette is seen against the red sky as she looks towards her home.

In the scene showing the siege of Atlanta, Steiner uses fragments of southern folk melodies to depict the destruction of the South. Melodies which are usually major and diatonic are given a darker mood by using minor keys or chromatic harmonies as Scarlett sees the hundreds of injured and dying soldiers waiting for help. As the camera pulls back to show a tattered Confederate flag there is a crescendo and a broadening out of the music. By contrast the music for Scarlett is dominated by strings. The writing is intense and restless, with frequent chromatic passages and modulations reflecting the emotional turbulence of the characters, for example her agitations about getting help for Melanie. The music for Scarlett and Rhett's escape from Atlanta is fast and exciting, providing a commentary on the action as they encounter burning buildings and desperate soldiers.

Exercise 10

1. Summarise the main techniques used by Korngold in his music for *The Adventures of Robin Hood.* Describe at least two extended scenes in detail to explain how his music enhances the drama.

2. Explain the success of at least two European composers for the Hollywood movies of the 1930s. Use examples from a film score by each composer to illustrate your answer.

3. Compare the use of timbre and instrumental colour in Korngold's score for *The Adventures of Robin Hood* and Philip Glass' score for *The Hours,* explaining how they contribute to the effectiveness of the film.

Vertigo

Vertigo

Universal Pictures, 1958

Directed by Alfred Hitchcock

Starring James Stewart (John 'Scottie' Ferguson), Kim Novak (Madeleine Elster/Judy Barton), Barbara Bel Geddes (Midge Wood)

Music by Bernard Herrmann

Conducted by Muir Mathieson

Bernard Herrmann (1911–1975) studied in New York with the Australian composer Percy Grainger. As a student he was attracted by the music of native American composers such as Charles Ives and Aaron Copland. He founded the Young Composers' Group to perform and promote works by himself and other composers who shared the experimental and uncompromising attitudes of American composers (such as Charles Ives, Carl Ruggles and Henry Cowell). After the group had broken up Herrmann got a job for CBS, working on the music for radio programmes. His involvement with Orson Welles's notorious radio adaptation of *The War of the Worlds,* which caused a panic by listeners who believed a Martian invasion was really taking place, led Welles to ask him to compose the music for his first film, *Citizen Kane* (1941).

Herrman's style of composing was too conservative for him to gain much more than modest success as a serious composer. His opera *Wuthering Heights* and his cantata *Moby Dick* are impressive works but are not often performed. But in terms of film music, his style was regarded as adventurous, even avant-garde. He orchestrated his own scores, experimenting with unusual sonorities to create the sounds required for the drama. Considered to be difficult to work with, Herrmann had a clear vision of what he wanted to achieve and strong views about the role of music in films. He regarded his film music equally as valuable as his other compositions, and he was very dismissive about attempts by directors to downplay the importance of the film composer. He believed that the role of the composer was to get inside the story and understand the psychology of the characters. This matched the approach of the director Alfred Hitchcock, whose films were renowned for their exploration of psychological themes. In addition to *Vertigo*, Herrmann's nine-year partnership with Hitchcock produced well-known films such as *North By Northwest* (1959) and *Psycho* (1960). Not only are these among the finest examples of film music but also demonstrate the close artistic empathy between director and composer.

Vertigo is now considered to be one of Hitchcock's – and cinema's – greatest achievements, but it was poorly received when it first appeared. The film is based on *D'Entre les Morts* (1954) by Pierre Boileau and Thomas Narcejac, written with Hitchcock in mind.

The story

Scottie is a detective who is forced to retire because of acrophobia – a fear of heights. He is hired by Gavin Elster to follow his wife, Madeleine, who is behaving as if possessed. Scottie falls in love with her. He takes her to the San Juan Bautista Mission, which has figured in her dreams, to prove that she has nothing to fear. She runs up the bell tower at the mission. Scottie's acrophobia prevents him from following her and she falls to her death. He suffers a breakdown. He becomes so obsessed with Madeleine that when he finds a girl, Judy Barton, who looks like her he insists that she has a full makeover so that the likeness is exact in every detail. He realises that Judy has been part of a plot by Gavin Elster to murder his wife. He forces Judy to revisit the Mission and climb the bell tower, with the same tragic consequences.

The film is more than just an ingenious and entertaining detective story. Through the story and the medium of film, Hitchcock explores various themes about reality, illusion and romantic love. The double structure of the story has Scottie falling in love with the same woman and losing her both times. He sees Judy as an ideal woman, a re-creation of the perfection that was Madeleine. When he discovers her deception he is both attracted and repelled by her. The story has similarities with the Greek legend of Orpheus, who goes to the Underworld to recover Eurydice from death only to lose her again because he breaks his promise not to look back as she follows him.

There are also strong connections with the story of Richard Wagner's opera *Tristan und Isolde* (1865), which deals with overpowering romantic love which is fulfilled through death.

Bernard Herrmann's music avoids Wagner's leitmotif-based symphonic style which Korngold used in *The Adventures of Robin Hood*. Instead, his style is much leaner, responding to the psychological implications of the drama rather than providing an illustrative commentary on the action. Most of the music cues are centred on the characters of Scottie and of Madeleine, who has her own theme. Midge does not have her own music: she is more often associated with diegetic music (music which is played as part of the action). She plays a recording of J. C. Bach in her apartment, and a Mozart symphony is used as part of Scottie's therapy. The Mozart has no effect on Scottie's condition. There is a dramatic distinction between the use of the pre-recorded music to represent

A strike by American musicians forced the recording of the music to be switched to London and Vienna, under Muir Mathieson, who conducted the music for many British films of the time.

the real world and Herrmann's music which represents the world of Scottie's emotions.

Tonality and harmony

Herrmann uses a number of dissonant chord formations to support the drama. The two most characteristic of these chords are the so-called **Hitchcock chord** (which he also used in *Psycho*), a minor chord with a sharpened 7th, and the **Vertigo chord,** a bitonal combination of two triads with roots a semitone apart. In the example *left* the triads for the Vertigo chord are E♭ minor and D major.

The chromatic nature of the Vertigo chord makes it very difficult to decide which key it is in. In *Vertigo*, the use of successions of chromatic chords, which resolve in a variety of ways, creates an unsettled feeling throughout passages of the music. Dissonant chords can also be used in parallel formations, not resolving at all. For example, listen to the music for the mysterious scene in which Scottie and Madeleine examine the sequoia trees, scored in parallel 7th chords in second inversion.

Herrmann seems to have been particularly influenced by *Tristan und Isolde* and he employs a variety of chord voicings which are similar to the Tristan chord (shown *below*). A number of commentators have suggested musical parallels between sections of the film and passages from *Tristan*. In Wagner, the richness of the chromatic harmonies are combined with frequent modulations, suspensions and appoggiaturas to disguise the tonality. In the opera, the doomed lovers Tristan and Isolde live in a permanent state of longing. To reflect this, Wagner's music creates a feeling of constant yearning by denying the ultimate fulfilment of reaching a tonic chord.

Wagner, *Tristan und Isolde* (opening)

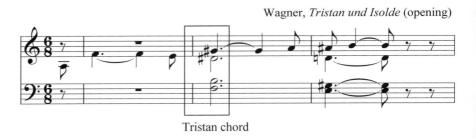

Tristan chord

Herrmann's use of suspension is seen in Madeleine's theme, the first four bars of which is quoted here.

Madeleine's theme

It is worth listening to parts of *Tristan und Isolde* to hear which elements of Wagner's style have been taken up by Herrmann in *Vertigo*. A good place to start would be the orchestral excerpts known as the *Prelude and Liebestod* (from the beginning and end of the opera). There is more information on Wagner and *Die Walküre* in the chapter on Music for the stage.

Beginning of the film

Timing	Action on screen
0:22–3:12	Title music
3:12–4:47	The chase across San Francisco rooftops
4:46–7:11	Scottie and Midge – diegetic music
10:36–10:49	Flashback to the rooftop, Scottie falls
16:34–21:47	Madeleine at Ernie's restaurant. Follows her: flower shop, Mission Dolores, Carlotta Valdes's grave.
24:43–26:31	Portrait of Carlotta

The dramatic and urgent title music is very different from the rest of the score. The opening is based on arpeggios of E♭ minor with a sharpened 7th (the Hitchcock chord), arranged so that the dissonances on the strong beats are emphasised:

The timings above are for guidance only. Different DVD editions can produce different timings for the same film.

The trombone motif (two pairs of notes: D–C and E♭–D) is typical of a score in which many melodic motifs and chords appear in pairs, particularly falling or rising in step.

The changes in the chords and their instrumentation are timed to synchronise with the title sequence, for example the E♭ minor sharpened 7th chord on 'James Stewart' and 'In Alfred Hitchcock's', separated by A♯ minor on 'Kim Novak', and a more dissonant combination of the two chords at the title 'Vertigo'. Ascending trills in the violins match the upward fade of the title and the spiral which grows in the eye. The human face disappears and the titles focus on the spirals. The first appearance of the more legato and romantic 'love motif' (as David Cooper labels it) suggests that the inner workings of the mind are going to be as important to the film as the outward action.

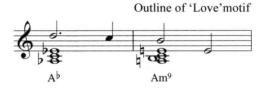

Outline of 'Love' motif

The reappearance of the two sets of material, although compressed the second time, with a short coda give the prelude an overall ABABA shape. The arpeggiation of the opening section makes only a brief appearance in the rest of the film – when Judy's outward appearance is being changed so that she looks like Madeleine.

Without a break we are immediately into the action on the rooftop. The rushing semiquaver ostinato accompanying slow octave leaps in trombones and tuba generate excitement and menace as Scottie and another policeman pursue their suspect. When Scottie slips and looks down, we hear the 'Vertigo' chord for the first time. The forceful superimposed chords of D major and E♭ minor are

Chase across rooftops

arranged for trumpets, woodwind and vibraphone, with two harps (each tuned to different scales a semitone apart) in ascending and descending glissandi. This chord alternates antiphonally with a quieter but equally dissonant combination of A♭ minor and G minor triads in a low register (listen for the sound of the Hammond organ among the strings and brass of this chord).

Striking though these chords are, the music is completely immobilised by them – these dissonant chords are unrelated to the previous key. The rhythmic momentum has also been lost. The static nature of the music, with unresolved chords which can only be juxtaposed, matches the dramatic situation: Scottie is hanging by his fingertips, terrified and unable to move.

Ernie's restaurant

The character of Madeleine is first introduced in Ernie's restaurant. Her long melodic theme, with its slow and regular harmonic movement, is different from the short, unconnected phrases of much of the rest of the score. Although the strings are muted (Herrmann generally preferred the veiled tone of muted strings), there is more warmth and vibrato in the string writing than usual.

When Scottie is following her in the car, the music reverts to a motivic pattern, with an ostinato in clarinets and bass clarinet supporting variations on the initial five-note motif in the violins. The violins disappear with Madeleine as she enters the shop through the back door. Note the parallel chords in the clarinets as Scottie walks through the gloomy back room. Madeleine's theme is heard for the second time as she is revealed in a full-length shot. The romantic nature of the music tells us that Scottie is not just observing her actions as a detective: he is attracted by her.

The graveyard

The next time we hear Madeleine's theme is in the graveyard, strangely and sparsely orchestrated with the melody in the high register of the violins, with only low clarinets in 5ths accompanying. He follows her to the gallery, where she sits looking at the portrait of her ancestor, Carlotta Valdes. The mysterious new theme features low 3rds on flutes, with a habanera rhythm in the harp, linked to the Spanish ancestry of the subject of the painting.

Madeleine's death

Timing	Action on screen
65:45–66:04	Scottie walking in the city at night
66:19–68:50	Madeleine's dream
68:50–75:26	Journey to the Mission, the Livery Stable, the Tower
80:04–82:01	Scottie visits Madeleine's grave, the nightmare

A brief link between scenes is provided by a shot of the city at night with the figure of Scottie walking in the dark to the accompaniment of the love motif, played three times in different registers. The Habanera rhythm returns as Madeleine recounts her dream and describes the bell tower. The same music is used again for the scene at the Mission. Sitting in the Livery Stable, Madeleine tells Scottie of her 'memories' of her previous existence in the Mission. The habanera rhythm is now in low flutes, with the violin melody in nine four-bar phrases, each different. The section is beautifully orchestrated to suggest the distant memories, with rich harmonies and a slow yearning melody. The romantic string music breaks the spell of the dream for a moment, but Madeleine rushes towards the tower. The music breaks into a waltz version of her theme, with the motifs altered and extended until the love motif develops out of the theme.

The tower

Scottie realises that she is going to climb the tower. As he follows her up the tower, the fast music from the scene on the rooftops returns, a contrast to the slow tempi of most of the score of *Vertigo*. Unusually Herrmann closely synchronises the music with the different shots in the sequence, creating a disjointed feeling of panic: there are separate chords, each with a different register and instrumentation as Madeleine breaks into a run, he looks up at the tower, realises where she is going, stands in the interior of the church, looks at the font, then at the bottom of the stairs of the tower. The juxtapositions of the 'Vertigo' chords – each of them scored differently – are synchronised with Scottie's view down the stairs, an effects shot which simulates a feeling of dizziness. The paralysing effect of the dissonant and distant chords shows his inability to take any action that will save Madeleine's life.

The nightmare

The nightmare scene begins with a repeated tremolo string figure, ascending chromatically which reflects the disturbance in Scottie's mind. As the images from the story of Carlotta appear there is a loud, distorted version of the Habanera. The music sounds much more forceful and dance-like, with the addition of castanets and tambourine strengthening the Spanish element in the music. The nightmare ends as Scottie's silhouette falls to the sound of the 'Vertigo' chords.

Exercise 11

1. Look at the scenes when Judy is made to look exactly like Madeleine. Explain the role of the music in reflecting the conflicting emotions of Scottie and Judy.

2. Compare the scene of Madeleine's death with the corresponding scene at the end of the film.

3. Make notes on Herrmann's use of instrumentation and timbre in one of the scenes from the film.

Related repertoire

Further reading

Bernard Herrmann's Vertigo: A Film Score Handbook by David Cooper (ISBN: 978-0313314902, Greenwood Press 2001). A detailed and readable account, including music examples and descriptions of the various cues.

Overtones and Undertones: Reading Film Music by Royal S. Brown (ISBN: 978-0520085442, University of California Press 1994). A general survey of film music, including a section on *Psycho* and Bernard Hermann.

American Film Music by William Darby and Jack DuBois (ISBN: 978-0786407538, McFarland & Co new edition 2000). A useful general survey, including information on both Korngold and Herrmann.

On the Track: A Guide to Contemporary Film Scoring by Fred Karlin and Rayburn Wright (ISBN: 978-0028733104, Routledge 2nd edition 2004). An invaluable guide to the practical aspects of writing for films, intended for composers. Includes many detailed examples from a range of well-known modern film scores.

You are expected to be familiar with other films which show the integration of music and drama.

Large-scale orchestral scores fell out of fashion during the 1950s and 1960s. Producers and directors looked to jazz and more popular styles for films with contemporary settings, reserving the orchestral style for period dramas. The symphonic style tended to be regarded as too melodramatic for modern audiences. At times directors felt that music could weaken scenes that were intended to be realistic by introducing an inappropriate theatrical feeling or emotion into the scene.

Composers such as Bernard Herrmann led the way in experimenting with 20th-century composing techniques, which were increasingly accepted by audiences in the concert hall. In the 1960s, younger composers were introducing a more rhythmic and dissonant style when it was required by the film. Scores such as Elmer Bernstein's for *The Great Escape* (1963) and Jerry Goldsmith's for *Patton* (1970) show how composers continued the practice of providing memorable theme tunes for their films (in both cases marching tunes suitable for films set in World War II). At the same time, they were able to respond to the dramatic needs of the film. In *Patton*, the music is used sparingly, with only about half an hour of music in a three-hour film. Goldsmith uses an echoing trumpet motif to suggest Patton's belief in reincarnation and that his career as a general is a continuation of previous triumphs in history.

The Taking of Pelham One Two Three (1974) is a thriller in which a gang of armed men hijack a subway train in New York. Composer **David Shire** creates a dissonant jazz style from a 12-note series. He organises his row (see *below*) into four motifs of three pitches. Over a syncopated bass ostinato, the melody in the brass (bars 2–9 of the example) uses all 12 chromatic notes in the set order. Leaps of 3rds and 7ths give the melody a distinctive rhythmic and melodic profile which is similar to bebop influenced jazz writing – this gives the score its urgent, urban feel. Note also the use of the row to make up the syncopated chords for the full band.

12 note row

The End Title, *The Taking of Pelham One Two Three*

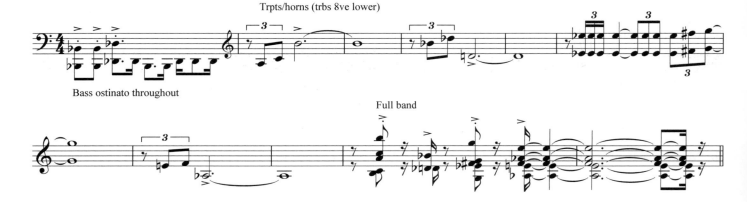

Apart from the opening sequence, most of the music is in the second half of the film. There are short cues, for example when the ransom money is tipped out onto the floor of the train – the three-note motifs are heard distinctly in single harp notes. As the train with its hostages starts to move for the first time the full theme is heard, fading out as the train passes through the station. The rhythmic repeated notes of the 3rd motif (bar 6 in the example) adds to the tension ('Pelham 123 is in motion') as the gang change clothes and attempt to escape.

Exercise 12

1. Explain how Bernard Herrmann has used aspects of melody, harmony and tonality in his music for *Vertigo*. Show in at least two extracts how the dramatic effectiveness of the film has been enhanced by the music.

2. Explain the different approaches to writing music for a film used by Bernard Herrmann in *Vertigo* and by Erich Korngold in *The Adventures of Robin Hood*. Discuss at least one extended extract from each film to compare the techniques which the composers used.

3. Describe how composers of music for films since 1950 explored new methods of creating dramatically effective scores by using new techniques or new sounds. You should choose examples from at least two films which you have studied.

The Hours

Philip Glass (b. 1937) is one of the pioneers of Minimalistic music which developed in the United States in the 1960s. Glass had travelled to Europe to study and work with the Indian sitar player Ravi Shankar. In common with many composers he was stimulated by the different approach to music found in non-Western cultures. These seemed to be more emotionally connected to the listener than the atonality of much contemporary music. On his return to the United States he set up the Philip Glass Ensemble, with which he experimented in a new style of composition based on repetition and gradual modification of acoustic and amplified sound. He is a well-known composer of eight symphonies, other concert works and operas, including *Einstein on the Beach* (1976) and *Satyagraha* (1980). He has written music for many films, including *Kundun* (1997), *The Thin Blue Line* (1988), *Dracula* (1999) and *Mishima* (1984).

The Hours begins with Virginia Woolf's suicide in 1941. Her novel *Mrs Dalloway* is the inspiration for Michael Cunningham's book on which the film is based. Woolf's story takes a day in the life of one woman, Clarissa Dalloway, who is arranging a party. Cunningham's novel *The Hours* provides the basis for David Hare's screenplay. It is the story of three women, set in three different times and places: Virginia Woolf in 1923 in Richmond, Surrey; Laura Brown in 1951 in Los Angeles; and Clarissa Vaughan in 2001 in New York.

The scope of the action is very limited. Not much happens between the two suicides. One of Virginia Woolf's particular contributions to the development of the English novel is her narrative technique,

The Hours

Paramount Pictures and Miramax Films, 2002

Directed by Stephen Daldry

Screenplay by David Hare

Based on the novel by Michael Cunningham

Starring Meryl Streep (Clarissa Vaughan), Julianne Moore (Laura Brown), Nicole Kidman (Virginia Woolf)

Music by Philip Glass

See Philip Glass's website for more information: www.philipglass.com

often referred to as 'stream of consciousness'. In the opening pages of *Mrs Dalloway*, we gain an impression of the story of the novel through the thoughts and feelings of the main character, not necessarily in a logical order because her mind darts from one thought to another. There is no conventional narrative which describes objectively what is happening.

In a film the effectiveness of the drama depends on showing the audience what is taking place, but the screenplay retains much of the subtle interplay of thoughts and emotions which are in both *Mrs Dalloway* and *The Hours*. The expressive and restrained emotion of the music provides additional information about the characters, which the audience might miss if they were relying on visual clues only.

A temp-track is pre-existing recorded music used to test the sort of music needed for the film.

The music plays an important part in establishing the continuity between the three stories. The makers of the film tried various 'temp tracks', and their test of Glass' music was the most successful because it avoided the sort of emotional commentary that film music often provides. The director wanted music that contributed expressively to the film without creating unwanted suggestions about the dramatic or emotional significance of what the music was accompanying.

The music responds to the dramatic elements in the film – the scenes in which Laura leaves Richie and goes to the hotel are discussed below. However, Glass uses a largely consistent musical style throughout the film, tying together the different scenes to achieve a feeling of one story. A number of musical techniques are used to do this:

➢ The instrumentation of piano and strings

➢ Consistent use of broken chords or arpeggios in quaver or triplet patterns

➢ Variations on repeating patterns of chords

➢ Triadic harmonies, favouring minor keys but freely using chromatic major triads (e.g. flattened supertonic A♭ major in the key of G minor)

➢ Chords changed gradually by metamorphosis (altering one note of the previous chord at a time)

➢ No modulation

Only a small orchestra is used: piano, strings, harp, celesta, glockenspiel and triangle.

➢ No extremes of tempo – moderate tempi preferred, with regular quaver movement.

The style of music avoids any suggestion of a particular period in time – 1920s-style music, for example, would not suit the later periods in the story, and there is no attempt to switch musical styles between scenes. In an interview on the DVD extras, Glass says that he chose the piano because it crosses periods easily. The individual, personal quality of the solo piano contributes to the feeling that the music is about the three individual women and what they have in common. There is no music associated with the other characters, no attempt to provide child-like music for

Richie or Vanessa's children, still less any leitmotif-style response to important characters such as Leonard or Richard.

Like Korngold, Glass also reuses some of his earlier music. The music for the melody of six semibreves (see the example on page 105) is taken from his opera *Satyagraha* ('Protest', Act 2 Scene 3), while other music is based on *Metamorphosis Two* for solo piano. The diegetic music which Louis Waters interrupts when he calls at Clarissa's apartment is Richard Strauss's *Four Last Songs*. The screenplay specifies the singer, Jessye Norman, but not which of the four songs. The third song, *Beim Schlafengehen* (text in German by Hermann Hesse), is about sleep freeing the soul from the weariness of the day. Strauss was in his 80s when he composed these songs, which are all on the theme of the calm acceptance of death. He died a few months later.

Beginning of the film

Timing	Action on screen
1:56–3:36	Virginia Woolf at the river
3:37–5:40	Title music – Los Angeles, 1951 – Dan arrives home Richmond, 1923 – Leonard arrives home
5:41–8:53	New York, 2001 – Sally arrives home Linking Virginia, Laura and Clarissa
12:50–14:45	Laura: breakfast in Los Angeles
15:56–18:06	Clarissa: the flower shop, Richard's novel
20:34–22:57	Richard for the first time
25:47–27:07	Clarissa leaves Richard's loft Virginia writing
30:06–32:04	Virginia walking, thinking through her ideas

The Hours begins without music, using Virginia Woolf's suicide as a prologue to the drama. The underscore begins as we see the river for the first time. The music subtly suggests the current of water in the undulating movement of the strings (see example overleaf). The harmonies alternate between the tonic chord (in the example G minor) and the flattened submediant 7th (Eb^7). These chords are closely related – only the Eb needs to be added to the G minor chord. The chord pattern extends over 14 or 16 bars, with more contrasting chords (F major and the dominant, D^7) used at the end. The music is calmly expressive – note the dissonant Eb against the dominant chord in the final bar of the example. There is no attempt to underline the drama of Virginia Woolf's death in the romantic style of earlier film music.

The timings above are for guidance only. Different DVD editions can produce different timings for the same film.

The Poet Acts (2:31–2:59)

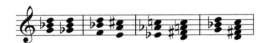

The solo piano is introduced in the title sequence from 3:36. The contrasting settings of the film are shown but also the similarities: the three partners are introduced first, followed by shots of the three central characters in bed. There are alarm clocks, mirrors, each woman thinking, and there are flowers. The repeating sequence of chords uses a chromatically descending pattern (shown *left*) to move towards the dominant chord and return to the tonic.

The first time this sequence is heard the music is in two-bar phrases separated by pauses, but there is continuous quaver movement for the rest of the music. Each variation of the chord sequence reflects the action in the film in its instrumentation or texture:

Dan goes into the house	More continuous left-hand movement in the piano
Laura is sleeping	In ¾, violins added
Leonard arriving home	Low strings, no piano
Talking to the Doctor	Slower, no quaver movement
New York subway, Sally	Louder strings, arpeggio 7ths in piano

Apart from the scene with the doctor, for which the music is unobtrusive, there is no dialogue. The music is forwardly balanced, with the sounds of the action heard in the background. The role of the music is to help establish the dramatic link between the characters. It builds to a climax as the three women are thinking and the vases of flowers are picked up or adjusted. As the next scene begins with Virginia and Leonard's dialogue, there is a diminuendo and the texture is reduced to broken octaves in the left hand of the piano and detached octaves in the violins. The music fades out quickly.

The longer scenes have no underscore: the music begins as a significant point is reached in the dialogue, continuing through any short scenes and fading out as the next long scene begins.

The next cue, following the title music, begins after our glimpse of the false normality of Dan, Laura and Richie's family life. Laura and Richie are left alone in the house. The broken-chord accompaniment is again based on closely related chords. The use of A minor in second inversion gives an unsettled feeling – the chord only finds root position when the six semibreve melody (two descending 4ths and a diminished 5th) appears later in the bass.

I'm Going to Make a Cake (13:14–13:25)

The music plays through into the next scene, fading as Clarissa enters the flower shop, so that the dialogue there is not underscored. The music resumes again in response to Barbara's perception that Clarissa is the woman in Richard's novel, linking to Virginia Woolf's voiceover: 'A woman's whole life in a single day … and in that day, her whole life'.

The flower shop

A different approach is used in the scene in Richard's loft. The music is an underscore to important dialogue (Richard is talking about himself as a writer) instead of providing continuity between scenes. The music is a pianissimo rearrangement of the music of the Virginia Woolf's suicide, with the melody in the violins and the lower strings *sotto voce* so that the dialogue is clearly heard. The next cue repeats material from Laura and Richie's scene (the melody of six semibreves quoted in the example *above*). The repeated chords in the strings crescendo as Woolf's ideas become more clearly formed, only to be cut off by Nelly's interruption. When she goes out to escape from the distractions of the house, the music becomes more expressive in its chromatically shifting harmonies as she realises that her character must die.

Richard's loft

The hotel

Timing	Action on screen
57:01–61:57	Laura and Richie in car – leaving Richie, driving to the hotel
62:40–65:38	Laura reading – Virginia Woolf's voice over – Laura imagines drowning
66:40–69:06	Virginia and Vanessa kiss – Vanessa and Louis leave

As Laura and Richie get in the car, leaving the cake on the table, the texture of the music consists of two strands, the string broken-chord figure alternating between A minor and A♭ minor and the high sustained octaves separated by rests in piano and violins. When she leaves Richie, doing her best to hide her feelings from him, a third layer of lower sustained chords is added. More expressive chord combinations are used, including the G minor – G♭ augmented – B♭ major pattern first heard in the title music. Richie struggles with Mrs Latch and the music becomes less diatonic: the piano/violin octaves are more dissonant against the broken-chord harmonies, including use of false relations (for example an E♭ in the melody clashing against an E♮ in the bass). Laura speeds towards the hotel, her feelings reflected in the clash of quavers and triplets in the strings (using the chord pattern of the title music). Richie is building a house. The piano hammers out the melody in a high register, followed by repeated spread chords with the strings playing repeated chords in quavers and then in semiquavers. There is a sudden change to *piano* as she enters the hotel, and the restless music stops as Laura is alone in her room.

Voice-over The music restarts as she thinks of the cake. The music establishes the connection between her and Virginia Woolf, changing only for the harp, celesta and glockenspiel scales which depict the water which floods Laura's room.

The kiss The six semibreve melody returns as Virginia and Vanessa kiss, beginning in a high register and passed through lower registers until it reaches the bass. The repeated chords in the strings and the forward balance of the recording as the dialogue ends shows the intense emotion of Virginia and Clarissa as their guests depart. The music pauses for them to exhale a breath of relief before the final chord of the cue.

Related repertoire

You should be familiar with other contemporary film music which adapts techniques of composition such as Minimalism or leitmotif. **John Williams**' work for the directors Stephen Spielberg and George Lucas did much to revive the large-scale orchestral score as a medium for film music in the 1970s and 1980s. He uses many of the symphonic techniques that Korngold and Steiner used but also incorporates elements of harmony and rhythm of early 20th-century composers such as Prokofiev and Stravinsky. John Williams has a gift for writing memorable melodies which has made his music popular among general audiences. He is particularly associated with the *Star Wars* and *Indiana Jones* series.

E.T.: The Extra-Terrestrial One of the most successful of his early Spielberg scores is *E.T.: The Extra-Terrestrial* (1982). The opening titles use electronic sounds, but the rest of the score is for a large orchestra. Herbert W. Spencer's orchestrations are refined and detailed. The opening scene, as E.T. explores the forest, uses string glissandi and chromatic decoration on celesta. Passages in bare octaves suggest the mystery of the forest at night. As the view of the city is revealed the music briefly opens out into a major key, but the ominous sounds of woodwind and brass are heard as the sinister government agents arrive. The appearance of the sinister man with the keys – we do not see his face – is accompanied by a fanfare motif with a dotted rhythm on a single note.

This motif plays an important part in the final scene, in which Elliott and E.T. escape to meet the spaceship in the forest. John

Williams wrote an extended music cue in which many of the leitmotifs reappear at the dramatic climax of the movie. A series of hit points in the music (for example the healing light at the end of E.T.'s finger, the rainbow in the sky as the spaceship takes off) proved difficult to coordinate with the running of the film, so Spielberg re-edited the film to match the action with the music cue.

Howard Shore uses a system of leitmotifs in his score for *The Lord of the Rings: The Fellowship of the Ring* (2001), the first of Peter Jackson's trilogy based on J. R. R. Tolkien's epic fantasy of 'Middle Earth', filmed in New Zealand. There are over 80 leitmotifs to characterise the various cultures, characters and ideas in the three films. Like the leitmotifs in Wagner's Ring (see *Die Walküre* in the chapter on Music for the stage) and in Korngold's *The Adventures of Robin Hood*, Shore uses relationships between the motifs to suggest dramatic ideas. The motif of a stepwise ascending 3rd (major or minor) represents the Ring's influence on the story and works its way into a number of the themes in the score. It appears in the second and fourth phrases of the 'Fellowship' theme. The theme is modal (aeolian) but harmonised using major chords:

The Lord of the Rings

Howard Shore, *Fellowship theme*

In addition to the leitmotifs, the separate races of elves, men, dwarves and hobbits each have their own musical sound. The hobbits, for example, are associated with rustic-sounding music on dulcimer, fiddle and Celtic instruments (bodhrán, Irish whistle, Celtic harp). The elves of Lothlórien – less connected to the human world than the elves of Rivendell – have Eastern-sounding melodies on the ney flute, drones on the monochord and the resonating strings of the sarangi.

As the Fellowship sets out from Rivendell we hear the full Fellowship theme at its most heroic, scored in full brass in A major. The trumpets climb up to a concert A for the final note, and the quaver accompaniment in the strings is continued as Gandalf's voiceover gives us the plan of the journey. As the crows are seen approaching, the tension of the situation is reflected in the breathless ostinati figures and the building up of a dissonant chord note-by-note. The crows return to Saruman's industrial setting with its machine-like five-beat rhythm and rattling metal chains. Listen for the minor 3rd steps of the Ring's theme in the boys' voices tempting Boromir as he picks up the Ring in the snow.

At the entrance to Moria, Shore contrasts the minor key with the use of major triads (D, E and F♯ in voices and high strings for the light on the gate. The attack of the monster in the water is presented by dense glissandi chords. The composer often writes glissandi that spread out until all notes of a chord are covered, but here he allows more of an aleatoric element with the players allowed to decide which of his selected chromatic notes to sustain or repeat. The effect is to suggest the wriggling mass of arms which are attacking from the water.

The journey through Moria uses male voices for the chanting of the underground culture of the dwarves, using choirs of Maori men and grunting sounds from rugby players. The ostinati patterns are used throughout the scene as danger closes in, using both the minor 3rds motif and the five-beat pattern of the orcs. The Fellowship theme is urgent and heroic in full orchestra as they make their escape.

Exercise 13

1. Explain how the use of tonality and harmony in Philip Glass's score for *The Hours* contributes to the effectiveness of the film. Your answer should include a discussion of examples from at least two extended scenes.

2. Compare the music of *The Hours* with either *The Adventures of Robin Hood* or *Vertigo*. Assess to what extent the music contributes to the audience's understanding of each film.

3. Show how film composers have adapted composing techniques such as leitmotif, minimalist or serial procedures. Discuss examples from two film scores composed since 1980.

Resources and further reading

Philip Glass's music from *The Hours* is published as a piano solo arrangement by Hal Leonard (ISBN: 0-634-06579-3).

Doug Adams has written detailed notes on Howard Shore's *Lord of the Rings* scores, particularly for the booklet of the complete soundtrack (Reprise Records 49454-2).

Topic 4:
Music and belief

The three prescribed works in this topic represent differing musical expressions of belief over a period of nearly four hundred years. Byrd has been chosen to represent the great flowering of choral polyphony within England during the Renaissance era. His Mass for four voices is a highly personalised outpouring of Catholic belief in a turbulent age which witnessed a return to Protestantism.

The St Matthew Passion by J. S. Bach is a work of considerable magnitude and draws upon the largest performing resources in this topic by a significant margin. Bach, working in the Baroque period, was composing at a time when the issue of musical patronage came to the forefront. Much of Bach's religious output of this period was written to order for the weekly services at the *Thomaskirche* in Leipzig and an enormous amount of choral cantatas started life in this way. The depth of expression in the Passion, though, suggests that Bach was not composing for purely pragmatic reasons and at the very least that he was sympathetic to his text.

Stockhausen's *Stimmung*, from the 1960's, is typical of that era's interest in exploring religious traditions outside of Christianity. Stockhausen developed his own esoteric version of spirituality in which all religions were subsumed into a single, overarching system. The 'magic names' from *Stimmung* represent deities from many world religions and the chant-like intonations, the long time-scale and the use of overtone singing also draw on different religious traditions. He believed that the effect of music and sound on humans was a profoundly spiritual experience, with the human ear acting as what he thought of as a 'radio receiver' for vibrations from the cosmos. He felt that this spiritual effect was intensified if the music was structured through mathematical schemes, which perhaps explains the many interlocking systems for organising pitch, rhythm and timbre in *Stimmung*.

Mass for four voices

William Byrd (c. 1540–1623) is commonly regarded as the greatest English composer of the 16th century. His work spanned both the last great period of Catholic Church music in England and the Elizabethan age of secular and instrumental music. The four-part mass was written near the end of Elisabeth I's reign

By the late 16th century, Protestantism had become firmly established in England, and the small numbers that held fast to the old Roman Catholic faith faced persecution. However, Byrd's Catholic sympathies seemed to have been met with tolerance by the monarch. In the 1590s he produced three settings of the Ordinary of the Mass, including the four-part Mass (c. 1592). This period also coincides with Byrd's move to Essex under the patronage of Sir John Petre – a wealthy Roman Catholic. The Masses, then, are not believed to be an expression of protest but rather a pious attempt to sustain Catholic life into the future.

The Mass as a genre

The Mass is the Eucharistic liturgy of the Roman Catholic Church. The full sung form of this service is known as High Mass and there are countless musical settings of the text in existence between the medieval and modern periods. The two main elements of the Mass are as follows:

The Ordinary: these are the set of texts that do not usually vary.
The Proper: these texts change according to the Church calendar.

These are the sections of the Ordinary:

➢ Kyrie (Eleison)

➢ Gloria (in Excelsis)

➢ Credo

➢ Sanctus

➢ Agnus Dei

➢ Ite Missa Est*

* Although this is strictly part of the Ordinary, it is rarely set by composers.

The Kyrie, Gloria, Credo, Sanctus and Agnus Dei form the sections of Byrd's four-part setting.

The score

Check which edition you are using to study the Byrd Mass. In this guide we will be referring to the Henry Washington Edition published by Chester Music – a widely used edition of the work. It transposes Byrd's original down a tone to F minor (it was originally composed in G minor) and reduces 16th century note values by half with a time signature of $\frac{4}{4}$.

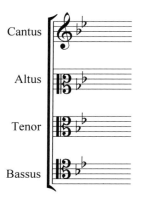

Byrd's original score however, would have looked slightly different and in the example *left* you can see the original clefs he would have used. The lower three parts use the C clef, which can sit anywhere on the five-line stave. The join between the two semi-circles in the middle of the clef indicates the position of middle C. It also shows the original key signature (G minor). You will also notice the names of the parts are different: **altus**, **tenor** and **bassus** sound like their modern equivalents (alto, tenor and bass). The word **cantus** was a medieval and Renaissance word for melody, and referred to the highest voice in a polyphonic composition.

Polyphonic texture and imitative counterpoint

The 16th century is regarded as a golden age of polyphony, and Byrd's imitative setting is typical of both the time and genre. All the voice parts are of equal importance. Each movement begins with a head motive that is then imitated by the other parts in varying degrees of strictness, normally at the interval of a 5th. At the beginning of each movement or section the texture therefore gradually builds up from a single voice to all four parts.

The study of Renaissance counterpoint could fill a text book in its own right and a detailed account is beyond the scope of this guide. However, look at the opening of the Kyrie and examine the first two bars of each voice entry:

Kyrie (bars 1–10)

Notice that the cantus begins in imitation of the altus head motive, but then deviates in its second bar. You will also see that the altus part begins with the notes F and C – the tonic and the dominant. In imitative polyphony, it is the convention to answer this pattern with the reverse – the dominant followed by the tonic. This is what happens at the beginning of the cantus part and it explains why the initial interval is now a 5th rather than the 4th heard at the beginning of the movement. The tenor part then enters with a more faithful imitation of the original pattern – the intervals and rhythms of the altus part are preserved. In the fifth bar, the bassus enters completing the four-part texture with the head motive first heard in the altus, but then quickly deviates in the following bars.

Tonal language

The modern tonal system was starting to emerge when Byrd wrote this Mass. This is particularly evident in the above example, in which V–I progressions in F minor occur in bars 3^2–3^3, 6^4–7^1, 7^4–8^1 and in the final cadence. The last of these ends on a major chord (known as a tierce de Picardie) because it was to be another century before composers felt happy to end minor-key sections on what they felt was the unstable sound of a minor tonic chord.

Equally tonal is the way that the second section of the Kyrie (Christe Eleison) ends with a V–I progression in C (the key we would now recognise as the dominant of F minor). However, the influence of the old modes lingered on, as can be seen in the third note of the alto part in the previous example – a pitch that we would now regard as the leading-note if the key is F minor and which, because it rises to the tonic in the next bar, would normally be raised to E♮ in tonal music. Here, though, Byrd is content to leave it as a very modal-sounding E♭.

Byrd's use of dissonance, often through the use of suspensions is also striking. Suspensions are governed by the following conventions:

➢ **Preparation:** the note is sounded in a consonance context on a weak beat

➢ **Suspension:** on the following strong beat the note is repeated or held over a new chord and so becomes a dissonance

➢ **Resolution:** the dissonant note is resolved by step to a consonance, on a weak beat.

All suspensions contain these three elements, and they can be seen twice in the following example from the Kyrie:

Kyrie (bars 19–22)

The first suspension in the above example is particularly expressive and piercing. It is made all the more so by the tenor part's unexpected leap from G to E which raises the tenor part above the altus.

Structure of text and word painting

The lengths of movements in the Ordinary of the Mass vary greatly. Whereas Byrd's continental counterparts often spun out the material for shorter texts such as the Kyrie, Byrd does not use much word repetition or other extending techniques.

The lengthiest texts are the Gloria and the Credo, and these can frequently cause difficulties for composers in deciding how they should be divided. The Gloria's divisions are not entirely conventional in this work. A usual breaking point is just before the words 'Qui tollis', but Byrd opts for the double bar and new section a phrase earlier. This could possibly be a reflection of the way in which Byrd was taught to read and punctuate the Gloria text. Alternatively, it might be a means of highlighting the words 'Jesu Christe' which, as a result, fall at the end of the previous section.

There are a number of examples throughout the Mass where Byrd pays particular attention to the sense of the words. One of the

Byrd's continental contemporaries include:

Giovanni Pierluigi da Palestrina (c. 1525–1594).

Orlande [Roland] de Lassus (c. 1530–1594).

Thomás Luis de Victoria (1548–1611).

most vivid examples is the last section of the Agnus Dei, where the words 'dona nobis pacem' are set over an 18-bar extended passage. These bars form an almost continual chain of suspensions and is all the more notable in an Agnus Dei that has been largely consonant until this point. A number of these suspensions involve the expressive interval of a major 7th – for example the C in the cantus in bar 43 against the D♭ in the bassus. All of the suspensions resolve onto a minor chord, until the final major chord of the Mass. Byrd's use of dissonance, and his predilection for minor harmony, is highly expressive and seems an appropriate way of highlighting this prayer for peace.

Although this passage is reminiscent of the expressive dissonance in the Kyrie (mentioned earlier), there is little sense of thematic cross-referencing within Byrd's Mass. The only real exception to this is his use of similar head motives to open the majority of the movements namely the Kyrie, Gloria, Credo and Agnus Dei. Compare the themes of these openings (shown *right*) and you will see that they are clearly derived from one another.

Case study: the Credo

The first section of the Credo presents a good opportunity for an exploration of Byrd's polyphonic technique. It opens with strict imitation between the altus and cantus parts, the latter entering a 5th higher than the altus. The tenor part enters at the end of bar 5, imitating the second phrase from the altus and cantus parts. When the bass enters at the end of bar 8 however, it introduces a new musical idea which is subjected to free imitation among the other parts. Byrd introduces more strict imitation in the subsequent bars. For example, the cantus entry at the end of bar 14 is imitated exactly in the bassus part a bar later. This creates a **canon** between the outer voices. This passage is also notable for the extent of its vocal range: the tenor part climbs to a high A♭ in bar 19; meanwhile the bass part falls from D♭ down to low C over the space of five bars (bars 18–22). Byrd also uses the technique of diminution between imitative entries in the first section of the Credo. Look at the tenor line in bars 39–40, this is imitated in the cantus part from the end of bar 41 but with the last four note values of 'consubstantiálem' diminished.

The end of the first section (the double bar at bar 53) again shows Byrd employing an unorthodox division in the text. A number of composers have preferred to place emphasis upon the Incarnation and make the section break with the words 'Et incarnatus est'. Byrd however, brings forward the section break, preferring to end with 'per quem ómni a facta sunt' and subsequently does not highlight 'incarnatus' with a particularly expressive setting.

The passage from 'Et resurrexit' introduces some high vocal ranges in the tenor part (top B♭ in bar 99) and a top F in the bassus in bar 101. These high notes are the culmination of an octave climb under the words 'et ascendit in caelum' ('and ascended into heaven') – one of the more overt pieces of word painting in the Mass. It also leads to some polyphonically dense writing in bars 102–103, where the note values divide into quavers and semiquavers. These give the effect of some pace under the prevailing $\frac{4}{4}$ metre.

This level of polyphonic intricacy is carried through much of the remainder of the Credo and generally it is the most melodically decorated of the movements in the Mass. The movement ends with a **melismatic** setting of the word 'Amen' and is made more expressive for its pungent suspension in bar 184 where there is a compound major 7th between cantus and bassus. The final chord of the movement is an F major chord forming another **tierce de Picardie**.

A melisma is where there are multiple notes set to one syllable of text, creating a decorated vocal style.

Related repertoire

Your related repertoire should be drawn from the substantial body of motets and anthems composed in England between the late 16th and early 17th centuries. One of the most important figures of this period was **Thomas Tallis** (c. 1505–1585). In 1575, he collaborated with Byrd over the production of a printed collection of motets and hymns entitled *Cantiones Sacrae*. The two composers dedicated this work to the Queen (Elizabeth I) in recognition of the monopoly they had been granted for the printing of music and music paper.

Tallis' Lamentations were probably composed in the mid to late 1560s at a time when the idea of making musical settings of the Holy Week readings from the Old Testament Book of Jeremiah was popular. However, it is believed that these motets were never intended to be used in Church and the Tallis scholar Paul Doe has gone so far as to suggest they were composed for recreational singing by loyal Catholics.

Modern performances and recordings will often link the two Lamentations together, but it is unlikely that this was Tallis' intention. They are written in different modes, which suggest they were conceived quite separately.

Tallis Lamentations of Jeremiah I

The texts form the first two lessons from the Maundy Thursday Matins (sometimes known as Tenebrae). Tallis set not only the biblical text but also the announcements, the Hebrew letters that separate the verses and a short refrain at the end of each lesson. The text for the first lesson is shown in the following table. Tallis' varying approach to choral textures is one area of investigation for this work.

	Original text	English translation
Announcement	Incipit lamentation Ieremiae prophetae	Here beginneth the lamentation of Jeremiah the prophet
Hebrew letter	Aleph	(first Hebrew letter)
Lesson	Quomodo sedet sola civitas plena populo	How doth the city sit solitary, that was full of people!
Refrain	Ierusalem, Ierusalem, convertere ad Dominum Deum tuum	Jerusalem, Jerusalem, return unto the Lord thy God

The score used in this analysis was edited by Philip Brett and published by OUP Tudor Church Music Series. Be aware that you may come across different editions for higher voices and/or in different keys.

The vocal scoring is unusual: unaccompanied ATTBB (1 alto, 2 tenors and 2 basses). Most modern performances will use male voices for all parts (although it possible that the top part was sometimes sung by a falsetto or low treble). The first motet begins in the phrygian mode (the mode that uses the white notes on a keyboard from E to E) and the opening announcement is **canonic** – the bass I part follows the tenor II part, imitating at the interval of a 5th, half a bar later:

Tallis subsequently brings in all five entries in strict imitation.

The harmonic language is intense and the main reasons for this are:

➢ The low tessitura (range) used by Tallis

➢ The use of false relations.

An example of a false relation occurs in bar 11, where a C♮ in tenor II immediately follows a C♯ in the alto (beats 3–4). An example of a simultaneous false relation can be found in bar 10 (beat 2) where a G♯ is sounded directly against a G natural.

The effect is richly pungent and regular occurrences of this kind of dissonance gives the work its distinctive flavour. False relations are characteristic of much Elisabethan music and generally arise from conflicts between modality and emerging tonality.

Try making a structural plan for the motets – the first one may begin like this:

> The absence of a soprano part gives the music a darker feel.

Bars	Section	Comments
1–22	Announcement	Canonic opening Use of false relations and dissonance Ends with fermata (pause) on a plagal cadence
23–37	Hebrew Letter (Aleph)	The Hebrew letter is repeated several times The vocal setting is far more melismatic and ornate than other parts of the text in the motet
37–68	First part of lesson	The first word 'quomodo' is dovetailed into the previous section – there is no sectional break The word setting is more syllabic than the previous section The texture is more homophonic – more counterpoint appears later, though it is much freer in its level of imitation
69–75	Hebrew letter (Beth)	The Hebrew letter is repeated several times This time the alto part sings a long pedal note with the lower parts moving in pairs beneath It is highly ornate and melismatic It ends with a fermata and section break
76–124	Second part of Lesson	This section begins around B♭ major harmonies, forming a tritone relationship to the opening in the mode of E

124–end	Refrain	Tallis' refrain is dovetailed into the previous material
		He sets up an antiphonal relationship between the alto and the rest of the choir which answer in a homophonic block
		Tallis makes a great deal of these words in both motets (the second is more elaborate still) and as a Catholic in a Protestant country they may have held some special significance for him

Exercise 14

1. Try to make a structural plan for the second motet. In this, you can also observe some highly expressive examples of word-painting, for instance the long downward canonic movement under the text 'nec invenit requiem' (she findeth no rest).

2. Compare the word-setting techniques demonstrated by Byrd with at least one other composer of the period.

3. Examine Byrd's approach to choral textures in his Mass for four voices. Make detailed reference to at least one extended passage of music.

4. Compare and contrast the harmonic language used by Byrd and Tallis.

5. How does religious belief shape the work of English composers in this period?

Further reading

The Oxford History of English Music by John Caldwell,
(ISBN: 0198161298, OUP 1998).

The New Grove High Renaissance Masters: Josquin, Palestrina, Lassus, Byrd, Couperin, Rameau by Jeremy Noble and Reese
(ISBN: 978-0333382387, New Grove Composer Biography 1984).

St Matthew Passion

The Passion is the story of the crucifixion as told in the four Gospels of the New Testament by Matthew, Mark, Luke and John. As a musical genre, it is a setting of Christ's Passion, which reached its grand apogee with J. S. Bach in the middle of the 18th century. It had existed since the Middle Ages, when the story was presented in plainchant, sung by the priest. Composers became increasingly adventurous with the genre through the Baroque period, and experimented with the introduction of instruments and non-gospel texts. Bach took the gospel text as his starting point, but embellished his Passions with a number of oratorio characteristics. These include the use of accompanying instruments and the interspersion of arias and chorales into the Gospel narrative.

His two best-known Passions were both composed in the mid 1720s – St John in 1724 and St Matthew in 1727 – following his move to Leipzig in 1723. Bach had been appointed to one of the most prestigious musical posts in Germany: the role of Kantor at the Thomasschule. The school was closely connected to the more famous establishment – the Thomaskirche – where the St Matthew Passion was first performed on Good Friday in 1727. Bach himself was the Kappellmeister at the first performance.

Kantor: chief musician at an establishments

Thomasschule: St Thomas School

Thomaskirche: St Thomas Church

Kapellmeister: The person in charge of music-making

The Passion employs enormous choral and instrumental forces: solo voices, double choir and double orchestra. In a 1736 revision by Bach, he also included two organs in the instrumentation. It uses a libretto by Picander and sets chapters 26 and 27 from St Matthew's Gospel. The biblical text is set primarily in recitative, but the insertion of poetic texts allows Bach to cultivate a more lyrical, aria style by way of contrast. His aria writing also often assumes a meditative or reflective perspective on the narrative that has preceded it.

Picander was a pseudonym for Christian Friedrich Henrici (1700–1764), a German poet and librettist who also provided the text for a number of Bach's Leipzig Cantatas.

The Evangelist: a tenor who sings the narration of the Gospel text in recitative.

Other named parts include: Jesus, Judas, Peter, two high priests, Pilate, Pilate's wife, two witnesses and two maids – though these parts do not all necessarily need to be sung by different singers.

St Matthew Passion is a vast work, running to well over three hours in full performance. A full commentary on the work is therefore beyond the scope of this chapter, but we shall instead examine selected aspects of Bach's writing in the Passion.

Recitative is a device found in both opera and oratorio, and is an efficient means of covering a large amount of narrative text, without resorting to spoken dialogue. Bach's setting is not untypical in that his recitative follows the natural rhythm and shape of the words. However, it is far from devoid of expressive input and there are countless examples of where Bach added poignancy to the harmony or the melodic line.

Recitative

The author has used *The New Novello Choral Edition of the St Matthew Passion*, edited by Neil Jenkins (ISBN: 0-85360-802-4). Be aware that if you are using a different edition the numbering of the recitatives, arias and chorus may be different.

No. 24 (Recitative) – Da kam Jesus mit ihnen zu einem Hofe (Then cometh Jesus with them unto a garden)

This recitative section begins with the Evangelist singing a predominantly arpeggiated vocal line. The rhythmic movement is mostly in quavers, reflecting the natural nuance of the text. The word 'Gethsemane' is slightly pointed by virtue of its distinctive dotted rhythm. The central part of this recitative sees a move from major to minor tonality. Significantly this occurs with the words 'began to be sorrowful and very heavy' (*und fing au zu trauern und zu zagen*). In bar 9, Bach gives further expressive emphasis to the word 'sorrowful' by using a Neapolitan 6th chord in the continuo accompaniment (the G♭ major chord). The pace of the accompaniment increases towards the end of this recitative, moving into repeated quavers. Bach ends the passage using the conventional language of recitative accompaniment: a perfect cadence after the narrator has finished singing.

Another feature of Bach's recitative writing that can be seen in this example is the addition of string instruments at the points when Jesus sings. This technique of characterisation was a convention that had been established for nearly one hundred years. Surrounding the words of Jesus with a halo of string sounds dates back at least to a setting by the composer Schütz in 1645; many other Passion composers followed suit through the 17th and 18th centuries. The Evangelist and minor characters, meanwhile, are supported by a plainer accompaniment of continuo.

Bach makes a point of dramatic significance out of this towards the end of the Passion when Jesus calls out in despair on the Cross. In No. 71 (Recitative) *Und von der sechsten Stunde an* (Now from the sixth hour onwards), Jesus proclaims the words in Hebrew which mean 'My God, my God, why hast Thou forsaken Me?' Not only are these marked with a slower Adagio tempo, but the string halo is conspicuously absent. Bach is making a dramatic musical reference to Jesus' sense of abandonment.

Arias

The viola da gamba is a member of the viol family. Popular in the 16th and 17th centuries, it is a bowed and fretted string instrument which was played in an upright position and held between the legs. In the St Matthew Passion there are two viola da gambas, one in each orchestra.

The other aria to include the viola da gamba is No. 66 *Komm, süßes kreuz, so will ich sagen* (Come Healing cross).

The arias of St Matthew Passion are highly varied and diverse in their instrumentation. No. 41 (Aria) *Geduld! Geduld!* (Endure! Endure!) is significant for being one of two arias in the Passion that includes the viola da gamba. From bar 2, it plays a highly decorated bass line, setting up a distinctive dotted rhythm with incessant upward and downward leaps. This idea recurs throughout much of the aria. The vocal line, in contrast to the recitative style is significantly more florid and Bach makes use of extended melismatic passages, for example bars 25–27.

A wider vocal range is also exploited. A particularly expressive passage is exemplified from bars 10–17 (see music example at top of next page), where the vocal part has a range in excess of an octave. In bar 11 there is an upwards leap of an octave, followed by a downward fall of a 7th. This passage also contains some piercing dissonances (for example at the beginning of bar 11, the clash between the vocal E – prepared in the previous bar – and the accompanying D minor harmony).

Geduld! Geduld! (bars 10–17)

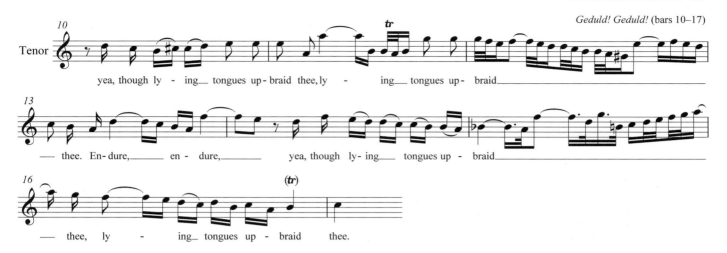

Tonally and chromatically, the aria is highly active, moving frequently between different key areas. In bar 22, E♭ major harmony is introduced, which is far removed from the home tonality of A minor.

Chorales

A chorale was a well-known hymn tune of the Lutheran Church, sung by the congregation, though it is debatable whether the Leipzig congregations would have joined the performers at this point in the Passions. However, given the familiarity of these tunes, it was a means of involving the congregation on a more devotional level. Therefore, although the chorale tunes themselves were rarely composed by Bach, he invests them with striking harmonisations and sometimes multiple different harmonisations within the same work. These have become models for the study of strict four-part harmony.

The most well-known of these chorales is the Passion Chorale 'Herzlich tut mich verlangen' (usually associated with the words 'O Haupt voll Blut und Wunden' – O sacred head sore wounded). It is used five times within the St Matthew Passion itself and also appears in Bach's Christmas Oratorio and the cantatas Nos. 135, 159 and 161.

The Passion Chorale appears in the following places:

No. 21: *Erkenne mich, mein Hüter* (Receive me, my Redeemer)

No. 23: *Ich will hier bei dir stehen* (Here would I stand beside me)

No.53: *Befiehl du deine Wige* (Commit thy way to Jesus)

No. 63: *O haupt voll Blut und Wunden* (O sacred head, surrounded by crown)

No. 72: *Wenn ich einmal soll scheiden* (Be near me, Lord, when dying)

Two of its more interesting appearances are in close juxtaposition – Nos. 21 (*Erkenne mich, mein Hüter*) and 23 (*Ich will hier bei dir stehen*), separated by a short recitative section. The two versions use identical harmony, but the first is in E major and the second in E♭ major – a semitone lower. This dramatic tonal shift is facilitated during the intervening recitative and between bars 10 and 12 of No. 22 there is a move from E minor to C minor. A chromatic note (A flat) on the word 'die' expressively points the way towards the new key. The unsettled mood of the disciples at the thought of the impending denial is highlighted by this dramatic shift of tonality.

The most chromatic and expressive setting of this chorale tune appears in No. 72 *Wenn ich einmal soll scheiden* (Be near me, Lord, when dying) and this is more than appropriate to the text which talks of death, anguish, pain and woe. The chromatic harmony in bars 5–8 is especially poignant and worthy of further examination.

Choruses

The choruses provide the epic quality for St Matthew Passion, and as part of his performing resources Bach calls for two SATB choirs. These *turba* passages (from the Latin word 'turba' meaning crowd) are written for either or both choirs in a variety of different choral

Polychoral music is music for two or more choirs of voices and instruments and often employ antiphonal effects.

Cori spezzati literally means 'separated choirs' and was a common spatial technique practised by Italian composers of the Renaissance and Baroque periods such as Monteverdi.

A **cantus firmus** is literally a 'fixed song', and it is where a pre-existing melody forms the basis of a polyphonic composition.

textures. The extended chorus at the end of No. 33 *Sind Blitze, sind Donner in Wolken verschwunden* (Have lightnings and thunders forgotten their fury?) coincides with Jesus' arrest and only includes a minimal amount of text. However, the choral setting is highly dramatic. In bar 65, the two choruses share the same material which is presented in imitative counterpoint – each entry a 4th higher than its predecessor. The word 'Donner' (thunder) is set to a highly ornate melisma in the bass part, extended over 12 bars from bars 73–84. The choruses split in bar 81 which leads to **antiphonal writing** between the two groups, not unlike the *cori spezzati* techniques of the Venetian polychoral style.

Following a dramatic general pause in bar 104, each chorus resumes with a more homophonic texture – while one chorus sings, the other holds a long chord. These spatial alternations become increasingly rapid from bar 122, before all eight vocal lines culminate with a homophonic statement setting the darkest part of the text: 'The treacherous betrayer, the murderous blood' (*den falschen Verräter, das mördrische Blut*).

The kinds of complex antiphonal exchanges that we see in this chorus are even more evident in the short choral passage at the end of No. 43 *Weissage, Weissage* (Now tell us, Now tell us). In just eight bars, Bach presents a highly elaborate vocal texture, with interlocking dialogue from the altos, tenors and basses, and two independent soprano parts that soar above with florid melismas.

By way of contrast to these large-scale polychoral textures, No. 59 *Sie schrieen aber noch mehr* (But they all cried out the more), merges the two choruses into one SATB choir. The writing is deeply expressive, and it is a feature of Bach's style in the Passion that words such as 'crucify' are set to more chromatic melodies. The passage between bars 2–9 sees all the voices entering in imitative counterpoint.

The most significant choruses in the entire work, though, are the ones which frame the Passion at the beginning and end. They are monumental and, at the time, unprecedented in their scope and ambition. The opening movement: *Kommt, ihr Töchter* (Come, ye daughters) is a choral fantasia; its imitative counterpoint is disguised by the entry of all the vocal parts at the outset. The soprano and bass, however, have two different head themes in bar 17 which are imitated by the alto and tenor respectively in the following bar. The choral texture is further complicated by the introduction of a cantus firmus part in bar 30. Bach introduces the choral melody of *O Lamm Gottes* (O Lamb of God most holy) at this point, and it is sung by a separate treble choir.

The final chorus – *Wir setzen uns mit Tränen nieder* (We bow our heads) of the Passion is well-known in its own right. In common with the final movement of Bach's St John Passion, the chorus depicts Jesus' burial and farewell. Both movements also share the same key – C minor – and similar metres and tempos. The rhythmic feel is that of a Sarabande – a stately triple-time dance from the Baroque period. The vocal style is more homophonic than we have seen in many of Bach's choruses.

Bach's genius lapsed into relative obscurity following his death in 1750, and it was not until well into the following century that his work was revived by Mendelssohn. The first work to be subjected to this revival was the St Matthew Passion. It was performed in Berlin in March 1829 to universal acclaim and eventually led to a full restoration of Bach's place in musical history. Bach's own devotion to the Passion text is suggested by his underlining of the scripture texts in red ink in the manuscript. While it is first and foremost a highly devotional work, it goes much further than that. The musicologist Arthur Loesser summed up the achievement of St Matthew Passion by describing it as 'an act of worship which has the animation of a play'. In short, it was a spectacular union of the Church and the theatre.

Related repertoire

Your choice of related repertoire should be drawn from Handel's oratorio and smaller-scale Baroque works for voices and instrumental combinations.

George Frederick Handel (1685–1759) was born just six weeks before J. S. Bach. Although a German composer by birth, he spent much of his adult life in England and became 'composer of music for the Chapel Royal' in 1723.

An oratorio, like Bach's Passions, is a large-scale work for orchestra, choir and soloists. Its subject matter is usually sacred and composers would normally take their stories from the Bible. Both oratorios and Passions share features with opera – they both use recitative, arias, ensembles and choruses. However, the fundamental difference is that opera was a secular work intended for the stage, while the majority of Handel's oratorios were sacred works for concert performance.

Handel wrote nearly 30 oratorios and the most popular of these is undeniably *Messiah* (1741). This work therefore forms a good starting point for study, but there is no reason to restrict your listening exclusively to this.

> Other oratorios you might wish to listen to include *Israel in Egypt* (1738), *Samson* (1741) and *Judas Maccabaeus* (1746).

Messiah

Messiah was written over a period of just 24 days in 1741, and had its premiere in Dublin, Ireland. It uses a libretto by Charles Jennens, which tells the story of Jesus' life and its Christian significance, drawing predominantly from the Old Testament. Although the vocal and instrumental forces are large, they seem rather modest in comparison to the St Matthew Passion. Handel uses four soloists, SATB chorus, two oboes, bassoon, two trumpets, timpani, strings and continuo.

> Note that trumpets did not appear in Bach's Passion, as these would have been considered out of place in celebrating the Passion story.

Handel took a particular interest in word painting – a musical technique that attempted to convey the sense of the text in a pictorial fashion. There are numerous examples throughout the work, and the following are a launch pad to further investigation:

> ➤ The first aria (No. 3, 'Ev'ry Valley shall be Exalted') presents a wealth of word-painting possibilities, particularly the passage from bar 24. Here the music rises up and down a sharp contour over the words 'And ev'ry mountain', the word 'low' is set to a low pitch and the word 'crooked' is set on alternating quavers.

Handel, like other Baroque composers, has a tendency to use vocal melisma to highlight words of expressive importance. This can be seen on the word 'exalted' later in the aria, which undergoes two passages of extensive decoration.

➤ No. 16 Recitative ('And suddenly there was with the Angel') is unusual by recitative standards for its metrical regularity. However, it has been suggested that these repeated patterns in the string accompaniment are to depict the beating of the angels' wings – an unusually expressive gesture for recitative too.

➤ No. 48 ('The Trumpet shall Sound'). In this aria, the trumpet is evoked both literally (with the inclusion of an accompanying trumpet) and more subtly with the fanfare dotted rhythms and opening arpeggio motif from the bass soloist.

Handel's ability to create grand choral gestures is also worthy of further examination. One of the most famous examples of this is the Hallelujah Chorus which concludes Part II of the oratorio. This chorus contains a variety of homophonic, polyphonic and unison writing. After a short introduction, the choir enters in homophony that draws attention to the word 'hallelujah', which is repeated ten times. Handel then brings the choir together in bare octaves for the words 'for the Lord God Omnipotent reigneth', suggesting that he wanted to set these with particular emphasis.

There is a little imitation in this first section, but the more intricate counterpoint begins with the words 'and He shall reign for ever and ever'. This section opens with a fugato passage led by the basses and shortly answered by the tenors a 5th higher. The alto and soprano parts subsequently enter, stating the subject and answer respectively. This passage does not develop into a fully worked-out fugue though, we only hear the presentation of the subjects and answers, as in a fugal exposition.

This is followed by a return to more homophonic choral writing with the tenors, basses (and eventually altos) moving in together under long pedal notes in the soprano parts. These notes become progressively higher in pitch and longer in length. The culmination of Part II of *Messiah* sees the entire orchestra and choir come together in homophony for the final 'hallelujah'. For these last chords, Handel employs a plagal cadence – often associated with the 'amen' at the end of hymns in earlier times – and surely recalled here to give an impression of sacred grandeur.

In his 1901 biography on Handel, C. F. Abdy Williams provides an interesting perspective of the relationship between Handel's and Bach's treatment of the Passion story (which appears in Part III of *Messiah*):

'In Bach's Passions, the Evangelist narrates the events, which are emphasised by the chorus, who represent Jews, apostles, and so forth, and the Saviour Himself speaks. The music for the soloists and congregation represents the emotion that is aroused by the events narrated. In *Messiah*, the congregation takes no part, the soloists are impersonal, and they and the chorus carry on the

Further listening

Bach's Magnificat in D major BVW 243 and Cantata No. 147 *Herz und Mund und Tat und Leben* ('Heart and mouth and deed and life') BWV 147.

This cantata was written in the early period of Bach's residence in Leipzig, and is scored for small orchestra and SATB choir. It contains the well-known movement, which is today better known as 'Jesu, Joy of Man's Desiring'.

narrative by means of passages of Scripture bearing the story. The Passion is a religious service; *Messiah* is a sermon.'

Further knowledge may be gained by listening to a selection of Bach's smaller-scale works for vocal and instrumental combinations from his Leipzig period. One of the responsibilities of his new post was to supply cantatas for performance each Sunday. During the first five years of his tenure, he composed three annual cycles of cantatas (around 150) and his Magnificat (BVW 243) in D major, which is scored for five solo voices, five part-chorus, orchestra and continuo, and numerous other motets and sacred pieces.

> **Further reading**
>
> *Bach* by Malcolm Boyd (ISBN: 978-0-19-530771-9, OUP Master Musicians Series 2006).
>
> *Baroque Music in Focus* by Hugh Benham (Rhinegold Publishing 2007 ISBN: 978-1-906178-13-0).

Exercise 15

1. Examine Bach's different approaches to text-setting for dramatic effect in the St Matthew Passion. Refer to at least two extended sections from the work.

2. In what way is the St Matthew Passion representative (or not) of large-scale choral music of this period?

3. Compare and contrast Bach's text setting with another oratorio from this period.

Stimmung

The German Karlheinz Stockhausen (1928–2008) was one of the leading avant-garde composers of the second half of the 20th century. A student of Olivier Messiaen, he first came to the fore in the early 1950s by applying the serial techniques of Schoenberg not only to pitch but also to rhythm, articulation and dynamics, a technique that became known as total serialism. He went on to develop many other ways of organising music around mathematical schemes, including 'group composition', in which collections of musical events, rather than individual notes, were treated in a serial way; 'formula composition', in which melodies and whole pieces were generated from a mathematical formula; and 'indeterminate music', music in which some elements were based on chance elements and improvisation.

At the same time, he was the leading pioneer of electronic music, developing compositions using 1/4 inch tape at the Studio für Elektronische Musik in Cologne. This experience led him to analyse how raw sounds, for example radio hiss, were put together and to create new sounds, both through the use of synthesis (in the same way that present day synthesisers work) and by modifying recorded sounds by means of varying the speed and direction in which the tape was played, using filters, ring modulators and other devices. He wrote pieces for tape alone, for instance *Hymnen*, and compositions which combined live performers and a tape recording, such as *Kontakte*.

His music was highly controversial among the classical-music establishment as it seemed to ignore every principle upon which Classical music up to that time had been based: tonality, harmony, melody, rhythm and structure. However, his experiments were highly influential on other composers such as Boulez, Ligeti, and Xenakis, and from the 1950s onwards, young composers flocked

He was also highly regarded by some popular music groups: Stockhausen's tape compositions inspired similar experiments on the Beatles' album *Sergeant Pepper*, and Stockhausen's face appears on the album cover.
If you want to find out more about *Sergeant Pepper* and the Beatles go to the chapter on Popular Music.

to the Darmstadt Summer School where he taught, to discuss and listen to the latest experimental music.

From the late 1960s, Stockhausen's standing as a key musical innovator began to wane as his musical style mellowed and as he espoused highly unorthodox spiritual beliefs: he believed that he was educated on the star Sirius. The period from 1977–1998 was devoted to the composition of a huge cycle of seven operas, *Licht*, which was based on his spiritual beliefs. Stockhausen died in 2008, with his place as one of the great 20th-century musical innovators still intact.

Genre

Stimmung (meaning 'tuning' or 'state of mind') is a 75-minute vocal work for six solo voices: 2 sopranos, 1 alto, 2 tenors and 1 bass. These voices are amplified by microphones and all the singers sit in a circle around a loudspeaker, from which a chord built from the harmonics of a low B♭ are continually sounded. Apart from spoken sections, everything the singers sing is derived from this chord. In one sense, *Stimmung* is an unaccompanied sacred choral piece, having parallels with chant-like traditions such as plainsong, Russian Orthodox chant and Buddhist chanting. In another, however, it is an electro-acoustic composition, very much focusing on the timbral composition of the sounds themselves: the phonetic sounds of the consonants and vowels of the texts and the overtones produced by the singers. *Stimmung* was more influential on works composed subsequently. The slowed-down sacred minimalism of composers such as Arvo Pärt and John Taverner, although from a different tradition, created a similar effect, with its long timescale and slow-moving harmony, while the amplified small vocal ensemble became a popular medium in the 1970s, with groups such as the Swingle Singers attracting avant-garde composers like Luciano Berio. A group of composers known as French Spectralists later developed the idea of using overtones in music.

Style and influences

Stimmung (written in 1968) draws on several musical concepts that were in vogue at the time. Because it is based on a single chord, it is often described as a **minimalist** piece, related to the American composers LaMonte Young and Terry Riley's early compositions, which repeated patterns over a long time scale. The degree of choice in the music, where singers choose which order to sing sections of their music, draws on the **aleatoric** (or chance-based) philosophies of John Cage. As mentioned above, the attention to minute details of timbre allies it to the electronic compositions of Stockhausen himself. The use of **overtone singing** allies it to the traditional overtone singing of various cultures, such as the Inuit, Tibetan Buddhist monks and peoples of Tuva. Finally, the tight control Stockhausen imposes on the structure of the piece through the use of highly detailed schemes and performance instructions shows the influence of Stockhausen's total serialist pieces of the 1950s.

Try searching for 'overtone singing' on YouTube to see overtone singers in action.

Overtone singing is a technique where a singer sings a held note and adjusts the position of their lips, tongue and throat in such a way as to create an overtone (or higher note) above the note they are singing. Overtones are pitches from the **harmonic series** of the **fundamental**, or lower note. With a lot of practice, singers are able to produce many different overtones from the same fundamental and make these relatively loud. The performers of *Stimmung* therefore have to be highly skilled in overtone singing. The notes sung by the singers are themselves from the harmonic series based on B♭ below the bass clef. Stockhausen specifies which overtones the singers are to produce in their models. The following example shows which overtones are produced by the bass in section 1 of the Paul Hillier recording of *Stimmung*.

Harmonic series used in Stimmung (the notes in black are the only pitches to be sung conventionally by the singers)

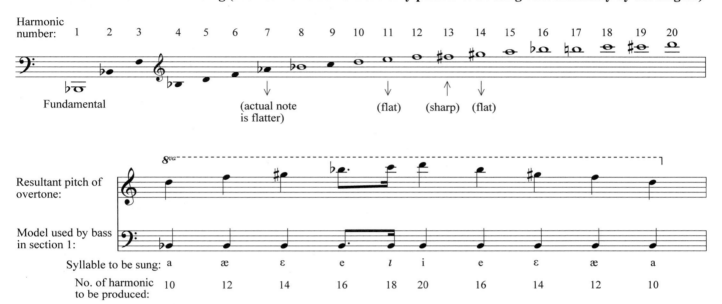

The score of *Stimmung* only loosely resembles that of a conventional musical score. Each singer is given the following items:

The score

➤ A **form-scheme**. This is a single sheet of paper and is the closest thing to a musical score. It is divided into 51 sections, each of which loosely resemble bars. The form-scheme shows which note each singer sings for each section (written out on a stave), which singer is the 'leader' for each section (indicated by a thick horizontal line), points where a magic name is to be called out (shown by a letter 'N'), places where a singer is to change what they are singing to match that of the model-singer gradually (a letter 'T') and places where the singers may vary the tuning slightly.

➤ A sheet of **models**. Each singer cuts out their models and reassembles them in a different order. Male singers are given nine models each and females eight. Each model has its own tempo, rhythm and metre, and the syllables to be sung or said, which are written out using the phonetic alphabet, and the overtones that are to be sounded. For example, one model contains the syllables 'ø i ø i ø i ø i ø i føniks', which is to be sung to the rhythm of 12 quavers and two semiquaver

➤ A sheet of **magic names**. The magic names are religious figures from all over the world and from different eras. Examples are 'Allah' (Islam), 'Vishnu' (Indian), 'Dionysos' (Ancient Greek), 'Osiris' (Ancient Egyptian), 'Sedna' (Eskimo) and 'Turkura' (Australian). As with the models, each singer cuts out their magic names and reassembles them in a random order.

> ➤ A set of **performance instructions**. This tells the singers how the piece works – so explains how to interpret the form-scheme and how they are to use their models and magic names. It also stipulates that they should perform cross-legged in a circle on a raised platform with a single light above them and that they should wear 'light-coloured, simple clothing, barefoot'.

Although this may suggest a rather random, haphazard effect, in practice the instructions are so detailed that performances are surprisingly similar. The main element that varies is the order in which the models and magic names are used, and once a performing group has decided upon an order that works (which was often developed under the supervision of Stockhausen himself), they tend to use that order in all their subsequent performances. Thus there is a 'Singcircle version' and a 'Theatre of Voices' version of *Stimmung* in which the models always follow the same sequence.

Section 1 of the form-scheme indicates with a horizontal thick line that the bass is the leader and so should sing their first chosen model to the note B♭. Tenor II has a thin horizontal line which tells them to copy what the bass is singing, also on a low B♭. The bracket above the soprano part tells the singers that they may vary the tuning of their note slightly. The bass therefore sings their B♭ to the rhythm of the model, to the tempo indicated (30 b.p.m), using the text shown in the box. The numbers above and below the text show which overtones are to be produced. Tenor II copies what the bass is singing as exactly as they can. When they have finished, they carry on repeating the music enclosed by repeat marks. Towards the end of section 1, tenor I enters on a higher B♭, again copying the model used by the bass. After several repetitions, the bass gives a sign to the next section leader (the alto) to start section 2 by introducing the next model.

For **section 2**, the thick line in the form scheme shows that the alto is the leader, who sings the repeated section of her chosen model to the note 'D'. Tenor II copies the alto's model straight away, to the note 'F'. However, as there is a 'T'' written above the tenor 1 line in the form-scheme, tenor 1 gradually transforms what they were singing in section 1 (i.e. 'a æ '...' etc.) into the rhythm, tempo and syllables of the alto's model of section 2 (i.e. u ɪ u ɪ u ɪ u ɪ), which in the recording takes about 20 seconds. Stockhausen refers to this process as 'reaching identity'. Soprano I enters on a C at about 29 seconds, closely copying the alto's model. 44 seconds into the section, the singers move on to the second section of the model, which contains breathy noises and the sung material 'vishnu', then go back to repeating the first section.

As section 2 has an 'N' above it in the form-scheme, this means that one of the singers may introduce a 'magic name'. So, at 1 minute, one of the male singers says 'Abassi-Abumo' in an evocative way. All the singers immediately adjust what they are singing so that they are singing 'Abassi-Abumo' to the rhythm of their model, but using the same lip movements they used for 'u ɪ u ɪ u ɪ'. Gradually, they change the syllables until they get back to 'u ɪ u ɪ u ɪ' and the alto signals to the leader of the next section, soprano II, to introduce her model.

The way in which the performance instructions work in *Stimmung* can be seen in the first three of the 51 sections taken from the *Paul Hillier Theatre of Voices* recording on Harmonia Mundi, HMU807408. Note that the text below will not match with any other recording.

In **section 3**, soprano I, tenor I and tenor II each gradually transform what they were singing at the end of the previous section into the rhythm, syllables and tempo of the soprano II model. These parts all reach identity at around 33 seconds, by which time they are all singing the same rhythm. However, the alto carries on singing the model from the previous section – they have no 'T' above their part in the form-scheme so do not change what they are singing. Notice that the model used for section 3 includes the word 'Monday' (at 39 seconds): all the days of the week appear during the course of the piece and are particularly significant for Stockhausen. As with section 2, section 3 is a 'magic name' section, so the word 'Shiva' is introduced at 50 seconds. All the voices then incorporate 'Shiva' into their music, gradually moving back to the word 'Monday' of the model by 1'22".

The ensuing sections of the work carry on in the same way, with a wide variety of rhythms and vowel sounds explored in the models. Additionally, Stockhausen states that, instead of magic names, his own erotically charged poems, which are in German and included with the score, may be substituted. In the Paul Hillier recording, they appear at tracks 28, 32 and 43. Unlike the magic names, however, they do not affect how the other singers sing their model.

Form-scheme for sections 1 to 3

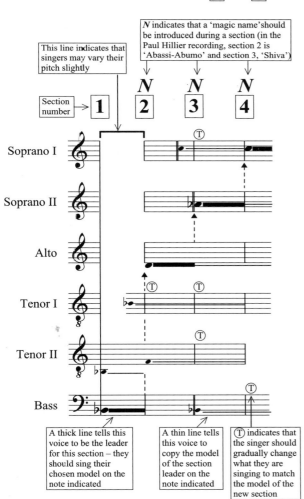

Model used for Section 1 (leader: Bass)

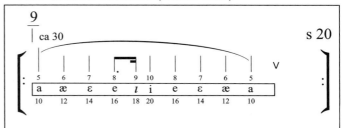

Model used for Section 2 (leader: Alto)

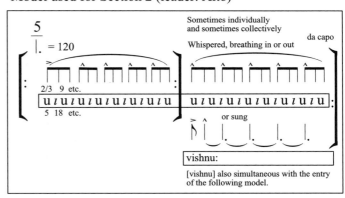

Model used for Section 3 (leader: Soprano II)

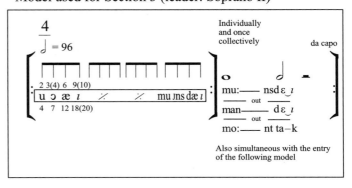

Tonality

Owing to its highly original nature, *Stimmung* is very hard to compare with traditional music. Harmonically, it is based on a single chord of B♭ major with an added 7th and 9th. These notes are taken from the **harmonic series** based on the B♭ below the bass clef. As not all the singers sing all the time, and move from one note to another for different sections, the harmony is not static, with F (in section 2) or D often forming the root note of the chord instead of B♭. The thickness of the chord is often varied too, so there might be just one note present for some sections (such as section 1), or as many as six (for instance section 3). So, although the harmony is generally very static and geared towards inducing a trance-like state, there is sufficient variety within it to maintain a listener's interest over 75 minutes.

Texture

Again, *Stimmung* cannot be described in traditional terms. From the recording it is clear that the voice parts interact in a very complex way, reacting to each other either immediately or gradually. This creates two broad types of texture:

➤ A texture with 'strong group identity'. This is where all the parts are doing the same thing. This creates a clear, homophonic texture

➤ A texture with 'weak group identity'. This is where the parts are doing different things. This creates a complex, multi-layered texture.

Stimmung can be thought of as a continual process of transition between strong and weak group identity.

Timbre and word setting

The timbres in *Stimmung* consist of the huge variety of syllables and vowel sounds used, the tonal contrasts (such as nasal sounds) created by the singers, the overtones they create and the spoken material of the magic names and Stockhausen's own poems. The speech patterns of the syllables are more important to Stockhasuen than either word painting or expressive use of the text, which derives from his fascination with phonetics.

Stockhausen had studied phonetics (the study of the sounds used in speech) at Bonn University in the early 1950s, and he created his own 'vowel square' of vowel sounds, which is included in the instructions for *Stimmung*. This classifies vowel sounds like the pitches in a musical scale. So for Stockhausen, the sequence of vowels in the words 'shoe', 'door', 'car', 'care' and 'big' would form the equivalent of an ascending scale. His main aim in *Stimmung* is therefore to make interesting sounds, patterns and shapes from these syllables rather than to try to depict musically what they might mean. This explains why much of the text makes no sense on its own.

Stockhausen, Stimmung and belief

Stockhausen was originally a Roman Catholic, but left the faith after an extra-marital affair in the early 1960s. His subsequent spiritual beliefs were based on a number of different principles, some of which are reflected in *Stimmung* and other works.

He expressed a desire 'to create a music which would clearly express my relationship to God [...] the proportions in my music have always been related to everything I learn from the nature of the stars and the galaxies [...], from the atoms and molecules, and the cells. Everything in my music is an extension of what I experience as Creation – how Creation is composed.'

In other words, Stockhausen felt that the laws of science, nature and music were all related to creation and thus to God. So the cycles and processes in *Stimmung* could all be seen as reflecting this relationship with God: the days of the week, the vowel square, the use of the overtone series and the organisation of the different sections in the form-scheme. In his other music, his use of total serialism, formulae and group composition were probably also an extension of this theory.

Another belief is that of all religions and cultures ultimately having a common source. He wrote, 'the next step is the untangling of the particular religions. A new orientation has to occur, which embraces all of humanity and in which no one feels excluded…'. This would account for his use of the magic names from many different religions and cultures and epochs in *Stimmung*. Importantly, when the magic names are spoken, they are repeated by the singers and then gradually absorbed back into the repeated phonetic sounds of the models, which perhaps represent the overriding, universal religion that Stockhausen envisages.

Stockhausen also felt that when he composed music, he was receiving what he called 'cosmic rays' from across the universe and that his music should therefore reflect this. 'I believe that […] the pure, abstract arts acquire a new purpose […] to connect man with the mysterious vibration structures of the entire cosmos.' The meditative tone and repeated rhythms and vowel sound patterns in *Stimmung* might have been Stockhausen's way of trying to 'tune in' to these, like tuning a radio to pick up certain frequencies.

Finally, he believed that erotic love was an essential part of the spiritual equation. His composition *Momente*, for example, contains the lyrics 'Hear the Moments – Music of Love […] the Love which holds together the entire Universe'. This accounts for Stockhausen's inclusion of his own erotic love poetry in *Stimmung*.

Related repertoire

Any repertoire you choose will invariably highlight how unique *Stimmung* is, so you should choose a selection of music that gives an impression of the range of choral music that was being created in the 1960s and 1970s. Choices could include the sacred minimalist style of Arvo Pärt, John Tavener and Henryk Górecki, minimalist vocal works by La Monte Young, Terry Riley, Morton Feldman and early Steve Reich, and avant-garde choral music by György Ligeti, Iannis Xenakis and Luciano Berio.

Arvo Pärt (b. 1935) is an Estonian composer who spent his life until 1980 in the former Soviet Union, before moving to the west, settling in Berlin. Pärt originally composed in a neoclassical style but in the 1960s was the first Estonian to use serial techniques. There was then a creative silence of seven years, during which time he studied the Gregorian chant from which the musical tradition of the Russian

Associating number systems with God was not a new idea: Medieval and Renaissance composers often used the 'holy ratio' of the golden section in their musical structures, while Bach made extensive use of the number 3, symbolising the Holy Trinity, in his B minor Mass.

In another piece, *Inori*, he uses mimes of prayer gestures from around the world, and in *Hymnen* he uses recordings of national anthems from around the world.

A repertoire list is given at the end of this chapter.

Arvo Pärt

Tintinnabuli means 'little bells' and uses a simple technique which combines plainsong-like melodies and bell-like harmonies that move together in note-against-note counterpoint.

Orthodox Church stems. In 1976 he produced his first 'Tintinnabuli' piece, *Für Alina* and has composed in this style ever since.

Missa Syllabica

Missa Syllabica (1977) is one of only a handful of Pärt's works that can be used liturgically (or in other words as part of a church service). In the Russian Orthodox tradition, all words delivered in services are sung, with the exception of the sermon, so they take on a ritualistic quality that could be compared to *Stimmung*. Although *Missa Syllabica* is very different from *Stimmung*, it nevertheless has striking similarities, as the comparison table below shows.

Stimmung	Missa Syllabica
Scored for unaccompanied, amplified voices	Scored for unaccompanied choir, unamplified
Uses only pitches from the harmonic series of B♭	Uses only pitches from the dorian mode based on D
Homorhythmic in passages of 'strong group identity'	Homorhythm used almost completely throughout the work
Structured in sections which follow continuously from each other	Structured in sections separated by silences
Uses overtone singing, speech and extended vocal techniques	Uses only standard vocal techniques
Uses many different texts and languages	Uses only one text and one language, Latin
The tempo is different in each section	The tempo of each movement is fixed
The rhythm, metre and structure are derived from the texts used	The rhythm and metre are derived from the number of syllables and stress patterns of the words and the structure from the structure of the text
The work uses several mathematical systems, including overtone series and the vowel square	The piece uses the system of 'tintinnabuli'
Based on a mystic, universal faith of Stockhausen's own creation, which incorporates all faiths	Based on a single, specific faith, that of the Russian Orthodox church

Here is an extract from the Kyrie of Pärt's *Missa Syllabica*. This displays several features that are typical of his style from the late 1970s to the present day.

Notice the following:

➤ The music is divided into bars according to the text, with one note to a syllable, and one word to a bar. As the words have different numbers of syllables, the metre changes from bar to bar.

➤ Each phrase of text is separated by a six crotchet rest and each new section of text by a nine crotchet rest. The structure of the music is therefore completely derived from that of the text.

➤ Tenor 2 has a mostly stepwise melodic line in the dorian mode on D, while tenor 1 sings the notes of a D minor triad. This demonstrates Part's tintinnabuli technique, which combines a stepwise melodic line or lines in a single mode with one or more parts that use arpeggio-based lines on a single chord.

➤ The overall texture is very economical. Unlike much Classical music of the time, which tended to explore more and more complex timbres, rhythms, textures and harmonies, this music returns to the simplest musical building blocks.

Exercise 16

1. What makes Stockhausen's *Stimmung* so novel in comparison to other choral music of its time? Refer to specific examples from the music to support your answer.

2. Compare Stockhausen's musical treatment of text in *Stimmung* to that of another composer of the same period.

Further listening

Lux aeterna (1966) by György Ligeti (16-part choir)

Nuits (1967) by Iannis Xenakis (12 singers)

Rothko Chapel (1971) by Morton Feldman (soprano, alto, mixed choir, instrumentalists)

Dream House (1973) by La Monte Young (performed by the Theatre of Eternal Music)

a - ronne by Luciano Berio (1975) (8 singers)

The Liturgy of St John Chrysostom (1978) by John Tavener (SATB chorus)

Miserere (1981) by Henryk Górecki (unaccompanied choir)

Search for 'Overtone Singing' and 'Stockhausen Interview' on YouTube.

Topic 5: Music for the stage

Music and drama have always been closely linked. Modern stage music began with the invention of opera and the development of recitative. From Monteverdi's *Orfeo* (1607) onwards composers have recognised the need to add choruses, arias, dances and instrumental pieces to create a more compelling musical experience. The challenge for composers writing for the stage has been to create a work which is successful both as music and drama.

The three prescribed works span nearly 300 years, offering a snapshot of three very different styles. All three are in their own ways strongly characteristic of their countries of origin, but all three made clear and distinct changes to the typical style of the stage works of the time. Purcell's *Dido and Aeneas* (c. 1689) is a short, compact opera, written when spoken drama dominated the English stage. *Die Walküre* (1870) represents Wagner's attempt to create a wholly new form of German opera, the music drama, addressing fundamental philosophical issues through the retelling of myth. Bernstein's *West Side Story* (1957) builds on the American 20th-century musical, imagining Shakespeare's *Romeo and Juliet* set in the violent West Side of New York. It combines the popular format of the musical with elements of contemporary jazz and Latin-American dance.

The role of the text or libretto

Nahum Tate (1652–1715) was born in Dublin and was known as a poet, lyricist and hymnist. In 1692, he became England's poet laureate.

A **ground bass** is a repeating phrase in the bass, over which the rest of the music changes. Purcell frequently uses this form, often referred to as a chaconne.

Nahum Tate's text for *Dido and Aeneas* provides Purcell with a structure of short verses, with short rhythmic lines which use rhyming couplets and other rhyming patterns. Repetition is used to extend passages, but characters rarely sing uninterrupted for more than a few lines. It is a short opera in which the action moves quickly. There are a few longer numbers in which there is musical expression of emotion – the arias 'Ah! Belinda' and 'When I am Laid in Earth' are splendid examples of Purcell's skills in exploiting the expressive potential of the ground bass.

Wagner wrote his own libretto and, in a conscious effort to reassert the importance of text in opera, had it published before he wrote the music. The traditional division of opera into separate numbers was replaced by an attempt to create a continuous symphonic texture, with the orchestra carrying much of the musical argument. The pacing of the drama is very different, with more concentration expected of an audience listening to a work of over four hours. Individual acts are constructed over a long time span. Rather than tell the story as a series of arias or choruses which are each a musical highpoint, in *Die Walküre* the drama patiently builds to a few overwhelming climaxes, exploiting the richest harmonies and orchestral textures available.

The lyrics of *West Side Story* are largely by Stephen Sondheim, who became a well-known composer of musicals such as *Sweeney Todd*

(1979). The structure of the work was the product of collaboration between Leonard Bernstein, Stephen Sondheim, Arthur Laurents and Jerome Robbins. Like most musicals of the time, the work is divided into distinct numbers separated by spoken dialogue. Much of the action is developed in the dialogue. There are few numbers for the chorus, which consists of the two gangs and the Jet girls. The input of contemporary dance techniques by choreographer Jerome Robbins leads to the greater use of dance to express the opposition of the two gangs.

Dido and Aeneas

As a boy Henry Purcell (1659–1695) was a chorister at Westminster Abbey, where he later became organist. Instrumental works such as the 'Fantasias for the viols' (1680) shows the influence of English polyphonic composers such as Byrd and Tallis, while the 'Twelve Sonatas of Three Parts' (1683) shows the more modern influence of Italian music for strings. His choral works for the Chapel Royal reflect Charles II's preference for the French style and its homophonic choruses. Purcell's genius was recognised by his contemporaries and after his early death many of his stage works continued to be performed at the Theatre Royal, Drury Lane and some volumes of his music were published. There was a considerable revival of interest in his work in the 19th century, and the influence of his music is seen in the work of 20th century English composers such as Britten and Tippett.

The Young Persons Guide to the Orchestra by Britten is based on a theme by Purcell.

The first performance of *Dido and Aeneas* is thought to have been held at Josias Priest's girls' school in Chelsea, probably in the spring of 1689. The libretto, adapted by Nahum Tate from Virgil's *Aeneid*, tells the story of the Trojan hero Aeneas, who escapes the sack of Troy to found a colony in Italy that would eventually become Rome. Virgil's story was meant to glorify Rome's imperial destiny. Tate's version focuses instead on the tragedy of Dido, the Queen of Carthage, who is let down by the faithless Aeneas. Although the opera was not performed again in Purcell's lifetime, it represents a breakthrough in his career as a composer for the stage. After *Dido and Aeneas* he was much in demand as a composer of music for plays and semi-operas.

Note: There is an on-going debate over for whom this work was written and when and where the first performance took place. The commonly held view that the first performance took place at Josias Priest's girls school in Chelsea was challenged in a 1992 article 'Unscarr'd by turning times' (Early Music Journal), by Bruce Wood and Andrew Pinnock.

Opera struggled to become established in England at this time. While the Italians were pioneering attempts to integrate music and drama, the dominant English tradition was that of the **masque**, a mixture of drama, scenery, dance, poetry and music. Early masques made successful attempts at writing dramatic recitatives in the continental style, but there was little public demand for this type of dramatic music. The preference in the English court was for stage machinery and spectacle. The London theatre public was more interested in plays, with songs, dances and complete masques frequently inserted. Indeed the first public performance of *Dido and Aeneas* in 1700 was as part of an adaptation of Shakespeare's *Measure for Measure*.

Purcell's later large-scale stage works, such as *King Arthur* (1691) and *The Fairy Queen* (1692), based on Shakespeare, are known as dramatic operas or semi-operas. The music was largely additional to the main action, with the principal characters in the play acting rather than singing. This was very different to the closer integration of music and drama in Italian or French opera, in which the characters in the story expressed their personality and motivation in the arias and recitatives.

Perhaps because it was composed with a school in mind, *Dido and Aeneas* is unusual compared to other English stage music of its time:

➤ It is a short opera, lasting just under an hour and is made up of many short numbers

➤ The songs are fairly simple in vocal technique

➤ Recitative is used instead of spoken dialogue

➤ The main characters sing the principal numbers, so the drama develops through the music

➤ The production demands only strings and harpsichord in the orchestra, and there is no elaborate scenery.

Aspects of style, structure and technique of *Dido and Aeneas*, can be found in earlier works, most notably John Blow's masque *Venus and Adonis* (c. 1684). Purcell would have also been aware of the music of Jean-Baptiste Lully (1632–1687), who dominated opera in France and whose *Cadmus et Hermione* was performed in London in 1686. While Italian opera was developing the extended solo aria which took the emotional burden of the drama, French operas tended to favour short airs and more melodic recitatives. The simple plots based on classical (Greek and Roman) stories provided plenty of opportunities for display, scenery and machines, with ballets, choruses and instrumental symphonies.

The score

Further listening

Here are two contrasting recordings of *Dido and Aeneas*:

The English Chamber Orchestra conducted by Anthony Lewis, with Janet Baker as Dido (Decca, 1962).

Academy of Ancient Music and Chorus conducted by Christopher Hogwood with Catherine Bott as Dido. This recording casts a bass for the role of the Sorceress – David Thomas (Decca, 2006).

Only the libretto of the 1689 performance survives. The earliest surviving copy of the music is known as the **Tenbury manuscript**, probably dating from 1775 and thought to be copied from now lost material used for the third performance in 1704. The 1689 libretto includes the text of a Prologue (an allegory on the accession of King William and Queen Mary) and additional dances.

Modern performances face problems in interpreting the sources. It is worth listening to more than one recording if you can. Older recordings tend to have slower speeds and heavier voices. Not all agree if the Sorceress should be sung by a bass, and it will be a matter of taste if the Witches should distort their voices or sing normally. Some recorded performances include extra dances at the points indicated in the 1689 libretto.

The story

Belinda and the chorus persuade Dido to declare her love for Aeneas. The Witches plan her downfall: they brew up a storm to force the lovers to shelter in a cave, then one Witch, disguised as the god Mercury, persuades Aeneas to abandon Dido and leave for Italy. About to board his ship, Aeneas's explanations are dismissed by Dido. She is left to die of a broken heart.

Individual scenes in the opera are made up of recitatives, airs or arias, choruses and dances, commonly in that order. The rapid succession of shorter numbers allows the drama to move quickly, with the longer numbers such as the ground-bass arias adding contrast and emotional weight.

Main characters:

Dido (also known as Elissa), Queen of Carthage	Soprano
Belinda, her sister	Soprano
Second Woman	Soprano
Aeneas, a Prince of Troy	Tenor
Sorceress	Mezzo-soprano, often sung by a bass
Two Witches	Soprano
Spirit	Mezzo-soprano
A Sailor	Soprano or tenor

Tonal scheme

A clear scheme of keys is used to underline the dramatic shape of each scene.

Act 1 is in C minor, moving to C major as Belinda and the court convince Dido to 'fear no danger' and pursue her love for Aeneas. Aeneas' key is E minor ('If Not for Mine, for Empire's Sake), hinting despite his words, of the uncertain nature of his love. The act however, ends in the optimism of C major.

Act 2 introduces the Witches' in the key of F minor, but their scene also moves to the tonic major (F major), with a brief diversion to D minor for the duet 'But Ere we this Perform' before concluding in F major with a chorus and a dance. The second scene of Act 2 has a similar tonal scheme, progressing from D minor to D major, with A minor for the Spirit's attempt to divert Aeneas to Italy. Here the act ends, although it is possible to argue that like the previous Act, this scene should also end with a chorus and dance in D major or D minor. If it exists, any music for the rest of the scene is lost.

Act 3 begins with the sailors and witches in B♭ major, with G minor for the concluding scene of Aeneas' departure and Dido's death.

Act 1

Purcell models his overture on the French style established by Lully. In C minor, it opens with a slow and stately introduction with dotted rhythms, followed by a fast section which begins imitatively. The first scene opens with Belinda urging Dido to 'Shake the Clouds from Off your Brow'. The short lines of text in Tate's libretto are set in a series of short phrases, two or three bars long, with the words set syllabically, apart from melismas on words such as 'shake' and 'flowing'.

The clear melodic style continues into the chorus 'Banish Sorrow', which sets two lines of text. The homophonic style, with the melody in the sopranos, allows the text to be set in two, two-bar phrases. When it is repeated the second line is extended into three-bar phrases by the use of imitation between sopranos and basses, which provides some variety for the texture.

In the following aria, 'Ah! Belinda' the ground bass is four bars in length, played 21 times. The song is entirely in C minor apart from bars 29–36, which is in the key is G minor. Purcell avoids the tendency of the ground bass to be repetitive by changing the lengths of phrases in the voice part, overlapping rather than coinciding with the four-bar pattern of the bass. The table below details the phrase lengths and how they correspond to the bars of the ground bass.

Line of text	Length	Bars of the ground bass
Ah! Ah! Ah! Belinda	4 bars	2, 3, 4, 1
I am press'd with torment	3 bars	2, 3, 4
Ah! Ah! Ah! Belinda	4 bars	1, 2, 3, 4
I am press'd with torment not to be confess'd	5 bars	1, 2, 3, 4, 1

The subsequent passage establishes a regular pattern with the text 'Peace and I are strangers grown' – the voice begins in the fourth bar of the bass, with the repetition of 'strangers' allowing the bass and voice to end the section together. The aria ends with a short instrumental ritornello, in which the first four notes of the ground bass are taken up as the main feature with imitative string entries.

After Dido's long, contemplative aria, the action returns to the rapid succession of changing styles: a four-bar recitative ('Grief Increases'), a nine-bar song, and a 13-bar chorus ('When Monarchs Unite'). The chorus begins with two regular phrases of four bars each, but Purcell's ability to be flexible and unpredictable with phrase lengths can be seen in the way he uses the repetition of 'they triumph' to make a satisfying concluding phrase of five bars.

In the recitative 'Whence Could So Much Virtue Spring', Dido's love becomes apparent. Purcell shapes the melody to represent the words. There are melismas on 'storms', 'valour' and 'fierce'. The repetition of the words 'How soft' contrasted with the repeated 'How fierce' gives a clear musical shape to the recitative, which makes it more than just a method of setting dialogue. There is a clear direction to the vocal line, for example in the ascending scale from the low C on storms to the high G on sing and in the setting of 'How soft in peace, and yet how fierce in arms!' Purcell makes the most of the contrast between 'soft' and 'fierce'. The use of the minor key and the accented dissonance on 'soft' make the word more expressive. Note also the brilliant ascending semiquavers on 'fierce' accompanied by the sudden use of descending quavers in the bass and the modulation to C major.

In Roman legend, Aeneas was the son of Anchises, a Trojan prince, and Venus, the goddess of Love.

Belinda's response is gently mocking – note the appoggiatura on 'strong', echoed a bar later in the semitone change from minor to major on 'woe'. Purcell's recitative has strong musical qualities, with a clearly shaped melody and bass line. Dido's 'Mine with storms' begins in the upper register, the melody descending until 'distress'd'. For 'Mean wretches' grief can touch' the voice descends to a lower register. From there follow the ascending scale which builds to a climax with the expressive repetition of 'But ah' (appoggiaturas again). Note contrary motion between the constant pull of the bass in a downward direction with the ascending melody.

The tension is broken by the C major duet, sung in 3rds by Belinda and the Second Woman. The inverted dotting (also known as Lombardic rhythm or the Scotch snap) is characteristic of Purcell's approach to setting English words, but it is also a feature of the homophonic, dance-like choruses of French opera.

Act 3

Act 3 begins with the music of the sailors, a dance in triple time with imitative entries in the strings, leading to the solo and chorus 'Come Away, Fellow Sailors'. Whereas most of the airs have a structure based on the repetition of material (most often AAB or ABA), unusually each of the six lines of this air are set to different music. Note also the irregular phrasing of the First Sailor's melody – five-bar phrases are used at the beginning and the end, the Scotch-snap rhythm for 'never', and the modulation to G minor (the relative minor) for 'Take a boozy short leave of your nymphs of the shore.' The sailor's cheerful disregard for the girls left behind could be interpreted as a warning for the young ladies of Chelsea.

The Witches appear to express their gleeful delight at the success of their plans. The 'Ho, Ho!' duet changes the Sorceress' recitative into more of a song. In her air 'Our Next Motion' the repeat of the opening seven-bar phrase gives the air its regular AAB shape. Dotted rhythms feature in the bass continuo, taken up by the voice for 'storm' and 'bleeds'. The chorus 'Destruction's Our Delight'

The Witches' Dance is also known as the Jack of the Lanthorn Dance. The stage instructions for the Witches Dance from the 1689 libretto reads: 'Jack of the Lanthorn leads the Spaniards out of their way among the Inchanteresses.'

alternates the homophonic choral writing with an imitative 'Ho ho ho ho!' in 3rds. The Witches' Dance also uses G minor rather than the dominant F major as the secondary key to B♭ major, anticipating the use of G minor for the final scene.

The opera concludes with Dido's chromatic ground-bass aria 'When I am Laid in Earth' and the sorrowful final chorus 'With Drooping Wings'. The music is given more time to express the emotion and tragedy of the drama. The sorrowful mood is mirrored in the persistent use of descending melodic shapes, either chromatic or minor scales:

Recitative: 'Thy hand, Belinda'	The voice descends bar by bar through most of the notes of the chromatic scale as Dido accepts that Death is her fate
Aria: 'When I am Laid in Earth'	Chromatic ground bass, descending from G to D. Five bars long, played nine times and twice in the ritornello
	Descending scale of G minor for 'Remember me, but ah! Forget my fate'
	In the ritornello, the strings' imitation is based on the descending chromatic pattern from the ground bass
	The first violins extend their phrase by playing a one-bar motif of three minims, which descends in semitones through the complete chromatic scale (except for A♭, which is omitted)
Chorus: 'With Drooping Wings'	Chorus entries on a descending scalic motif
	'Keep here your watch', builds to a high G in the soprano melody, with the shape of the next six bars outlining a descending scale to the final G an octave below

Related repertoire

Your choice of related repertoire should be drawn from court masque and theatre music in England. **John Blow**'s *Venus and Adonis* (c. 1684), written for the court of Charles II, is the most significant of the works that preceded *Dido and Aeneas*. It is a masque in three acts and a prologue without spoken dialogue. Blow's writing for voice shows sensitivity in setting English words, and his music combines influences from English music, French opera and the Italian cantata. You should also be aware of *The Beggar's Opera* (1728) written by **John Gay** and with music arranged by Johann Pepusch. This satirises the immorality of politicians of the day, quoting well-known tunes and highlighting the absurdity of Italian opera.

Acis and Galatea

He made a further version *Acis and Galatea* in the 1730s, when it became his most performed work.

Handel's *Acis and Galatea* (1718) demonstrates a more Italianate approach to the English court masque. It was written for the Duke of Chandos at his newly built mansion, Cannons in Middlesex, where Pepusch was the director of music. The text was by John Gay, Alexander Pope and John Hughes, based on a story from Ovid's *Metamorphoses*. Only five voices and a small orchestra were required to perform the work: the choruses were originally sung one voice to a part.

Handel was born and brought up in Germany, but he spent a few years in Italy and was a master of the Italian style. He enjoyed success in London with his Italian opera *Rinaldo* in 1711 and two years later, settled permanently in England shortly before his German employer, the Elector of Hanover, became King George I. He was engaged to write a series of operas for the Royal Academy of Music, a group of aristocrats and wealthy men who aimed to present Italian opera to the London public.

The numbers in the first part (in some editions known as Act 1) of *Acis and Galatea* are in a gentle, pastoral mood, introducing us to the lovers: the shepherd Acis and the nymph Galatea. The recitatives are short, with less melodic variety than those of Purcell. The accompaniment is sustained chords, with none of the rhythmic movement in the bass which made some of Purcell's recitatives closer in style to the arias. They typically begin with a first inversion chord, and there is a clear perfect cadence at the end of sections. Although expressive, the short recitatives are there principally to link the arias, which are almost all large-scale da capo structures in the style of Italian opera. The attention is focused solely on the voice.

The pastoral scene is vividly drawn in Galatea's aria, 'Hush, Ye Pretty Warbling Choir', in which she responds to the singing of the birds. The picturesque 17-bar introduction in F major features recorders and violins in 3rds and trills, which form the basis of the accompaniment throughout the song. The four short lines of text are freely repeated in the A section, with the sung section taking up 43 bars, followed by a further 13 bars of the music from the introduction to complete the section. The B section is short (only 18 bars), in the relative minor (D), modulating to A minor, and setting two new lines of text ('Cease your song and take your flight, Bring back my Acis to my sight'). The da capo instruction requires the repeat of the A section, the standard dramatic convention of the time. The music is attractive and delightful, but the B sections add only a little in terms of dramatic development. The drama develops more through a series of contrasts between arias. Agitated dotted rhythms in the contrasting key of C minor introduces Acis's aria, 'Where Shall I Seek the Charming Fair?', which follows immediately.

In the second part (Act 2) the introduction of the monster Polyphemus, who wants Galatea for himself, brings more tension to the story. The increased dramatic action is reflected in the longer recitatives. In the chorus 'Wretched Lovers!' (see example overleaf) Handel contrasts the dissonant suspensions and imitative textures of the chorus' warning to the lovers with faster counterpoint for Polyphemus. The word painting of 'ample strides' as detached notes (each quaver separated by a quaver rest) and 'giant roars' as semiquavers in the bass create a vivid picture of the monster. A further dramatic touch is the antiphonal exchange of the word 'hark' in the other voice parts.

The da capo aria is in three sections, ABA. The B section is short, in a related key and uses moderately contrasting material. The 'Da capo' marking appears is at the end of the B section, instructing the performer to repeat the A section. Customarily the singer would introduce a certain amount of ornamentation into the performance of the repeated section.

Acis and Galatea, 'Wretched Lovers!' (bars 72–75)

Other voices:

roars, hark, hark, hark, hark, hark, hark,

Bass:

roars,_____

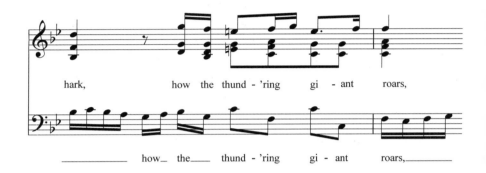

hark, how the thund - 'ring gi - ant roars,

_____ how_ the___ thund - 'ring gi - ant roars,___

Exercise 17

1. Compare Handel and Purcell's writing for the solo voice. Make a list of similarities and differences.

2. What were the characteristics of Italian opera seria? Why was it a target for satire in *The Beggar's Opera*?

3. Explain how Purcell uses harmony and tonality to illustrate the drama in *Dido and Aeneas*.

4. Describe the main features of setting English texts in two musical works for the stage before 1750. Your answer should refer to at least one extended scene from the work of two different composers.

5. Assess the importance of Purcell's contribution to the development of stage music in England, using examples from at least two scenes from his work.

Further reading

Henry Purcell's Dido and Aeneas, by Ellen T. Harris (ISBN: 978-0193152526, OUP 1987). A detailed and informative account of the historical background, music and performance history of the greatest operatic achievement of the English 17th century.

The Oxford Illustrated History of Opera by Roger Parker (ISBN: 978-0192854452, OUP 1994).

Baroque Music in Focus by Hugh Benham (ISBN: 978-1-906178-13-0, Rhinegold Publishing 2007).

Resources

A score of *Dido and Aeneas* is published as part of Norton Critical Scores series, edited by Curtis Price (ISBN 0-393-95528-1, 1986). This includes the Tate libretto (including the 1689 Prologue) and useful essays on historical background, analysis and criticism. There are many recordings available, see page 134.

Die Walküre

'...whereas the public, that representative of daily life, forgets the confines of the auditorium, and lives and breathes now only in the artwork which seems to it as Life itself, and on the stage which seems the wide expanse of the whole World.'

Richard Wagner, *The Art Work of the Future* (1849).

In his essay *The Art Work of the Future*, Richard Wagner (1813–1883) presented his theory that opera would be the medium for combining all the arts in a single, unified work of art – a *Gesamtkunstwerk*, a 'complete art work'. He had already begun to put his ideas into practice by drafting the libretto of an opera *Siegfrieds Tod* which was to evolve into the cycle of operas known as *Der Ring des Nibelungen*. Wagner worked on The Ring over the next 25 years – with interruptions to write two large scale operas, *Tristan und Isolde* (1865) and *Die Meistersinger von Nürnberg* (1867). *Die Walküre* (completed in 1856) was first performed in Munich in 1870.

For the first performance of the complete cycle in 1876 Wagner had his own theatre, the Festspielhaus, built in the Bavarian town of Bayreuth, where his operas are still performed annually. Here he could put his ideas into practice. The auditorium was to be in darkness, the seating arranged as in an amphitheatre and the orchestra hidden in a large pit which ran under the stage. The entire focus of the audience was to be on the performance.

The first opera, *Das Rheingold*, introduces the world of Norse mythology. Under the river Rhine the dwarf Alberich (the 'Nibelung' of the title) steals the Rhinegold and makes a ring which will give him world dominion. When his Ring is stolen by Wotan, the chief of the Gods, Alberich curses it: whoever owns the Ring will live in fear, whoever does not will lust after it. Wotan gives up the Ring to the giants to pay for the building of the fortress Valhalla, but immediately the giant Fafner kills his brother to have it for himself.

The story

Der Ring des Nibelungen ('The Ring of the Nibelung') is a cycle of four operas:

Das Rheingold (The Rhinegold)

Die Walküre (The Valkyrie)

Siegfried (Siegfried)

Götterdämmerung (Twilight of the Gods)

Main characters:

Siegmund, a Volsung	Tenor
Sieglinde, his twin sister	Soprano
Hunding, her husband	Bass
Wotan, the Chief of the Gods	Bass-baritone
Fricka, his wife	Mezzo-soprano
Brünnhilde, a Valkyrie	Soprano
The Valkyries, her eight sisters	Soprano and mezzo-soprano

In **Act 1** of *Die Walküre* a hunted, exhausted man arrives to shelter from a storm. Hunding's wife Sieglinde looks after him, but when Hunding arrives home he realises that his guest is the enemy he is hunting. The laws of hospitality guarantee his safety until the morning. He is weaponless, but with her husband watching, Sieglinde is unable to tell Siegmund of her father's sword, buried in the tree around which the house is built. Siegmund's father had promised him a sword before he abandoned him. Having drugged Hunding to sleep, Sieglinde returns. They fall in love and realise that they are brother and sister, Siegmund and Sieglinde. Siegmund pulls the sword from the tree and they escape into the night.

In **Act 2** Wotan instructs Brünnhilde, the eldest of his nine Valkyrie daughters by the earth goddess Erda, to give victory to Siegmund in his battle with Hunding. Fricka, Wotan's wife, is outraged by the incestuous relationship between Siegmund and Sieglinde, Wotan's twin children by a human mother. Wotan intends Siegmund to recapture the Ring, which, by the laws written on his Spear, Wotan cannot do himself. He abandoned Siegmund as a child, he argues, so that his son could be an independent hero – then take away your sword, Fricka retorts. Wotan's plan is in ruins and he now instructs Brünnhilde that Hunding must win. She appears to Siegmund to tell him that he is to die a hero's death and go to Valhalla. She is moved by his refusal to abandon Sieglinde and decides to defy Wotan's instruction, but in the fight Wotan intervenes to ensure that Siegmund's sword shatters on Hunding's spear. Brünnhilde escapes with Sieglinde and the pieces of the sword.

Act 3 begins with the famous 'Ride of the Valkyries', as the Valkyries arrive with the bodies of the heroes who are to go to Valhalla. With Wotan in pursuit, Brünnhilde asks for their help, revealing that Sieglinde is pregnant with Siegfried. Sieglinde escapes to the forest where Fafner hides his gold. Wotan declares that Brünnhilde's punishment is to lose her divinity and become an ordinary woman who can be woken from sleep by the first man to find her. Alone with her father, she defends herself. She reveals that Siegfried will be born and pleads that in sleep she should be surrounded by fire which only the strongest hero can break through. Wotan relents and summons the Magic Fire to surround her until she is freed by Siegfried.

The orchestra

Wagner uses a very large orchestra, requiring over a hundred players. The score specifies:

> Strings: 16 first violins, 16 second violins, 12 violas, 12 cellos, 8 double basses, 6 harps

> Woodwind: 3 flutes (third flute plays second piccolo), piccolo, 3 oboes, cor anglais (plays fourth oboe), 3 clarinets, bass clarinet, 3 bassoons

> Brass: 8 horns (4 players play 2 tenor tubas and 2 bass tubas when needed), contrabass tuba, 3 trumpets, bass trumpet, 3 trombones, contrabass trombone

> Percussion: 4 timpani, triangle, cymbals, tenor drum, glockenspiel.

The tenor tubas and bass tubas are often known as **Wagner tubas**. These were oval-shaped instruments constructed to Wagner's own specifications for The Ring. As they were to be played by horn players, they took a horn mouthpiece and had their valves on the left hand side.

The traditional operatic overture is replaced by a shorter orchestra prelude, which sets the mood and runs without a break into the first scene. There are longer passages of orchestral music between scenes or as part of the action, for example the Magic Fire music at the end of Act 3. Some of these orchestral passages were arranged for concert performance, with the vocal lines left out or taken on by instruments.

The idea of thematic reminiscence – bringing melodic material back to create a non-musical association – was not new. Earlier examples include Berlioz's *idée fixe* in his *Symphonie fantastique* (see chapter on Programme music) and the use of Samiel's sinister diminished-7th motif in Weber's *Der Freischütz*. By the middle of the century thematic reminiscence was a well-established feature of Romantic opera.

For The Ring, Wagner developed the leitmotif into a much more systematic form of organising dramatic music than thematic reminiscence. A leitmotif is a melody, phrase or motif which is associated with a character, object, situation or idea in the drama. Since there are many characters, objects, situations and ideas in the drama, so there are dozens of leitmotifs in The Ring. Some motifs do not recur but are used as unifying musical material for a particular scene; other motifs are heard regularly through all four operas. Used in different contexts, many of the motifs reappear in different forms, for example reharmonised, reorchestrated, altered in rhythm or intervals or shortened into a motivic version of the original extended theme heard earlier.

Discussion of leitmotif can create the impression that the music simply responds to the text with the most appropriate leitmotif, but Wagner takes care to structure his scenes carefully into sections which have some element of repetition, contrast and development. The most used shapes are AAB ('Bar' form) or ABA ('Bogen' – arch form), varied with the flexible use of introductions, codas and linking passages which disguise the formal outline of the music. Wagner also uses long-term tonal planning, giving each act a long-term shape similar to moving from a dominant to a tonic. Act 1 starts in D minor and ends in G. Act 2 moves from an unstable A minor to end in D minor. Act 3 starts in B minor and ends in E major.

Act 1 Scene 3

The scene begins in A minor with Siegmund alone. The rhythm of Hunding's motif is first heard on C in the timpani, then moves to A over alternating chords of A minor and B^7. A dramatic F minor chord accompanies his first words – he needs his father's sword – and the A returns, now harmonised as a diminished 7th. As his thoughts turn to Sieglinde, the tender sound of the solo cello is heard, and the A becomes the 3rd of a F^7 chord, moving towards a passage in B♭ major. The richness of Wagner's harmonic language enables him to build up the tension using different harmonisations of the pedal A, changing chords twice a bar to begin with, then slowing the harmonic rhythm as the $B♭^7$ chord changes it's A to an A♭, sending the music to the distant E♭ minor ('Wälse!'). As the light

Leitmotif

The term 'leitmotif' was not Wagner's but his friend, Hans von Wolzogen, who wrote the first guide to The Ring in 1878. Nor was Wagner responsible for the labels attached to the various motifs (misleadingly, in some cases) when his works were published.

There is an analysis of Wagner's use of Bar and Bogen forms in Act 1 of *Die Walküre* in Gerald Abraham's *A Hundred Years of Music*.

'Hunding'

'The Sword'

'Valhalla'

of the fire catches the sword in the tree, the music modulates to the sword's key of C major. The C major section falls into two sections: the first is led by the orchestra, repeating the sword motif with the voice answering; the second has the voice leading in a more lyrical style, as Siegmund is still thinking of Sieglinde, with the orchestra's motifs answering the voice. Hunding's rhythm returns on the timpani, bringing the mood back to that of the opening bars of the scene.

Siegmund and Sieglinde's dialogue is in recitative style, the accompaniment a combination of held or detached chords and brief interjections between lines. The arioso style returns for the Sieglinde's back-story. The Valhalla motif in E major tells the audience that the one-eyed guest in grey is Wotan. Notice how the motif appears at first in a two-bar version, after which the second bar is repeated six times over changing chords. As Sieglinde describes the consoling effect of his glance on her, the music takes on a highly expressive, chromatic character before returning through a perfect cadence to E major:

Die Walküre, Act 1 Scene 3

The C major sword music stands out in the following passage, as she describes how the sword was thrust into the tree. The music returns to E minor for her references to Hunding's kinsmen, with a more rapid recitative style, then back to the Valhalla music, giving her speech a loose ABAB shape.

The excitement of Sieglinde and Siegmund at finding each other is reflected in the new motif which is introduced. This fanfare motif is used to unify the music in this section only; it does not recur later in the opera.

G major is to be the concluding key of the act, but Wagner is planning a patient build-up to a thrilling climax. The joyful and energetic G major is diverted by an interrupted cadence and a diminished-7th chord into a new section in B♭ major. The door flies open and the moonlight streams in. The *Winterstürme* melody feels more like a traditional aria, with Siegmund singing about love in a way that adds nothing to the plot, but demonstrates that Wagner's theories did not totally exclude traditional operatic gestures.

However he does avoid any aria-like return to the opening melody, instead developing a new section which begins with one of The Ring's most characteristic love motifs from *Das Rheingold*. In *Die Walküre* this motif first appears (see the bracket in the example) when Siegmund returns the drinking horn to Sieglinde and notices her for the first time. The scoring in the first scene is delicate and expressive, a striking passage for cello solo accompanied by a cello section divided into four desks and a desk of double basses.

Die Walküre, Act 1 Scene 1

The orchestra takes over more of the musical argument, with the *Winterstürme* motif introduced again at cadences. Sieglinde's reply picks up the love motif, which is also used when she names him Siegmund just before he takes the sword from the tree.

> The C minor motif which Siegmund sings here is the same as sung by Alberich when he renounced love in order to steal the Rhinegold, a similarity which has puzzled commentators.

As the act reaches the end Wagner uses his orchestra to create a rich polyphonic texture, combining rapid bowed arpeggios across all four strings in the violins and violas, cellos divided into four groups (the top group often doubling the voice), the woodwind and horns doubling the voice or playing first triplet quavers and then six triplet crotchets against the prevailing four beats in a bar. The interrupted cadences delay the ending several times until Siegmund reaches his final notes of the act with a dramatic cadence in E minor. The concluding 26 bars modulate from E minor to G major, the rapidly moving conclusion demonstrating Wagner's ability to bring the curtain down in an exciting manner and to create a mood of expectation for the rest of the drama.

Exercise 18

1. Study the passage after Siegmund draws the sword (beginning 'Siegmund, den Walsung siehst du, Weib!'). List the key changes and melodic material found here. Explain how they contribute to the mood of the drama at the end of Act 1.

2. How does the different dramatic situation at the end of Act 2 affect the music at the conclusion of that act?

Act 3 Scene 3

Brünnhilde and Wotan are perhaps the two most important characters in The Ring, both appearing in three of the four operas. This scene marks an important phase in their development as characters in the drama: Wotan begins to accept that the downfall of the Gods is inevitable; Brünnhilde takes control of her own destiny which is human rather than immortal. Wagner's theme – as in many of his operas – is the redeeming power of Love.

Brünnhilde is at her lowest point at the beginning of the scene, abandoned to Wotan by her sisters. The scoring features solo woodwind instruments: Wagner uses the singing, expressive qualities of the clarinet, cor anglais and oboe taking the melody in turn. Brünnhilde sings quietly, alone and unaccompanied. As she grows in confidence and begins to defend herself, semiquaver motifs in the strings are used consistently, conveying the turbulent emotion under the long phrases of the voice. On the word 'Liebe' (love) the music modulates into E major, broadening into one of Wagner's love motifs. Each of Brünnhilde's arguments to Wotan is supported by the introduction of the appropriate leitmotif in the orchestra. She informs him that Sieglinde will give birth to a hero – we hear the Siegfried theme. Wotan reveals that she is to sleep until woken by a man; let it be a hero, she counters – we hear Siegfried's theme again. In desperation she asks to be surrounded by fire, and the flickering fire motif (associated with Loge, God of Fire, from *Das Rheingold*) strikes up in the orchestra.

Wotan's change of heart is matched by the power of the orchestral writing. The opera ends with one of the greatest of operatic bass solos, Wotan's Farewell. The curtain closes slowly to the Magic Fire music and the sleeping Brünnhilde.

> **Further reading**
>
> *Aspects of Wagner* by Bryan Magee (ISBN: 978-0192840127, Oxford Paperworks 1998).

Related repertoire

Your choice of related repertoire must be drawn from contemporary Italian opera, a field dominated by the work of **Giuseppe Verdi** (1813–1901). Like Wagner, he wrote almost exclusively for the opera house, but Verdi's works were performed as soon as they were written, responding to public enthusiasm for opera in Italy, where every large town had an opera house.

The characteristic features of Verdi's style are:

➤ The texture is dominated by the voice, with the orchestra used to accompany vocal melody

➤ Although his operas become more continuous, there is still a clear division into numbers, with individual arias and choruses

➤ Fast-moving plots based on historical or contemporary drama, with real characters and theatrical contrasts of emotion.

Verdi *Don Carlos* (1867) was written for Paris, originally in French, although Verdi later revised it in Italian (*Don Carlo*) in four acts (1883, the version discussed here). The story is based on a historical play by Schiller about Don Carlos, son of Philip II of

Spain. Written at the height of Verdi's international reputation, it shows influences of French grand opera, particularly in the Act 2 choral historical spectacle of the Auto-da-Fé scene (the burning of heretics by the Spanish Inquisition).

Although Verdi does not use leitmotif systematically, he makes effective use of thematic reminiscence in a way that was common in 19th-century opera. The opening prayer motif of the chorus of Friars at the tomb of Charles V which juxtaposes chords of F♯ minor and F♯ major reappears in Act 4 pianissimo to set the scene at the tomb and at the end of the opera fortissimo as Charles V pulls Don Carlos into the safety of the tomb:

Don Carlo, Act 1

The duet March theme in 3rds, in which Carlos and his friend Rodrigo dream of freedom, reappears in Act 2 as Rodrigo takes Carlos's sword from him and in Act 3 as Rodrigo dies.

Philip's monologue at the beginning of Act 3 shows Verdi's approach to structuring material. The mood of loneliness is established in the prelude in D minor, which introduces two themes, the first on solo cello, the second a semiquaver motif which makes expressive use of appoggiaturas. Philip's first words ('Ella giammai m'amò') are on a repeated B♭ leading to a phrase over a perfect cadence which brings the prelude to a close, as if we are joining the action in the middle of his thoughts. The music from the prelude continues, combining the two themes polyphonically with the voice fitting in arioso-style, his words making it clear what he is thinking. The cadential phrase returns, with an interrupted cadence and a recitative with sustained chords and an ascending arpeggio figure in the cello. The modulation to F♯ minor suggests awareness at waking from his thoughts into the real world. The aria which follows ('Dormirò Sol') is back in D minor, with the middle section in B♭ (but moving to a dramatic D♭ chord at the climax). Verdi returns to the D major perfect cadence material of Philip's opening words to bring the scene to a close – the pause and a double bar allows room for applause from the audience.

Act 3

The scene which follows is a tense encounter between Philip and the Grand Inquisitor. The old, blind Inquisitor enters to a slow procession in F minor, the darkness of the orchestration (double bassoon and resolving pianissimo trombone chords) suggesting his age and the menacing power of his office.

Further listening

Das Rheingold (1869), *Siegfried, Götterdämmerung* (both 1876) by Wagner

Rigoletto (1851), *Un Ballo in Maschera* (1859), *Otello* (1887) by Verdi

Compare this scene with Wotan and Fricka's in *Die Walküre*.

Wagner's characters build up their arguments in long sections, whereas Verdi's arioso recitative has much more rapidly alternating dialogue of the type you would expect in a stage play. The Grand Inquisitor has a longer aria-like number in which he warns of the dangers to the Church and the throne. Both Fricka and the Grand Inquisitor appear only once and both composers return to the music which introduced the character at the opening of the scene for the character's exit at the end.

Exercise 19

1. Choose two scenes from *Die Walküre* and describe briefly the relationship between the voice and the accompaniment in creating the drama.

2. Describe some of the innovations in opera which were introduced by Wagner and their use in *Die Walküre*. You should take your examples from at least two extended scenes in the opera.

3. What were the main differences in style between German and Italian opera of the 19th century? Use examples from *Die Walküre* and one from an opera by a contemporary Italian composer.

West Side Story

Main characters:

Riff	Leader of the Jets
Tony	Riff's friend
Bernardo	Leader of the Sharks
Maria	Bernardo's sister
Anita	Bernardo's girlfriend
Doc	Owner of the drugstore
Chino	A member of the Sharks

The idea of the musical can be traced back to European comic operettas of the 19th century with spoken dialogue, including the works of Gilbert and Sullivan. The modern American version – often known as the Broadway musical, after the main theatre street of New York – was established with Jerome Kern's *Show Boat* (1927). The modern format was consolidated in the works of composer Richard Rogers and librettist Oscar Hammerstein II, particularly in their groundbreaking *Oklahoma!* (1943). Its main features were:

➢ A popular musical combining direct melodic appeal with harmonies in the late romantic style of the musical theatre

➢ A well-constructed plot which combined the features of a romantic comedy with colourful characters and setting, in this case the farmers and cowboys of Oklahoma

➢ Opportunities for solos, choruses and cheerful American country-dances

> ➤ A more serious ballet sequence, which uses contemporary dance and stage action to convey the psychological aspects of the plot.

In *West Side Story* (1957) the original concept of an urban musical based on *Romeo and Juliet* came from the choreographer-director Jerome Robbins, who approached Bernstein to compose the music and Arthur Laurents to develop the story and dialogue. The lyrics are by Stephen Sondheim, who became well known as a composer of musicals in his own right. Leonard Bernstein (1918–1990) had success with his first musical (*On the Town*, 1944) and was also building a reputation as a composer of more serious works for the concert hall. A highly versatile musician, he was the first American to become internationally known as a conductor. Despite his classical music training he was an admirer of jazz and enjoyed writing works which combined elements of lighter and serious styles.

The story

Act 1 opens with a Prologue introducing the two gangs, the Sharks and the Jets. Riff, the leader of the Jets, persuades Tony, who is losing interest in the gang, to help in the 'rumble' against the Sharks. Both gangs turn up to the 'Dance at the Gym', and Tony meets Maria for the first time. Against the background of the gangs' preparations for the fight, Tony and Maria pledge their love for each other in the bridal shop ('One Hand, One Heart') where Maria works. In 'The Rumble' Bernardo, Maria's brother kills Riff and in the confusion of the fight that follows Tony kills Bernardo.

In **Act 2**, despite the tragic events of the previous scene, Tony and Maria's love survives and they dream of a place where the violence of the gangs cannot touch them. Anita, Bernardo's girlfriend, discovers Maria's relationship with Tony but Maria persuades her to put aside her bitterness and recognise that she loves him. Anita takes a message to Doc's store intended for Tony, but she meets the Jets, who taunt and molest her. In anger she tells them that Chino shot Maria when he found out about her and Tony. Distraught at the news, Tony wanders the streets shouting for Chino to shoot him too. Just as he sees Maria, Chino fires and Tony dies in Maria's arms.

The link with Shakespeare's *Romeo and Juliet* is clear: Verona is now New York, the Montagues and Capulets are the Jets and the Sharks, Tony and Maria are Romeo and Juliet. There are parallels with other characters and with scenes from the play too. The Ball has become the 'Dance at the Gym', the Balcony Scene takes place on the fire escape of a tenement building. But there are also significant differences: Maria is left alive at the end, and there are no roles for Tony and Maria's parents. The adults – Doc, Shrank, Krupke and Glad Hand play only a marginal role – they have no music to sing and do not affect the course of the drama.

Following the success of the dance elements of *Oklahoma!*, American musicals were often directed by a choreographer, with dance playing an increasingly important role in telling the story. Jerome Robbins' choreography was based on the latest advances in American ballet techniques and made considerable physical and emotional demands on the performers. Bernstein uses a number of instrumental numbers intended for dance and mime at important dramatic points: the 'Prologue', 'Dance at the Gym', 'The Rumble', 'Ballet Sequence', and 'Taunting Scene'. The songs are more static in dramatic terms, and are used more to express the feelings of the characters than to move the story forward. Even in the 'Balcony Scene' the drama is in the dialogue with an orchestral underscore in between the passages of singing. Although in 'A Boy Like That' there is character development within the song: Anita's anger at Tony changes to understanding at Maria's explanation that she loves him.

Prologue

> Compare the Prologue with the different approaches of Purcell and Wagner. *Dido and Aeneas* has a separate overture in C minor, the key of the opening scene, which sets the mood. *Die Walküre* has a storm prelude which continues without a break into the first scene.

There is no overture in the original version of the show. Instead there is an instrumental Prologue accompanying action on stage. The immediate seriousness of the subject is clear – the fighting among gangs in an inner city contrasts with the traditional escapism usually associated with musicals. It was meant to provoke the New York audience into thinking about the uncomfortable issues of teenage society in their own city.

The Prologue creates a challenging multi-layered texture exploiting some dissonant features of both jazz and classical composition:

➤ Dissonant chords, with the 3rd of the chord clashing against the sharpened 2nd. The blues feel is increased by the swing rhythm and pushed chords that anticipate the strong beats of the bar

➤ The off-beat finger clicks from the gangs are written into the music – other examples of the integration of stage sounds with the music include the police whistle at the end of the Prologue, the juke box playing the mambo in the 'Taunting Scene'

➤ The unusual intervals in the melody – the range of a minor 9th between the highest and lowest note, and the interval of the **tritone**, which is a feature of the entire musical

Act 1, 'Maria'

Ma - ri - a!_____

Act 1, 'Cha-Cha'

Act 1, 'Something's Coming'

> The **tritone** was once known as **'diabolus in musica'** – the devil in music. A tritone is an interval of an augmented 4th, for example C–F♯. Later composers found its tonal instability useful for creating an unsettled mood. In *West Side Story* it is characteristic of the gangs, particularly the Jets. The interval can be found in the opening notes of 'Maria', in the melody and accompanying riff of 'Cool', and in the opening notes of the light-hearted 'Cha-Cha'. Even in the vaudeville-style comedy of 'Gee Officer Krupke' the tritone is present as the starting notes of each verse (E♯–B). Bernstein uses the tritone for dramatic effect in Tony's numbers 'Something's Coming' and 'Maria'. Here the tritone resolves upwards onto a consonance, as if to underline his wish to escape from the gang and find something better.

➤ Cross-rhythms – Bernstein uses a ⁶⁄₈ time signature for the melody, but the accompaniment is in a pattern of three beats, as if it were ³⁄₄ – this can be seen clearly from bar 21. In the fast section (bar 140, marked Più Mosso) he uses a melody in ²⁄₄ over an ostinato of seven quavers, creating a constantly shifting rhythmic pattern

➤ The opening melody uses a polytonal effect, exploiting the dissonances created by having the melody in one key (note the F♮s and C♮s) with an accompaniment in another key (using F♯s and C♯s)

Act 1

The final few songs of Act 1 demonstrate the range of musical techniques that Bernstein was able to exploit in telling the story. 'America' and 'Cool' each focus on one of the opposing sides in the story, providing some light relief before the drama continues with 'Tonight' and 'The Rumble'.

America

'America' is sung by the Shark girls with Anita and Rosalia light-heartedly competing to compare the merits of Puerto Rico and America. The Latin American style of music and dance is fully exploited. The introduction is in a moderate Tempo di Seis with the texture built up of different rhythmic strands, first set out in claves (a syncopated rhythm which is taken up by the bass) and guiro (triplet crotchets, to be taken up by the inner parts in 3rds) under the dialogue. When the singer starts, their rhythm is mainly in triplet minims. The fast and exciting Tempo di Huapango is based on a style from Mexico that alternates §8 and ¾ time signatures. The harmony uses six different major chords (C, F, G, E♭, B♭, A♭) over a C/G pedal.

Cool

In 'Cool', Riff prepares the Jets for the 'Rumble' that night. He wants them to be 'cool', meaning in control of their emotions. Although the song is in C major, the F♯ of the tritone motif is prominent with an E♭ giving a blues feel to the music. Bernstein's ability to combine ingredients of different styles of music is apparent in the fugal dance section. Here the intense semitone semiquavers of the fugue subject are combined with a jazzy countermelody in dotted rhythms. The tritone motif from the Prologue adds a third strand to the counterpoint. The climax features a syncopated version of the fugue subject in octaves alternating with drum breaks, which leads into a fortissimo orchestral repeat of the opening introduction music and a whole verse of the melody in big-band style, with the dotted-rhythm countermelody in the woodwind linking the phrases. When the Jet boys return to sing, their verse begins and ends with a controlled pianissimo – the gang are now as controlled as Riff was at the beginning.

> Bernstein had explored the potential for combining elaborate classical polyphony and popular idioms in an earlier instrumental piece *Prelude, Fugue and Riffs* (completed 1949, premiered 1955).

One Hand, One Heart

'One Hand, One Heart' is set in the wedding shop where Maria works. As she and Tony chat, the shop dummies are used to play the roles of their family and friends, underscored by the Cha-Cha version of Maria's music. There is an air of playfulness about the dummy guests at their pretend wedding, but the fragment of the 'Somewhere' theme at the change of key signature alerts us that their imagination is taking them into another world. Their wedding vows are solemn and heartfelt. As they speak their vows, the underscore is an intensely expressive passage for pianissimo strings. The key changes through C major, E major and A♭ major before finally settling in G♭ major, a key which Romantic composers regarded as particularly expressive. It also has a dramatic function: its distance from the 'real world' of C major – and the effort required to modulate into a key with six flats – emphasises that the lovers have lost themselves in their own world.

Act 2, Ballet Sequence

The instrumental underscore begins as Tony responds to Maria's tearful accusation, 'Killer, killer, killer'. The timpani repeat a rhythmic figure which turns into a two-note semitone motif. The characteristic resolving tritone version, first heard in the opening bars of 'Something's Coming', is never far away. The final bar of the underscore is a safety bar with a ½ time signature, to be repeated *ad lib* so that Tony can move without a break from speaking ('his voice gradually rising into song') into the first sung bars of the Ballet Sequence. Note the repetition of the resolving tritone motif on each minim beat. As the orchestra takes over the melody, the scene is transformed: the walls of Maria's apartment move back to reveal a city set, which the lovers break through to find a wide open-air place, the first sign of sunlight in an otherwise dark story.

The mood of the Scherzo is light and dance-like. The semitone of the two-note motif has been softened into a tone. The style of the writing owes a debt to Aaron Copland, whose ballet scores *Billy the Kid* (1938), *Rodeo* (1942) and *Appalachian Spring* (1944) had done much to create a distinctive American sound. The use of cross-rhythms and changing time signatures is very different from the regular time signatures of other musicals. The first full appearance of the 'Somewhere' melody (it was first heard in the accompaniment at the end of the Balcony Scene) is sung a by an unnamed Girl. Its first bars are hesitant accompanied only by single lines in the strings with imitative entries of the opening interval of a 7th. As the music grows in confidence, 'Someday, Somewhere' is set to the more optimistic tone version of the two-note motif. The motif is continued into the Procession, now as an interval of a 2nd resolving onto a 3rd, with a new slow melody. The violent music of the gangs interrupts, as there is a nightmare re-enactment of the fight between Riff and Bernardo.

Act 2, 'Transition to Scherzo'

Note: some of this music is cut in performances, and passages were also used to extend the Prologue music for the 1961 film version of *West Side Story*.

Related repertoire

You will need to study 'contrasting examples of stage musicals and/ or operas composed since 1945'. The period since the Second World War has seen a revival in native English opera, with **Benjamin Britten** (1913–1975) as its most successful composer. *Peter Grimes* (1945) explored themes of the outsider against the conventions of society, using an adventurous but tonal, post-romantic musical style. His other operas include large-scale works, chamber operas, operas for children, an opera for television, and works such as *Curlew River* (1964) for a small group of performers to be staged in a church.

Billy Budd (1951, revised in two acts 1960) is set in 1797 on a British warship during the Napoleonic Wars. The action on board HMS Indomitable is framed by a Prologue and Epilogue in which Captain Vere recalls his decision to condemn the sailor Billy Budd

The opera is based on a story by Herman Melville, adapted by the novelist E. M. Forster and Eric Crozier.

to death for the killing of the evil master-at-arms John Claggart, who had sworn to destroy Billy. The darkness and tension of the story of a struggle between good and evil aboard a 'floating republic' is reinforced by the use of an all-male cast, with a homosexual subtext which was important to Britten and Forster. A lighter contrast is provided by the action sequences, the sea shanties for the chorus, and some touches of humour in the score.

The opening of the Prologue sets up the conflict between two keys – B♭ major and B minor – which mirrors the conflict in the drama.

Billy Budd, Act 1 (bars 1–3)

Billy Budd, Act 1 (bar 5)

B minor is associated with mutiny, B♭ major with the idea of redemption. The Epilogue resolves the drama in the latter key, as Vere recalls how he was saved by Billy's self-sacrifice. Other keys represent other themes in the opera: Claggart's evil is in F minor, his defeat in F major. As Vere's memory goes back to 1797, the scene changes to the deck of HMS Indomitable. The music alternates between the brisk orders of a working ship and the chorus' refrain 'O heave, O heave away heave' using a motif of a 5th and a semitone which is a recurring melodic pattern in the score:

The use of the refrain gives a musical structure to the scene, but it also establishes the chorus as a 'character' in the drama – the sailors on whom the ship depends and among whom there is the potential to mutiny.

Billy Budd, Act 1

The chorus is used prominently throughout the opera. The Act 1 scene with the officers is punctuated by the sound of offstage chorus, which Vere can hear as he reads in his cabin. The following scene, below deck, picks up the same melodies at the climax of the orchestral interlude which is used to cover the scene change. The chorus also sings throughout the exchange of sea-shanties as Billy and the others make up words to fit the same tune. Later in the same scene in a powerful monologue, Claggart spells out his ultimate aim to destroy the goodness and beauty which Billy represents.

For more information on the tonal scheme in the opera see Mervyn Cooke's *Billy Budd* (Cambridge Opera Handbooks 1993).

There are many other examples of stage works that could be studied for this topic. The British musical has also been strikingly successful, even on Broadway. Andrew Lloyd Webber's *The Phantom of the Opera* (1986) and Claude-Michel Schönberg and Alain Boubil's *Les Misérables* (1985) demonstrate that musicals on serious subjects continue to appeal to audiences. There are also many examples of successful modern operas in English, by such diverse composers as John Adams (*Nixon in China*), Harrison Birtwistle (*The Mask of Orpheus*) and Thomas Adès (*Powder Her Face*).

Exercise 20

1. Describe the different musical styles used by Bernstein in his score for *West Side Story*. How do these contribute to the effectiveness of the drama?

2. Explain the techniques of harmony and tonality used in the operas or musicals of at least two composers writing since 1945.

3. To what extent can *West Side Story* be regarded as an innovatory work? Illustrate your answer with examples from at least two extended scenes.

4. Describe how Purcell and Bernstein approach the setting of English words, basing your answer on a scene from both *Dido and Aeneas* and *West Side Story*.

Further reading

Musicals in Focus by Paul Terry (ISBN: 978-1-906178246, Rhinegold 2008).

Benjamin Britten: His Life and Operas by Eric Walter White (ISBN: 978-0520048942, University of California Press 1983).

Resources

It is not easy to find a completely satisfactory version of *West Side Story*. Not all recordings include all the music, and the film version is different from the stage musical which is set for this topic. There is a good recording of the Leicester Haymarket Theatre Production conducted by John Owen Edwards (CDJAY2 1261).

A vocal score of *West Side Story* can be obtained from Boosey & Hawkes.

There is a marvellous recording of Britten's *Billy Budd*, conducted by Richard Hickox with the London Symphony Orchestra on Chandos (CHAN 9826).

Topic 6:
Popular music

Popular music, as distinct from the classical or art-music tradition, is music that is created with accessibility to the general public as its primary aim. It is also music that is designed with mass production and dissemination in mind, through recording sales and the media industry. In the 20th century, media dissemination was made possible through the invention of the television, radio broadcasting, CDs and audiocassettes. In more recent years, the internet has developed considerably and with it the opportunities for music distribution. This, combined with continually evolving approaches to the marketing of music, has changed the way in which we listen to and purchase popular music.

The distinction between popular and classical music may not be so conveniently straightforward. All three of the prescribed works in this topic draw upon a range of classical traditions (both eastern and western), be it instrumental, harmonic, structural or a particular musical technique. The Beatles, for example, blur the popular and classical boundaries through their use of solo string textures, while Freddie Mercury creates a pseudo-operatic section in one of his best-selling songs 'Bohemian Rhapsody'.

With just 40 years spanning the prescribed works in this chapter, it is a historically narrow topic. However, the sheer pace of stylistic evolution in the 20th and 21st centuries (popular or classical) somewhat disguises this fact, and there is enormous diversity in the repertoire – even if this does not develop along a straight-line continuum.

All three of the prescribed works are innovative and experimental in some way, and a bold statement of their creator's artistic individuality and freedom of expression. Production technology is a feature that they have all embraced in abundance; it is frequently the combination of state-of-the-art technology with an approbation of earlier composing models that makes the songs from these albums so distinctive. All three of the albums make regular recourse to the building blocks of popular music, such as the verse, chorus, bridge passage, instrumental solo and outro. Their individual way of approaching this should become a focal element of study, as these prescribed works are far from formulaic.

While mass appeal may not always equate to quality, *Sergeant Pepper* and *A Night at the Opera* have already passed a lengthy endurance test in popular music terms.

Sergeant Pepper's Lonely Hearts Club Band

This album was one of the most important ever to be produced, but it dates from a period when the public's obsession with the Beatles was beginning to wane. In fact, the band ceased touring in August 1966 and decided to become entirely studio-based. *Sergeant Pepper* was then recorded over a 129-day period beginning in December 1966. It has regularly been reviewed as one of the most influential albums, and *Rolling Stone* magazine ranked it as the greatest album of all time in a 2003 survey. It was produced by George Martin (b. 1926), who is sometimes anecdotally referred to as 'the fifth Beatle' due to his enduring association with the group. It was recorded at Abbey Road Studios in London.

The Beatles were a band from Liverpool that achieved considerable fame and commercial success from the early 1960s and earned more number-one albums than any other group in UK history. Although there were a couple of other members in early manifestations of the group, the famous line-up consists of:

➤ Paul McCartney (vocals and bass guitar)

➤ George Harrison (vocals and lead guitar)

➤ John Lennon (vocals and rhythm guitar)

➤ Ringo Starr (vocals and drum-kit).

Sergeant Pepper is sometimes described as a **concept album**. This is an album in which all the songs are related in some way. Paul McCartney's initial concept for the album was that it would be a recording by a fictitious band, i.e. 'Sergeant Pepper's Lonely Hearts Club Band', in which they could create an illusion for lonely people. It is this theme of loneliness, and how it is covered up, which links their songs in this album. The Beatles believed that by embracing this idea, it would give them greater opportunity for musical experimentation.

Harmonic style

The Beatles harmonic style is rooted in a tonal idiom, as would be expected from a pop or rock band, precedents for which may be found in a wide range of western tonal music. But there are also a number of more individual harmonic styles and adventurous chordal relationships, specific to the band.

The circle of 5ths, a harmonic sequence based on chords whose roots are each a 5th lower (or a 4th higher), is an example of their use of a more traditional harmonic technique. It is a progression that appears shortly before the D.S. al coda in the final song of the album 'A Day in the Life'.

This progression appears at 2:49, see table on page 158 for further details.

But somewhat less traditional harmonic schemes may be found in the songs 'Fixing a Hole' and 'Being for the Benefit of Mr Kite'. The latter uses a rather unusual chord progression for the verse, with the opening two bars moving through the following progression: Cm–G$^+$–B♭–Dm.

The melody is given coherence through its sequential writing:

Being for the Benfit of Mr Kite

'Fixing a Hole' uses a number of augmented chords, alongside added 6th, 7th and 9th chords. This arises due to the use of the blues scale in the vocal line for much of this song. Try playing the blues scale, shown *right*, based upon F, the key of the song and then compare it to the melody.

The notes that give the blues scale its particular flavour are the flattened 3rd and 7th degrees of the scale (A♭ and E♭ in the key concerned). These two notes are especially prominent in the melody of 'Fixing a Hole', with the exception of one passage where they are conspicuously absent (the words 'It really doesn't matter...'), which provides effective harmonic variety within the song.

The flattening of degrees of the scale, especially the 6th and 7th, is a harmonic theme which links a number of songs within the album. For example, 'With a Little Help from My Friends' is in E♭ major and one of its most distinctive chord progressions is the juxtaposition of E♭ and D♭ in the chorus. In 'Lucy in the Sky with Diamonds', the verses have a chromatic musical language and draw upon the flattened 6th and 7th scale degrees (F♮ and G♮ within A major). This leads to a chromatic bass line that tends to move as one note per bar in dotted minims.

Tonally, 'Lucy in the Sky with Diamonds' is also interesting for its use of three distinct key areas: A major for the verse, B♭ major for a linking passage and G major for the chorus. The chorus is not at all chromatic (in complete contrast to the verse) and instead uses the primary triads I, IV and V as the basis for its harmony.

There are a wealth of instrumental and vocal effects within the album, and a considerable amount of diversity with the instrumentation itself. But, as well as innovation, there is also a significant adoption of traditional sounds in some of the songs.

'When I'm 64' uses a clarinet trio – two B♭ clarinets and a bass clarinet – which is unusual in any context, but particularly remarkable for a popular-music genre. McCartney himself suggested that he tried to use the clarinets in a classical way, adopting a traditional sound to make it distinctive from the rest of the album. The style of the song recalls the British music-hall tradition of the late 19th and early 20th centuries.

In one of the few songs in which the Beatles do not play themselves – 'She's Leaving Home' – they opt for a traditional string sound. (A similar effect is achieved in the song 'Eleanor Rigby', and this would be a worthy comparison as related repertoire.) The string arrangement contains a variety of syncopation and other rhythmic effects. The vocals (sung by McCartney and Lennon) are also distinctive for their high, falsetto effects. The duet singing between the two is also notable as it is a rare feature of this album.

The Alice-in-Wonderland imagery used in 'Lucy in the Sky with Diamonds' was supposedly inspired by a drawing brought home by John Lennon's son. However, it has often been accused of rather less innocent associations, rigorously denied by Lennon.

Instrumentation

Paul McCartney was actually the son of a music-hall performer, Jim McCartney, and the tradition had a notable effect upon the Beatles. It referred to a form of variety entertainment including popular song and comedy and is often likened to its American equivalent – vaudeville. The music-hall tradition links the Beatles with Queen, who also experimented with the genre in the second prescribed work of this topic.

The song 'Being for the Benefit of Mr Kite' utilises a Hammond organ, Lowry organ, harmonium and harmonica (among others) – some of these instruments reappear in the Norah Jones prescribed work.

> The **Hammond organ** was invented by Laurens Hammond in the 1930s. It was initially a cheaper alternative to the pipe organ for Churches, but eventually became a regular contributor to jazz, rock and gospel ensembles.
>
> The **Harmonium** (not to be confused with harmonica) is a keyboard instrument. The sound is generated by air, via a foot-operated pump, that sets metal reeds into vibration. The sound is similar to that of an accordion.
>
> The **Harmonica** is associated with improvisations within rhythm and blues songs. Sound is produced by placing the lips over its individual holes – air is then blown in or drawn out.

The somewhat chaotic effect generated through this assortment of instruments is reinforced by the irregularity in the rhythm. Each stanza has seven lines of lyrics, which are divided into an irregular 2+2+3 grouping. Each of these subsections are then assigned different numbers of bars to them.

For the **middle-eight** section, which links back to the stanza, the Beatles created the sound of traditional fairground organs. This was assembled by recording a range of fairground sounds, chopping the tape into pieces, throwing them into the air and reassembling them in a random fashion. These sorts of **aleatoric** effects were much favoured by the experimental art music composers of the 1960s and 1970s too.

The momentum and excitement generated from a large number of instruments is recreated and heightened in the final song of the album, 'A Day in the Life'. This song uses two cacophonous crescendos which required the assembling of a 40-piece orchestra. The song is essentially strophic – though with some minor changes to the end of each verse – and the crescendos fit within the overall structure as follows:

Note that for this song, the piano score omits the orchestral crescendos and it is therefore better analysed in terms of its track timings.

Timing	Structure
0:00	Introduction
0:13	Verse 1 (verses written and performed by Lennon)
0:44	Verse 2
1:11	Verse 3
	These verses use predominantly the same music, although there are slight adjustments to the end of each
1:45	First orchestral crescendo
2:16	Middle section (written and performed by McCartney)
2:49	Circle of 5ths in harmony accompanied by vocal 'ahs'
3:19	Verse 4

Timing	Structure
3:53	Second orchestral crescendo – these crescendos are essentially improvised – the players are given the lowest and highest notes and a time frame during in which to play them
4:21	After a very short pause, there is a crashing E major chord played simultaneously on three different pianos – this persists for over 40 seconds – as the vibrations faded, the producer increased the recording level so that it was still heard
5:06	One of the more curious insertions in the album is a high-pitched tone – Lennon suggested that it was to annoy the listener's dog – followed by deliberately incomprehensible gibberish, spliced together with sections playing in both forward and reverse

Perhaps the most distinctive track on the album belongs to George Harrison – his somewhat opus magnum 'Within You, Without You'. At the time, this song was an unusually long pop record, although it was originally a 30 minute piece that had been trimmed down for inclusion in the album. It features George Harrison on vocals, sitar and acoustic guitar; none of the other Beatles are represented. It represents Harrison's immersion in Indian culture and Hinduism. He had a long association with Ravi Shankar who taught him the sitar.

Ravi Shankar (b. 1920) is one of the most famous musicians of the modern Indian era. He is the father of Norah Jones, singer-songwriter of the third prescribed work in this topic.

Harrison readily embraced Hindu mysticism and this song refers to *Dharma*, an ethical code within the religion. Harrison suggests that through mutual love, and the following of *Dharma*, the world can be saved from destruction. The rhythmic simplicity of the vocal part contrasts with the elaborate rhythmic extemporisations on the **tabla**. An extended pseudo-improvisatory passage in the middle creates a soundscape typical of Indian Classical music. There are also some effective moments of dialogue between the instruments. The tambura part (the drone instrument) is performed by Neil Aspinall, the only credited musician on the track; the same instrument appears in the song 'Lucy in the Sky with Diamonds' though this time it is performed by George Harrison.

Many of the vocal and instrumental ideas considered above represent the notion of experimentation and innovation. However, we shall link a few further ideas to the issue of recording technology that also plays a fundamental role in the album.

Experimentation, innovation and recording technology

Sergeant Pepper takes full advantage of **multi-track recording**, a technique somewhat taken for granted in the 21st century, but it should be borne in mind that Abbey Road was not in a position to install four-track recording machines until the beginning of the 1960s. The album also made wide use of **bouncing down**. This was a technique where the tracks were recorded across the four tracks of one recorder and then mixed down onto one track of the master four-track machine.

The Beatles themselves were keen experimenters and innovators with instrumental technology using devices such as a tape-based keyboard sampler and effects units like the **wah-wah pedal** and **fuzzbox**. The Beatles also precipitated one of the most important recording technology developments of the time, namely the invention of **ADT (automatic double tracking)**, which was developed specially for the group and quickly revolutionised the recording of popular music. The technique used tape delay to create a delayed copy of an audio signal that could then be combined with the original. The effect simulated the sound of the natural doubling of voices or instruments that could previously be achieved by double tracking – a practice disliked by Lennon due to its tediousness.

Examples of ADT's usage within the album include:

> 'Fixing a Hole' – the bass part is treated with this technique to simulate a fretless tone

> 'Within You, Without You' – used on most parts of the track

> 'Lucy in the Sky with Diamonds' – a flanging effect in the vocals, which is a variant upon this technique.

A more self-evident application of recording technology occurs in the song 'Good Morning', which includes a whole gamut of animal sounds towards its ending. The animals in this section are intended to increase in ferocity as the passage proceeds. Other technological innovations in this song include the creation of an aggressive instrumental sound by close microphone placement and heavy compression of the ensuing signal. The song is also innovative (at least for a popular record) in regard of its rhythm and metre – there are continual changes between $\frac{3}{4}$, $\frac{4}{4}$ and $\frac{5}{4}$ time signatures. The song ends as it began with a clucking-chicken sound effect, strategically placed so that it **segues** into the guitar on the next track, a reprise of the 'Sergeant Pepper' theme. The tendency towards track segues is another feature of *Sergeant Pepper* and a further pointer to its perception as a concept album.

Album cover The album's combination of innovation and its reverence towards traditional techniques and styles is perhaps best summed up by its cover. As an artistic design it was something of a revelation but it also alludes to the inspirations and influences absorbed by the Beatles. Known as 'People We Like', it featured 70 figures including Sigmund Freud, Oscar Wilde, various Indian gurus at the behest of Harrison, Karl Marx and (coincidentally) the experimental composer Karlheinz Stockhausen who features as a prescribed work in the Music and belief topic.

Related repertoire

Your related repertoire should be drawn from British popular music (by groups and solo artists) from the 1960s.

One of the most important and influential British groups of the 1960s onwards was the **Kinks**. The Kinks consisted of:

> Ray Davies (lead vocal, rhythm guitar and keyboard)

> David Davies (lead guitar and vocals)

> Peter Quaife (backing vocals and bass guitar)

> Mike Avory (drums and percussion).

Although *Pet Sounds* (1966) by the Beach Boys was acknowledged by Paul McCartney as a primary influence on *Sergeant Pepper*, the Beach Boys are an American band and hence do not fall within the remit of this topic, as defined by the specification.

Their third song 'You Really Got Me', written by Ray Davies, was the one that brought them to prominence in 1964 and it entered the charts directly at number one.

At a little over two minutes, 'You Really Got Me' is a short song, but it makes a powerful impression, primarily with the ground-breaking sound of its guitar playing. This was achieved by cutting into its amp speaker with a razor blade and poking pins into it, a typically rebellious and individualistic gesture of the time. The opening 'power chords' on the guitar form virtually all the song's underlying material. The song is structured as follows:

A **power chord** is a chord for guitar that omits the 3rd of the triad – it therefore contains a bare interval of a 5th.

Timing	Section	Comments
0:00	Intro	Four repetitions of the power-chord riff – the guitar is heard solo on the first two renditions, but is then joined by the drum-kit
0:08	Verse 1	The riff is heard as the accompaniment to the words a further eight times
0:22	Chorus	The use of the power-chord riff further links the verse with the chorus – this time it is heard in two transpositions, based upon the chords G–A and then C–D. It is followed by a short bridge passage at 0:39
0:43	Verse 2	Additional repeated piano chords are combined into the texture
0:57	Chorus	As above
1:16	Instrumental	A dynamic guitar solo dominates this section – this links into a shortened version of the intro which in turn links to a further verse
1:35	Verse 3	As above
1:48	Chorus	As above
2:07	Outro	Four power chords on the guitar conclude this song

Used in this way, the power-chord riff was an influential sound for rock groups, and the critic Robert Walser suggested that this song was 'the track which invented heavy metal'. This contrasts with the Beatles who were less inclined towards the heavy rock sound and hence made less use of riff material in their songs.

A further song from this collection, 'Waterloo Sunset', has been set as an Edexcel Anthology set work and is therefore well-documented in the *Edexcel A2 Music Study Guide* (Rhinegold 2009).

Further reading

The Beatles: The Complete Guide to their Music by John Robertson and Patrick Humphries, (ISBN: 0-7119-9882-5, Omnibus Press 2004). Contextual details and notes on all Beatles' albums.

The Beatles: Sgt. Pepper's Lonely Hearts Club Band, by Allan F Moore, (ISBN: 0-521-57484-6, Cambridge Music Handbooks, 1997) a scholarly account of the Beatles' album and in-depth analysis on each of the songs.

There is also a huge amount of information on this album available on the internet, but as always you should demonstrate critical judgement when evaluating this – making sure to separate the pop trivia from the musically insightful.

Exercise 21

1. To what extent might *Sergeant Pepper* be considered innovative?

2. Describe how the Beatles absorbed a number of external influences in the creation of the *Sergeant Pepper* album. Refer in detail to at least four songs.

A Night at the Opera

A Night at the Opera was released in 1975. It subsequently sold over 3 million copies and was number one in the album charts for nine weeks in the UK. At the time it was thought to be the most expensive album ever made and the track 'Bohemian Rhapsody' became Britain's third best-selling single of all time. 'Bohemian Rhapsody' was also one of the first singles to have a specially created music video. The album name itself is taken from the 1935 film by the Marx Brothers.

Queen was a British rock band who had formed in 1970 and consisted of the following members:

➤ Freddie Mercury (lead vocalist)

➤ Brian May (guitar)

➤ John Deacon (bass)

➤ Roger Taylor (drums).

A Night at the Opera was the fruit of considerable preparation and rehearsal, and was the most ambitious album of the band's career. It covers a wide range of musical styles, yet with Queen's distinctive sound pervading all the tracks. The band's own ambitions in regard of this album are also telling, Brian May articulating them in the words:

'We thought, this time, we're going for it [...] This one'll be our Sgt. Pepper'.

Musical styles and influences

The sheer range of musical styles is one of the distinctive features of *A Night at the Opera*. Although it is often associated with, or classified into, a progressive-rock genre, there is much more to the album than this alone. Influences that can be found in the album and would be worthy of further exploration, include the following:

➤ Heavy metal in 'Death on Two Legs'

➤ Music-hall associations of 'Lazing on a Sunday Afternoon' and 'Seaside Rendezvous' – perhaps recalling McCartney's approach in 'When I'm 64'

➤ Skiffle (and a concept of sci-fi sound) in '39'

➤ A Dixieland-style jazz band in 'Good Company'

➤ A pseudo-operatic approach in 'Bohemian Rhapsody'.

Skiffle is a type of folk music with jazz and country influences. It also typically uses homemade or improvised instruments such as the comb and paper or kazoo. Although these instruments are not a particular feature of '39', the kazoo appears in 'Seaside Rendezvous'.

We will revisit some of these ideas in the following sections of this chapter.

Vocal styles, instrumentation, harmony and structure

Although Freddie Mercury was the lead vocalist, all the band members contributed towards Queen's vocal sound. It is perhaps their regular interjections into the texture, in close harmony that gives the group its most distinctive sound. Instrumentally, their approach was also innovative for their the use of a banjolele, harp, koto and electric piano in a number of songs.

As a youngster in India, Mercury had received some formal piano training and it remained his chief instrumental interest. He played piano on a number of the tracks and one of his trademark flourishes of cascading arpeggios can be heard at the beginning of the first track, 'Death on Two Legs'. Although the piano style draws upon traditional idioms, the harmonic language is far from conventional:

$$E\flat \mid G\flat/D\flat \mid D\flat sus^4 \mid Fm/C \mid Em/B$$

As may be deduced from this, the bass moves downwards by step: E♭–D♭–C–B♮. This somewhat innocent-sounding introduction gives way to an intense, ostinato guitar-riff (shown *right*). The interval between the third and fourth notes – an augmented 4th or tritone – was a favoured ingredient for heavy-metal songs (another example is Led Zepplin's 'Immigrant Song') and gives it a dark quality to the music.

The opening to '39' also starts in an unusual way harmonically:

$$D\flat \text{ (+ supertonic of } E\flat) \mid B\flat m \mid F \mid B \mid E \mid A\flat$$

Considering the folk-like, even skiffle, feel to the song, this is a surprising opening and again demonstrates a tritone relationship with the shift from F major to B major. The song also contains a range of vocal sounds and effects. Taylor in particular demonstrates a wide register, singing high and low harmonies and also some **falsetto** effects. The unusual harmonies of the introduction are further developed in a bridge passage from 1:32. From this point the chord progression moves as follows:

Timing	Comments
1:32	E major (the melody moves between B–A♯–B–C♯, the A♯ again setting up a tritone relationship)
1:42	B♭ major (a tritone from E)
1:46	D♭ major
1:49	G minor – back to D♭ major (tritone again between G and D♭)
1:54	F major

This sort of experimental harmony is a typical feature of progressive rock, where dissonant intervals and unusual chord relationships tend to exist much more commonly than stereotypical I–IV–V patterns.

The somewhat abstract, sci-fi sound of '39' is in significant contrast with the song that precedes it on the album, 'You're My Best Friend'. This track is the only compositional contribution by bassist John Deacon and was written in dedication to his wife. Unusually for this album, it is a straightforward pop song without the more progressive or abstract sounds that characterise many of the other tracks. In contrast to '39', the harmony is mostly driven by tonic-dominant relationships. Furthermore, its economy of material suggests its skilful crafting and its structure is worthy of further analysis. The song also contains a number of vocal effects (sung by lead vocalist Mercury) such as ornaments and slides between notes.

Timing	Structure	Comments
0:00	Introduction	A four-bar introduction introduces the riff between two Cs (an octave apart) that characterises much of the song The bass line is therefore exclusively on C; in the third bar it becomes a pedal note under D minor harmony. The drums enter in bar 4
0:08	Verse 1	A ten-bar verse: the main chord progression is Dm/C–C and logically follows the harmonic shape of the introduction
0:28	Chorus	The chorus is dovetailed neatly into the verse and reuses some of the melodic material. The harmonic pattern is more adventurous with an increased harmonic rhythm. The secondary dominant chord (D major) is also used. Near the end of the chorus, there is an Fm^6 chord on which Queen's trademark close harmony can be heard. The vocal notes are D–F–A♭–C forming the Fm^6 chord
0:51	Bridge passage	Some reusing of melodic material from both the verse and chorus. There is extensive backing vocal accompaniment from the lead vocalists in this section
1:16	Verse 2	Music is the same as verse 1, with additional guitars and backing vocals
1:36	Chorus	As previously
1:58	Second bridge passage	Guitar solo with vocal harmonies, rather than lead vocal
2:30	Outro	Vocal phrases based upon verse material. Final bars contain a number of dominant-tonic resolutions

Innovation and recording technology

A *Night at the Opera* embraces innovation – as we have already seen in the previous section – and this extends to both the musical styles and the use of recording technology. The following list highlights some of the recording techniques used in the production of this album:

➤ 'You're My Best Friend' uses overdubbing techniques so that John Deacon could add two bass parts at a later stage (he performed electric piano on the recording itself)

➤ The tap-dancing effects in 'Seaside Rendezvous' were created by Mercury and Taylor 'drumming' on the mixing desk while wearing thimbles on their fingers

➤ The revving of the car at the end of 'I'm in Love with my Car' was produced by recording Taylor's car. This song also segues out of its predecessor – something of a trend on contemporary albums

➤ Stereo effects are also used extensively within the album.

Although stereo recording on LPs had been around for some time, it was becoming increasingly popular with the public. There are a lot of panning effects that exploit the effect of the sound moving between the left and right ears. This is best perceived with headphones and can be heard, for instance, in 'Bohemian Rhapsody' between 0:35–0:38.

The small technical reference to 'Bohemian Rhapsody' above belies the enormous production complexity surrounding this track. 'Bohemian Rhapsody' is perhaps the most famous individual song on the album and when it was released as a single it topped the UK charts for nine weeks, breaking various sales records of the time. One of the most noteworthy features of 'Bohemian Rhapsody' is the musical variety it contains within its six minutes. The structure encompasses five main different sections:

Timing	Section	Comments
0:00	Introduction	The first 15 seconds feature a capella singing in four-part vocal harmony. The primary melody is in the second highest part, a technique often employed by Barbershop groups. Much of the harmony is based around the circle of 5ths, for example the opening progression: Gm^7–C^7–F^7–$B\flat$
		The piano enters at 0:15. Shortly after this point, a more chromatic passage is heard in the harmony (lyrics: 'easy come, easy go') – the progression over these two bars is: B–B$\flat$–A–B$\flat$ | B–B$\flat$–A–B$\flat$
0:48	Ballad (+ guitar solo)	At just over two minutes, this is the most substantial section of the song. It opens with solo voice and piano/bass accompaniment, the drum-kit does not enter until 1:20
		This section is divided into two verses, the second of which begins at 1:55 and has some additional instrumentation including guitar. A word-enhancing effect occurs at 2:03 ('sends shivers down my spine') when May scratches the guitar strings
		Towards the end of the second verse, there is a build-up in intensity, which leads to a guitar solo providing a bridge between the two sections. This cuts out suddenly at 3:03
3:03	Pseudo-opera	This section, describing the narrator's descent into hell, begins with eight, A major chords on the piano, prior to the entry of the vocal part. The beginning of this vocal melody evokes the earlier line 'I'm just a poor boy from a poor family' with its use of rising and falling semitones
		The vocal effects are the most remarkable aspect of this section, and the 'choir' resulted in nearly 200 separate overdubs, using the 24-track technology of the day. It achieved Queen's aim of creating a wall of sound and exploits a enormous vocal range – from Mercury's low notes to the top falsetto B$\flat$ sung by Roger Taylor at 4:04
		Under the words 'Beelzebub has the devil put aside' – the chord progression is: E$\flat$–A$\flat$–D–Gm. The chords A$\flat$ and D are a tritone apart, and shows Queen's willingness to innovate with more exotic harmony
4:07	Rock	This section is a hard-rock interlude including a guitar riff created by Mercury. His vocals from 4:15 are double-tracked in order to give the sound more strength
4:55	Outro	This is a more reflective closing section and there are a number of musical features which reflect the sense of resignation in the words ('nothing really matters'):
		A slower tempo and quieter dynamics
		Less aggressive instrumental parts, for example the gentle arpeggios on the piano part
		The final sound heard is a quiet tam-tam (gong) effect that suggests the wind blowing – the last line of the song

Although 'Bohemian Rhapsody' is highly innovative in its production, the lesser-known 'The Prophet's Song' is perhaps even more adventurous. It is an epic track (over eight minutes long) and contains numerous changes in key and tempo. Written by Brian May, it allegedly came to him in a dream about the Great Flood and draws together a number of biblical references from the story of Noah's Ark and the Book of Exodus.

A canon is a contrapuntal device where one part is repeated a few notes later by another, while the original melody continues independently.

The most distinctive aspect of this song is the vocal canon which occupies just over two minutes in the middle of the track. Significantly, it comes after the words 'death awaits you', and sounds like some sort of surreal dream. It uses the technology of early tape-delay devices and initially features Mercury as a soloist with two delayed parts at the interval of four beats. Later it features Mercury, Taylor and May as a vocal trio. 'The Prophet's Song' is one of most eclectic on the album and shows the band's willingness to fuse traditional devices such as canon into a highly experimental production environment.

Related repertoire

David Bowie had an actual association with Queen – they collaborated for the song 'Under Pressure' in 1981.

Your related repertoire should be drawn from examples of glam rock from the 1970s and 'super groups' with international fame. Good examples of the latter include T. Rex and the Rolling Stones. One of 'glam rock's' most influential performers was **David Bowie** (b. 1947).

Glam rock, as a subgenre of rock music, is characterised by a combination of lyrical ballads, high-energy rock, and the experimental and progressive rock sound as cultivated by bands such as Queen. It was also synonymous with outrageous costumes, flamboyant antics on stage and a degree of sexual ambiguity, evident in Bowie's androgynous alter ego Ziggy Stardust.

Bowie was a renowned innovator and well-known for regular reappraisals of both his music and his image. The album *The Rise and Fall of Ziggy Stardust and the Spiders from Mars* (1972) (often known simply as *Ziggy Stardust*) draws together the above influences with a distinctly sci-fi theme (also evident in Queen's *A Night at the Opera* track '39').

Ziggy Stardust is a **concept album** in that it tells a story, albeit without any consistent narrative. Ziggy Stardust is the human persona of an alien, sent to humanity with a message of hope in the final years of its existence. Ultimately destroyed by his own excesses, Stardust is the archetypal rock star and through this album Bowie makes an important statement about the Messianic perception of our own rock idols. The album was released in 1972 and reached number five in the British album charts.

The eponymous track, *Ziggy Stardust* uses a range of vocal and instrumental effects within a relatively straightforward but slightly unusual structure:

Timing	Section	Comments
0:00	Intro	This begins with power chords, a lead guitar riff and cymbal crashes. Bowie enters with a falsetto effect, followed by one of his trademark exhalation noises at 0:20
0:25	Verse 1 and 2	Two verses follow each other consecutively and these contain a number of high guitar and distortion effects
1:13	Chorus	The chorus is underpinned by a stepwise progression of power chords, using the chord sequence A–G–F–G in a cyclic manner
1:36	Bridge	The bridge passage draws upon the music of the intro, in particular the lead guitar riff
1:48	Verse 3	A musical repeat of the earlier verses
2:11	Chorus	This time the chorus (unusually) has different words
2:36	Bridge	A further bridge using the intro riff
2:55	Outro	A rather indulgent vocal finish on the word 'guitar' which sees it extended for several seconds

A further song to study from the album would be 'Starman', also released as a single in 1972. This song forges a more traditional pop-rock sound, with its use of acoustic guitar and accompaniment featuring string instruments. Its chorus is loosely based upon Harold Arlen's classic ballad 'Over the Rainbow', which featured in the film *The Wizard of Oz* (1939) – suggesting Bowie's enthusiasm for drawing upon a range of eclectic influences.

Exercise 22

1. Why was *A Night at the Opera* such an important album? Refer in detail to at least four songs.

2. Queen suggested that *A Night at the Opera* would be 'their Sgt Pepper'. How was the Beatles album influential in their thinking?

Further reading

Queen, The Complete Guide to their Music by Martin Power (ISBN: 1-84449-871-9 2006, Omnibus Press).

www.queensongs.info – although there are huge amounts of Queen trivia and facts and figures available on the internet (which should generally be avoided for the purpose of A2 study), this site is a much more scholarly examination of the material. Note that some of the chord progressions quoted are transposed into easier keys.

David Bowie, The Complete Guide to his Music by David Buckley (ISBN: 1-84449-423-3, Omnibus Press 2004).

Not Too Late

Not Too Late, released in January 2007, is the third studio-based album by singer-songwriter Norah Jones. It reached number one in both the United Kingdom and USA. The album was produced by Lee Alexander, who had featured as a songwriter and bassist on Jones' previous albums.

Norah Jones (b. 1979) is an American singer-songwriter and versatile instrumentalist – the daughter of famed sitar player Ravi Shankar. Jones' career was launched by her debut album *Come Away With Me* in 2002 and since that point she has become one of the most successful recording artists of the 21st century, selling 36 million records worldwide.

In a similar way to the other prescribed works in this topic, Norah Jones' album transcends a number of musical styles and makes especially creative use of instrumentation – something that we will examine later in the chapter.

Harmonic language Jones' harmonic language has its roots in tonal, diatonic conventions but with a number of personal idioms. In fact her songs are harmonically varied to the extent that it is impossible to define the style of the album by any one of its tracks.

On occasions, Jones is highly economical with harmonic material, building songs out of just two or three chords, or a repeated chord progression. In these cases, there is normally a particular emphasis upon the melody. 'Until the End' uses a sparse harmonic vocabulary in such a way. The song is based predominantly upon two chords, although one of these is also used in an augmented version. The chords are C, C+ and F, though there is a short chorus-like passage that employs some additional harmony. This song is also unusual for its structure, being essentially through-composed in terms of its verse material which evolves throughout the track. The structure is as follows and is also notable for its lack of a regular phrase structure:

Verse 1	32 bars (vocal melodies are typically shaped in seven-bar phrases with an additional instrumental bar inserted)
Chorus	11 bars (though one of these is a $\frac{3}{8}$ bar insertion – effectively making the total 10.5 bars)
Verse 2	32 bars, based upon earlier ideas but significant changes in the melody
Chorus	As previously
Guitar solo	16 bars
Outro	11 bars of vocal material based upon verse and six bars of instrumental coda

Another song which uses harmony in a similarly economical way is 'Broken'. The accompaniment largely consists of a repeating four-bar chord progression: C | G | Dm^7 | F

This is a traditional progression, but it is modified on occasions by transforming the G major chord into its second-inversion form, such as in bar 10. The use of the second inversion is somewhat idiomatic to Norah Jones and also becomes a significant part of the harmony in the track 'Not My Friend'. The first ten bars of the song consist of a chord progression that oscillates between F major and Am/E (A minor in second inversion). By using the second-inversion chord so liberally, Jones is able to depart from the apparent traditional nature of her chord progressions.

The stepwise bass motion generated by the F–Am/E progression of the above example is also a theme of the track 'Sinkin' Soon'. The first 12 bars consist exclusively of E minor harmony but there follows a move to D^7, then C^7, then B^7 in the following four bars. If this downward movement is an oblique reference to the title of the track, then the music becomes more explicitly descriptive at the end of each verse with the words 'gonna be sinkin' soon'. Over the space of five bars, the melody moves down an octave in its range to the note E (below middle C) – particularly low in the female range and the lowest note on the album.

Both the melody and harmony of 'Sinkin' Soon' are closely modelled on the blues scale and Jones emphasises these blue notes in her performance. Manipulating the notes of the scale in this way makes a useful link with the Beatles who applied this technique a number of times in their *Sergeant Pepper* album (see earlier in the chapter).

Flattening the 6th and 7th degrees of the scale, for instance, was evident in the Beatles song 'With a Little Help from My Friends' and it is a harmonic idiom that Jones employs a number of times on the album.

'Thinking About You' is in E♭ major and it regularly uses the notes D♭ (flattened 7th) and C♭ (flattened 6th). Listen to two phrases (0:56–1:11) from the chorus of this track – there is a sliding harmonic progression (E♭–D♭–Cm) under the words 'But I'll be thinking about you', which is adjusted on the second half of the phrase to include the flattened 6th (E♭–D♭–C♭). Notice that the final note of each melodic phrase remains the same, but it sounds different on the second occasion because it is reharmonised with a C♭ major chord.

'Sinkin' Soon' is unusual on the album for its use of a minor key. Although most of the songs are written in a major tonality, the track 'The Sun Doesn't Like You' is rather more esoteric. For much of this song, the 3rd is omitted from the triad leaving some ambiguity as to whether the song is in the major or the minor. There are also hints of the transposed mixolydian mode with the appearance of C naturals and C major chords.

The mixolydian mode represents the white notes of a piano from G to G – this is the same as a major scale but with a flattened seventh. In 'Sun Doesn't Like You' it is transposed up to D and therefore features a C natural.

The tracks on the album span a range of harmonic complexity. Some are highly inventive such as 'My Dear Country' – note the range of diminished, augmented, 7th and 13th chords, while others are rather more prosaic. The final song on the album, 'Not Too Late', is harmonically understated and largely consists of a cycle of repeated chords, not dissimilar from the technique used in 'Broken'.

A track which draws together a number of harmonic ideas that we have considered so far is 'Wish I Could'. Written in D major, the song has a tonic pedal note (D) underpinning virtually all of the harmony – there are just a few short occasions when the bass note moves away from this. Other features that link this song harmonically with others on the album include a single chord for the introduction (although it is coloured with occasional suspensions); inversions and in particular some second-inversion chords; and chromatic adjustment of degrees of the scale. For example, in bar 17 an F major chord (flattened mediant) appears above the D pedal note. Although the song is in D major, the note C♯ is barely heard. Instead, the leading note is consistently flattened to produce C major harmony, for example in the progression that appears at the end of each verse. The use of a major key with flattened 7th again evokes the mixolydian mode (as in 'Sinkin' Soon'), but the case for it is made more strongly in this song.

'Wish I Could' is a strophic song where all six verses use the same music. However, Jones invests the music with considerable variety through her wide-ranging use of instrumentation and this becomes another theme for the whole album.

Word-setting and instrumentation

> On the Norah Jones album, the cello part is played by Jeff Ziegler, a cellist with the highly-eminent Kronos quartet. The Kronos quartet have demonstrated considerable diversity in their repertoire and are well-known for a recording of Steve Reich's minimalist work *Different Trains* (1988) which draws together a classical string quartet with electronic sampling.

The use of varied vocal styles, word-setting techniques and a diverse panoply of instrumentation characterises *Not Too Late* and links it to similar aspirations found in the Beatles' and Queen's prescribed works. The song 'Wish I Could', discussed above, achieves variety within its strophic structure through the use of differing instrumental and vocal techniques. The first four verses are structured as follows:

➤ Verse 1: solo vocalist and light guitar accompaniment

➤ Verse 2: addition of counter-melody played on cello

➤ Verse 3: vocalist multi-tracked to build up a more elaborate vocal texture

➤ Verse 4: cello solo, extemporising on earlier melodic material.

'Broken' experiments with a range of string textures including pizzicato and a bowed double bass. During the first instrumental bridge passage, the bowed bass enters and highlights the first quaver note (the root note of the chord) of each bar. This gives the accompaniment a somewhat fragmentary feel, and may even be designed to evoke the sense of the title. In the second instrumental bridge passage, Jones introduces further string effects such as glissandi in the cello's counter-melodies.

Further links to *Sergeant Pepper* can be seen in Norah Jones' deployment of keyboard instruments. For example, the track 'Thinking About You' features a Hammond organ and Wurlitzer, instruments that appear in *Sergeant Pepper*'s 'Being for the Benefit of Mr Kite'. 'Thinking About You' also contains noteable word-painting effects, such as the melismatic vocal setting of the phrase 'and the leaves were falling down softly' in bars 5–8.

All the tracks employ a range of keyboard sounds, from the traditional piano to the more unusual examples above. The final (eponymous) track of the album also features a Mellotron, a type of electro-mechanical keyboard devised in the 1960s which is also capable of playing back pre-recorded sounds.

Many of the tracks on *Not Too Late* are defined by their use of an extended instrumental solo. This may feature the acoustic guitar as in 'The Sun Doesn't Like You' and 'Until the End' where there is a passage of extended pseudo-improvisation (sometimes simply marked ad. lib in the score) above a light homophonic accompaniment. More diverse sounds are found in the track 'Sinkin'

Soon' which employs an unusually wide array of instrumentation. This song features:

➤ Piano

➤ Trombone

➤ Bass

➤ Mandolin

➤ Drums, slit drum, pots and pans

➤ Guitjo.

The trombone is particularly effective within the instrumental texture and it complements the blues style with its blue notes and swung rhythms. You can hear all kinds of timbral effects, such as the use of mutes on the trombone and the low note at the end of the song.

The range of musical styles and influences evident in *Not Too Late* suggests Norah Jones' enthusiasm for eclecticism. The incorporation of a classical string sound ('Wish I Could') and the use of blues elements ('Sinkin' Soon') is discussed above and these features can be found more widely in the album. Other ideas for exploration are as follows:

Musical styles and influences

➤ The use of traditional styles: there are elements of the traditional waltz in 'My Dear Country' with the use of regular phrasing, an 'oom-cha-cha' rhythm in the accompaniment, and a stately harmonic rhythm (although the harmonic language is much more complex than would be found in a traditional waltz)

➤ A strong country feel: in 'Wake Me Up' the syncopated guitar accompaniment, use of long sustained chords and the pitch-bending on the lap steel guitar contribute to this effect which is especially evident in the song's introduction.

Related repertoire

Your choice of related repertoire should be drawn from examples of music written and performed by contemporary singer-songwriters. One of the most eminent contemporary singer-songwriters is **Amy Winehouse** (b. 1983). Like Norah Jones, she draws upon a number of stylistic influences for her work. Her 2006 album *Back to Black* (following her debut album *Frank* in 2003) was the best-selling album in the UK during 2007.

'Rehab', the first song from *Back to Black*, was additionally released as a single in 2007 and it won the Ivor Novello award for 'Best Contemporary Song' in the same year. The lyrics of 'Rehab' describe the narrator's addictive drinking and refusal to enter a rehabilitation clinic. It almost certainly has a strong autobiographical element. Despite the contemporary and gritty subject matter of its lyrics, 'Rehab' has a distinctively retro feel, drawing particularly on Motown influence, a genre which celebrates its 50th anniversary in 2009.

Strictly speaking, **Motown** is the trademark of a record label founded in 1959 but has become a generic term for the associated musical sound. The Motown sound is a blend of soul, R & B with undertones of Gospel and is typified by one of its signature tracks – 'Dancing in the Street' (1964) recorded by Martha and the Vandellas.

'Rehab' is structured as follows and, in contrast to many other contemporary songs, has no discernible intro or outro:

Timing	Section	Comments
0:00	**Chorus**	The vocals enter first, followed immediately by the bass and percussion; there is no introduction. The beat, with its syncopated rhythms, drum-fills and off-beat handclaps is Motown-inspired The harmonic language is based upon 'rhythm and blues' using chords I, IV and V with a number of added 7ths
0:28	**Verse 1**	The verse uses a less conventional chord progression: Em | Am | F^7 | A♭ and this is repeated twice in a cycle There is also prominent use of the baritone saxophone which provides an off-beat riff. Like Norah Jones, Amy Winehouse draws upon a wide array of classical musicians in the production of this album
0:54	**Bridge**	A short bridge passage, where the second line is an augmented version of the chorus line 'But if my Daddy...'
1:07	**Chorus**	The texture is thickened with more brass instruments playing long crescendo notes
1:33	**Verse 2**	There are additional dialogue effects from the 'horns' in the band (the term 'horn' is used in the pop-band sense of the word, to refer to the saxophones)
2:01	**Bridge**	A repeat of the earlier passage
2:12	**Chorus**	This time the chorus is abridged, with only half the lyrics used. Some additional drum-fills are included
2:26	**Verse 3**	Additional instrumental effects are included, most notably a repeated riff on the keyboard
3:05	**Chorus**	A final repeat of the chorus. There is no outro or fade out – the song ends as suddenly as it began

'Rehab' makes for a constructive comparison to Norah Jones' album in its wide-ranging use of instrumental colour and engagement with other stylistic influences. Unlike many of Jones' songs, it does not contain an instrumental section, instead focussing on a more heavyweight vocal sound.

Exercise 23

1. Discuss Norah Jones' use of harmonic language in the album *Not Too Late* and compare it to at least one other contemporary singer-songwriter.

2. To what extent is instrumental colour used as a means of expression in the album *Not Too Late*?

3. Discuss the incorporation of classical traditions into the prescribed works of this topic. Refer to at least two of the prescribed works in detail.

> **Further reading**
>
> At the time of writing there is little or no published material (containing any analytical substance) on the works of Norah Jones. The following would be helpful by way of background on Amy Winehouse:
>
> *Amy Amy Amy: The Amy Winehouse Story* by Nick Johnstone (ISBN: 1847722423, Omnibus Press 2008).
>
> *Amy Winehouse: The Biography*, by Chas Newkey-Burden (ISBN: 1844545636, John Blake Publishing 2008).

Glossary

Absolute music. Music that is not about anything other than itself.

Aleatoric. Music that has elements created by chance, for example the rolling of a die to generate rhythm for a melody.

Anacrusis. The note or notes that form an upbeat (or upbeats) to the first downbeat of a phrase.

Antiphony. A technique where two instrumental groups or two choirs alternate in dialogue.

Appoggiatura. An ornamental note that falls on the beat as a dissonance and then resolves by step onto the main note.

Arpeggiando. A performance direction found in string music in which the performer is instructed to interpret printed chords as arpeggios. In some Baroque music, an example of the arpeggiation will initially be written out as an example for the remaining bars.

Articulation. The manner in which a series of notes are played with regards to their separation or connection – for example, staccato (separated) or legato (connected).

Atonal. Western art music, which wholly or largely does not use keys or modes. Many early 20th-century composers saw atonality as the inevitable outcome of the perpetual chromaticism and modulation of some late Romantic music.

Augmentation. The lengthening of rhythmic values of a previously heard melody (for example in a fugue), or the widening of an interval.

Auxiliary note. A non-harmony note which is a step above (upper auxiliary) or below (lower auxiliary) the harmony note and returns to it.

Avant-garde. (French for 'vanguard') A label applied to composers considered to depart radically from accepted styles of composition.

Ballett. A light type of madrigal, popularised in England by Morley and Weelkes. Usually in triple time it can be distinguished by its fa-la-la refrains.

Bariolage. Rapid alternations between a recurring pitch on an open string and one or more pitches on an adjacent string.

Binary form. Two-part structure (AB), usually with both sections repeated.

Bitonal/polytonal. Bitonal music uses two different keys simultaneously; polytonal can refer to music using any number of keys greater than one. Clashing keys can be used to symbolise conflict in a drama for example in Britten's *Billy Budd*.

Chord extension. Chords which add additional 3rds to the third and fifth degree of a triad, creating a 7th, 9th, 11th or 13th. Although technically dissonant, chord extensions become more commonly used from the 19th century

onwards. You will have encountered some of these in the instrumental jazz studied at AS level.

Chromatic. The use of non-diatonic notes (notes which are not in the current key). Chromatic notes or chromatic passages are often used for expressive purposes for example Bach's St Matthew Passion. In the 19th century, chromaticism played an increasing role for example in Wagner's *Die Walküre*.

Circle of 5ths. A series of chords whose roots are each a 5th lower (or a 4th higher) than the previous one. For example, Em–Am–Dm–G–C.

Cluster. A chord made up of adjacent notes.

Col legno. A string technique of playing with the wood of the bow.

Compound metre. Time signature in which the beat divides into three: $\frac{6}{8}$, $\frac{9}{8}$, $\frac{12}{8}$.

Con sordino. An instruction to the performer to play with a mute.

Consonant. Intervals or chords which are stable and sound pleasant (for example, unisons, 3rds, 6ths), as opposed to its opposite, dissonant.

Continuo. Short for 'basso continuo', the continuo instruments form the accompaniment in Baroque music. It may include instruments such as the harpsichord (capable of playing full harmony) and a cello or bassoon reinforcing the bass line.

Contrary motion. Movement of two parts in opposite directions to each other.

Counter-melody. An independent melody which complements a more prominent theme.

Cue. A section or number from a film music score. Film music usually consists of a series of separately composed cues which can vary in length.

Da capo aria. Common aria form of Baroque opera and sacred music. ABA shape, with Da Capo instruction at the end of the B section. The singer may add ornamentation during the repeat.

Diatonic. Using notes that belong to the current key.

Diegetic music. Music in a film which forms part of the action (e.g. played or heard by one of the characters), not part of the underscore.

Diminished 7th. A four-note chord made up of a diminished triad plus a diminished 7th above the root.

Dominant 7th. A four-note chord built on the dominant (5th) note of the scale. It includes the dominant triad plus a minor 7th above the root.

Double stopping. A string technique of playing more than one string at a time. Also triple and quadruple stopping.

False relation. A chromatic contradiction between two notes sounded simultaneously and in different parts. For example a G natural against a G sharp.

Falsetto. This involves the singing of notes above the normal range of the human voice, normally by male singers.

Galliard. Lively Renaissance dance, popular in the Elizabethan Court, written in triple time.

Gesamtkunstwerk. (Ger. 'complete art work'). See Music drama.

Glissando. A slide between two notes.

Ground bass. Repeating bass, usually four or eight bars in length, with changing music in the other parts. Popular in Baroque music.

Harmonic. Sometimes known as flageolet note, a technique of lightly touching the string (e.g. on a violin) to produce a high, flute-like sound.

Harmonic rhythm. The rate at which harmony changes in a piece.

Hemiola. The articulation of two units of triple time (*strong-weak-weak*, *strong-weak-weak*) as three units of duple time (*strong-weak*, *strong-weak*, *strong-weak*).

Hit point. Point in a film score where the music coincides with an event in the action (sometimes known as 'catching the action').

Homophonic. A texture in which one part has a melody and the other parts accompany. In contrast to a polyphonic texture, in which each part has independent melodic interest.

Imitation. A contrapuntal device in which a distinct melodic idea in one part is immediately copied by another part, often at a different pitch, while the first part continues with other music. The imitation is not always strict, but the basic melodic and rhythmic outline should be heard.

Leger line. Additional lines used above or beneath the stave to represent notes that fall outside of its range.

Leitmotif. A theme which is associated with a character, situation, mood, object or idea, especially in the operas of Richard Wagner and dramatic works/film music of later composers.

Libretto. The script or words for a dramatic work which is set to music (e.g. an opera, musical or oratorio).

Masque. Opera-like English court entertainment from the 17th and early 18th centuries.

Mediant. The third degree of a major or minor scale.

Melisma. A technique in vocal music, where a single syllable is set over a number of notes in the melody. Such a passage may be described as 'melismatic'.

Metamorphosis. Compositional device in minimalist music, aiming for gradual change achieved by altering one note of the previous chord at a time.

Metric modulation. A device for achieving a gradual change of tempo by setting a new beat which is a proportion of the previous beat.

Middle-eight. A passage that may be used in popular music forms, describing a section (usually consisting of eight bars and containing different music) that prepares the return of the main section.

Minimalist. A contemporary style of composing based on repetitions of short melodic and rhythmic patterns. Developed by American composers such as Steve Reich, Philip Glass and Terry Riley.

Mode. Seven-note scales that can be created using only the white notes of a piano keyboard. The dorian can be played beginning on D (i.e. D–E–F–G–A–B–C–D), the mixolydian on G, the aeolian on A and the ionian on C. These interval patterns can then be transposed to any other note. For example, dorian beginning on G (or G dorian) would be G–A–B♭–C–D–E–F–G.

The modes used in 16th-century church music came to interest later composers looking for an alternative to the major-minor tonal system. Often this was linked to a desire to imitate the sounds of church music or to use the modal styles of folksong to create a link with national identity for example, MacMillan's *The Confession of Isobel Gowdie*.

Modulation. The process of changing key. At AS level, modulation was usually to closely related keys. However, in the works studied for A2 you will see a more dramatic and expressive use of wide-ranging modulations, including keys which are distantly related. For example, Schumann's *Dichterliebe*.

Monophonic. A musical texture that uses a single melodic line.

Multi-track recording. A method of recording (normally for popular music) that allows sound sources to be recorded separately and later combined.

Music drama. Richard Wagner's term for his later operas, which attempted to combine music with the other arts to create a 'complete art work' (*Gesamtkunstwerk*).

Obbligato. Used in Baroque music to denote an instrumental solo part which must be included.

Octatonic scale. Literally an eight-note musical scale, this normally refers to a pattern of notes with alternating tones and semitones. Rimsky-Korsakov used it to exotic effect in *Scheherezade*.

Ondeggiando (ondulé). A string technique of rapidly alternating between two strings.

Ossia. An alternative passage, normally written above the stave, that may be played instead of the original music. This may be an easier alternative in virtuosic operatic arias, for instance.

Overdubbing. A recording technique where an additional musical part is recorded to a previously recorded track. This technique is often used by pop musicians to create additional sounds and add more instruments to an existing recording.

Pedal note. A sustained or continuously repeated pitch, often in the bass, that is heard against changing harmonies. A pedal on the fifth degree of the scale (known as the dominant pedal) tends to generate excitement, while a pedal on the key note (known as the tonic pedal) tends to create a feeling of repose.

Phrasing. In performance the execution of longer groups of notes which follow natural patterns of the music. 'Articulation' may be used to refer to phrasing over a shorter group of notes. Phrases may be indicated by the composer but the skill and judgement of the performer is also important in creating a successful performance.

Plainchant. Original monophonic music of the early Christian church.

Polyphonic. A texture consisting of two or more equally important melodic lines heard together. In contrast to a homophonic texture, in which one part has the melody and the other parts accompany. The term polyphonic has a similar meaning to contrapuntal, but is more often used for vocal rather than instrumental music.

Portamento. A slide between two notes.

Power chord. A term used in popular music to refer to a chord for guitar that omits the 3rd of the triad. It therefore contains a bare interval of a 5th.

Programme music. Music with a stimulus that comes from outside the music itself or depicts an extra-musical idea.

Recitative. A technique in opera and oratorio where the singer conveys the text in a speech-like manner. This is normally used to cover narrative effectively and contrasts with arias which are much more lyrical.

Ritornello. In Baroque music, the repeated tutti section used as a refrain; most often in the first or last movement of a concerto, or in arias or choral works.

Ritornello form. Standard form of first and last movements of the Baroque concerto, alternating tutti ritornelli with solo or ripieno (small group) sections.

Rubato. The alteration of rhythm, particularly in a melodic line, by lengthening and shortening notes but keeping an overall consistent tempo.

Sacred music. Music which is intended for worship or has a religious purpose.

Scotch snap. A two-note dotted rhythm which has the shorter note on the beat. Usually an on-beat semiquaver followed by an off-beat dotted quaver. Also known as lombardic rhythm.

Secular music. Music which does not have a religious purpose.

Segue. The continuation of one section or movement to another without a break. In popular albums, this refers to one track immediately following its predecessor.

Sequence. Immediate repetition of a melodic or harmonic idea at a different pitch, or a succession of different pitches.

Serialism. A system of composing atonal music, using a predetermined series of the 12 chromatic notes to guarantee equality of all pitches. For example, David Shire's jazz film score for *The Taking of Pelham One Two Three*.

Skiffle. A type of folk music with jazz and country influences. It also typically uses homemade or improvised instruments such as the comb and paper or kazoo.

Sonata form. Typical first movement form of the Classical and Romantic periods. In three sections – exposition, development, recapitulation – often based on two groups of melodic material in two contrasting keys (first subject, second subject).

Sprechstimme. A vocal technique which falls between speaking and singing.

Strophic. A song in which the music is repeated for each verse, for example a hymn.

Sul ponticello. A string technique of playing close to the bridge.

Sul tasto. A string technique of playing over the fingerboard.

Symphonic poem. Type of programme music for orchestra, depicting a character, mood or idea or telling a story. Also known as a Tone poem.

Syncopation. Placing the accents in parts of the bar that are not normally emphasised, such as on weak beats or between beats, rather than in the expected place on strong beats.

Tabla. A pair of hand-drums, used frequently in Indian Classical music performances.

Temp track. Temporary music track used in the early production of a film.

Tessitura. A specific part of a singer's or instrument's range. For example a 'high tessitura' indicates a high part of the range.

Threnody. (Greek thrēnos and ōidē) Wailing ode. A song of lament at a death.

Through-composed. A stage work (opera or musical) in which the music is not split into seperate numbers. Also a song in which there is different music composed for each verses.

Tierce de Picardie. A major 3rd in the final tonic chord of a passage in a minor mode.

Transcription. The arrangement of a composition for other instruments (e.g. a piano version of an orchestral piece).

Tritone. An interval that is equivalent to three tones (an augmented 4th or dimished 5th).

Underscore. Music which accompanies or represents the action on screen without being part of it. Also used for instrumental music accompanying dialogue in a musical.

Voicing. The arrangement of pitches within a chord to create a particular texture.

Word painting. A technique of setting text in which the sound or movement implied by a word or phrase is imitated by the music (e.g. a falling phrase for 'dying').

Index